MONOPOLIES AND MERGERS COMMISSION

Animal waste

A report on the supply of animal waste in England and Wales and in Scotland

Presented to Parliament by the Secretary of State for Trade and Industry by Command of Her Majesty September 1993

LONDON : HMSO

Cm 2340

£19·65 net

Members of the Monopolies and Mergers Commission as at 29 June 1993

Mr G D W Odgers *(Chairman)*
Mr P H Dean CBE[1] *(Deputy Chairman)*
Mr D G Goyder *(Deputy Chairman)*
Mr H H Liesner CB *(Deputy Chairman)*
Mr A Armstrong
Mr C C Baillieu[1]
Mr I S Barter
Professor M E Beesley CBE
Mrs C M Blight
Mr F E Bonner CBE
Mr P Brenan
Mr J S Bridgeman
Mr R O Davies
Professor S Eilon
Mr J Evans
Mr A Ferry MBE
Sir Archibald Forster
Sir Ronald Halstead CBE
Ms P A Hodgson
Mr M R Hoffman
Mr D J Jenkins MBE
Mr A L Kingshott[1]
Miss P K R Mann[1]
Mr G C S Mather
Mr N F Matthews
Professor J S Metcalfe CBE[1]
Mrs D Miller MBE
Professor A P L Minford
Mr J D Montgomery
Dr D J Morris
Mr B C Owens
Professor J F Pickering
Mr L Priestley
Dr A Robinson
Mr J K Roe
Mr D P Thomson
Professor G Whittington

Mr S N Burbridge CB *(Secretary)*

---

[1]These members formed the group which was responsible for this report under the chairmanship of Mr P H Dean.

Note by the Department of Trade and Industry

In accordance with section 83(3) and (3A) of the Fair Trading Act 1973, the Secretary of State has excluded from the copies of the report, as laid before Parliament and as published, certain matters, publication of which appears to the Secretary of State to be against the public interest, or which he considers would not be in the public interest to disclose and which, in his opinion, would seriously and prejudicially affect certain interests. The omission is indicated by a note in the text.

Contents

1 Summary

1.1. We have been asked to investigate the supply of animal waste in England and Wales, and in Scotland (see Appendix 1.1.)

1.2. This is our third report concerning the animal waste industry. The first report, submitted in January 1985, was on the supply of red meat animal waste in Great Britain as a whole (the 1985 report).[1] As a result of the report PDM (see paragraph 1.3) gave a number of undertakings concerning its future behaviour (the 1986 undertakings—Appendix 1.2). We are required to deal with England and Wales, and Scotland separately, and to include poultry waste. The second report, submitted in June 1991, was on the merger of Prosper De Mulder Ltd and Croda International plc (the Croda report).[2]

The monopoly situations

1.3. We find a monopoly situation in England and Wales in favour of Prosper De Mulder Ltd and certain subsidiary and related companies, which are all owned by the De Mulder family and are managed as a single entity. We refer to these companies as PDM. PDM processes about 64 per cent of red meat waste acquired for rendering in England and Wales and has over 80 per cent of the commercial market for poultry waste.

1.4. We find a monopoly situation in Scotland in favour of William Forrest & Son (Paisley) Ltd (Forrest) and its ultimate holding company, Hillsdown Holdings plc (Hillsdown). Forrest processes about 71 per cent of red meat waste acquired for rendering in Scotland. All poultry waste produced in Scotland that requires commercial rendering is processed in England.

The rendering industry

1.5. Red meat waste supplied to the rendering industry in 1992 amounted to almost 1 million tonnes in England and Wales and 150,000 tonnes in Scotland. Commercial renderers in England were supplied with approaching 300,000 tonnes of poultry waste.

1.6. The main categories of animal waste for commercial purposes are offal, fat, bones, blood, and poultry carcases and feathers. The main sources are abattoirs, some of which operate a gut-room where products of higher value are carefully segregated, and abattoirs sometimes contract out the operation to specialist companies.

1.7. The principal products from rendering animal waste (a mechanical and heat treatment process) are meat-and-bone meal, and tallow. An estimated 390,000 tonnes of

---

[1] *Animal Waste: a Report on the supply of animal waste in Great Britain*, Cmnd 9470, April 1985.

[2] *Prosper De Mulder Ltd and Croda International plc: a report on the merger situation*, Cm 1611, August 1991.

meat-and-bone meal (value £53 million) was produced in the UK in 1992 for use mainly in animal feed. Tallow production amounted to an estimated 195,000 tonnes (value £36 million) in that year. Tallows are variously used for soap manufacture, for animal feed, or in the production of chemicals. There are close substitutes for both meat-and-bone meal and tallow in most of these uses. Renderers operate under strict regulatory controls both as regards the safety of their products and the environmental effects of their plants.

Findings

England and Wales

Pricing

1.8. The main public interest issues concern PDM's pricing (including charging) policy and practices, and in this respect little has changed since the 1985 report. As before, we are concerned about the prices paid by PDM for high-grade waste and its charges for low-grade waste, and not about prices charged for its end products. We have received allegations from competitors that PDM engages in predatory pricing, and from suppliers that PDM takes advantage of its dominant position by imposing excessive charges for collecting material such as offal or paying unduly low prices for the better material such as bones and best fat.

1.9. There have been cases where PDM took contracts at a loss. It admits that it set charges/payments at a loss during the price war in 1992 but this fell short of predatory pricing in the cases we studied.

1.10. Our study of PDM's pricing also shows that PDM is able to set different charges/payments unrelated to cost differences. In short, PDM engages in discriminatory pricing. It might be thought that intermittent price wars are indicative of a healthy climate of competition in the rendering industry. It seems to us, however, that there is generally little competition amongst renderers. PDM admits that it does not normally compete for other renderers' supplies.

1.11. We conclude that PDM's practice of discriminatory pricing squeezes smaller competitors and restricts competition in rendering in England and Wales.

The 1986 undertakings

1.12. PDM has failed to fulfil certain of its 1986 undertakings: the carrying out of the accounting and budgeting arrangements regarding PDM's gut-room operations, and the pre-notification of PDM's acquisition of any animal waste business. In our view these failures are a serious matter.

Transparency and profitability

1.13. The financial results of PDM's rendering operations are not sufficiently transparent. Certain PDM companies which do not file accounts incur expenses on behalf of the rendering companies which they rebill with a mark-up. The existence of this mark-up depresses the reported profits of the rendering companies which do file accounts.

Efficiency

1.14. Our study of the comparative financial performance of renderers gives little indication that PDM is more efficient than the smaller renderers, and there must be at least some doubt whether it achieves the network benefit claimed from its multi-site operation.

Scotland

Pricing

1.15. Forrest has engaged in discriminatory pricing. This practice has the effect of squeezing its two smaller competitors, restricting competition in rendering in Scotland.

Profitability

1.16. Forrest's profitability reflects higher charges and lower payments for animal waste than would have been the case under more competitive conditions. This situation may be expected to continue.

Efficiency

1.17. Forrest's processing costs per tonne are significantly higher than those of the average of the smaller renderers included in our study of comparative financial performance. However, it earns the highest returns on capital employed of the renderers included in our study.

Recommendations

England and Wales

Remedying the adverse effects on competition

1.18. PDM should be required to publish weekly, together with detailed related information, a representative sample of prices and charges it has negotiated in the preceding week commencing with the week ending 9 October 1993, in a form approved by the Director General of Fair Trading (DGFT). In addition, PDM should be required to dispose of its moth-balled Market Harborough plant within six months from the publication of our report to a purchaser (not associated directly or indirectly with PDM) approved by the DGFT, and pending disposal the plant should be kept in good repair but not operated.

The 1986 undertakings

1.19. We make detailed recommendations for tightening the monitoring of PDM's gut-room operations. We add that if the DGFT is not satisfied that PDM is carrying on its gut-room business on an arm's length basis, or if there is a breach of any undertaking given by PDM in respect of its gut-room operations, PDM should be required to dispose of them to a purchaser approved by the DGFT.

1.20. As regards PDM's failure to pre-notify certain acquisitions of animal waste enterprises, PDM should be prohibited from making any such acquisition unless the DGFT has approved it in advance as being in the public interest.

Lack of transparency of published accounts

1.21. PDM should file with the DGFT, within nine months of the end of each accounting period, consolidated accounts for the whole of the PDM enterprise as defined in paragraph 3.6. These accounts should include detailed segmental information.

Scotland

1.22. Forrest should be required to publish weekly, together with detailed related information, a representative sample of prices and charges it has negotiated in the preceding week, commencing with the week ending 9 October 1993, in a form approved by the DGFT.

Overview

1.23. Despite the high levels of concentration, the evidence indicates that efficient smaller firms can continue not only to survive but to flourish in the animal waste industry. What is required at present is the minimum amount of additional regulation necessary to curb the over-zealous protection of their supplies of animal waste by the two monopolists, and to stimulate competition. The other renderers make a valuable contribution to the industry and should be encouraged to continue to do so; the preservation of competition for supplies of animal waste is likely to be the best way of ensuring that the public service performed by the industry is provided economically.

2 The rendering industry

Introduction

2.1. We use the term animal waste to refer to what is left of an animal after slaughter when meat and offal for human consumption have been removed. Hides and skins are, however, excluded from our definition of animal waste: they are processed separately and used to make quite different products. The terms of reference for this inquiry relate to animal waste that is acquired for processing in rendering plants, and we address this in paragraph 2.7.

2.2. Animal waste can be divided into red meat waste (from cattle, sheep and pigs) and poultry waste (from chickens, ducks, geese and turkeys). The main categories of animal waste for commercial purposes are fat, bones, offal, poultry carcases and feathers.

2.3. In this chapter we consider first the sources of supply of animal waste; we then look at the structure of the rendering industry, and its systems of transport and production; we consider the setting of prices for animal waste; we assess the market for the renderers' products; and finally we consider what barriers may exist to entry into the rendering industry.

Sources of supply of animal waste

2.4. The bulk of raw materials for rendering is obtained from abattoirs as a result of the slaughter of cattle, sheep and pigs, and from poultry plants as a by-product of the processing of chickens, ducks, geese and turkeys. Supplies, particularly from cattle, show a marked seasonal pattern, with lower volumes in late spring and early summer and higher volumes from late autumn to the end of the year. Other sources of rendering materials are:

(a) meat preparation plants supplying prepacked meat for supermarkets;

(b) meat preparation plants engaged in producing boned-out meat for food manufacturers;

(c) butchers' shops;

(d) hotels, restaurants and catering establishments; and

(e) knacker material obtained from farms, poultry rearers and hatcheries, zoos, hunt kennels and veterinary surgeons.

2.5. Diagrams of the sources and uses of red meat waste and poultry waste are shown at Figures 2.1 and 2.2. It should be observed that the by-products trades involved with poultry processing are far simpler than those concerned with abattoirs. The processing of poultry involves the removal of the feathers, heads, feet, fat and viscera, and except for condemned carcases, these items comprise the full range of products handled. At one time all these items were mixed with other animal waste to be processed into tallow and meat-and-bone meal, but following the salmonella concerns in 1988 (see paragraph 2.47), poultry waste and red meat waste are now processed separately.

5

FIGURE 2.1

Sources and uses of red meat waste

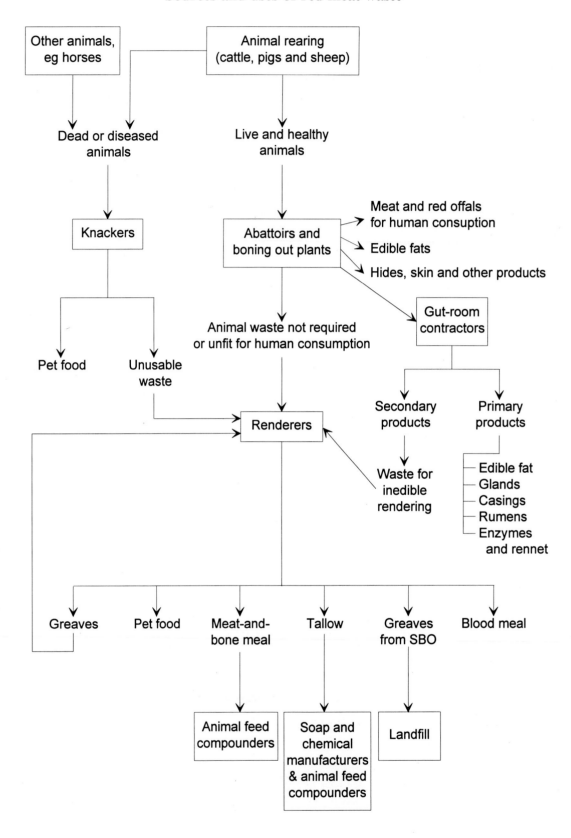

Source: United Kingdom Renderers' Association (UKRA) and MMC.

FIGURE 2.2

Sources of poultry waste

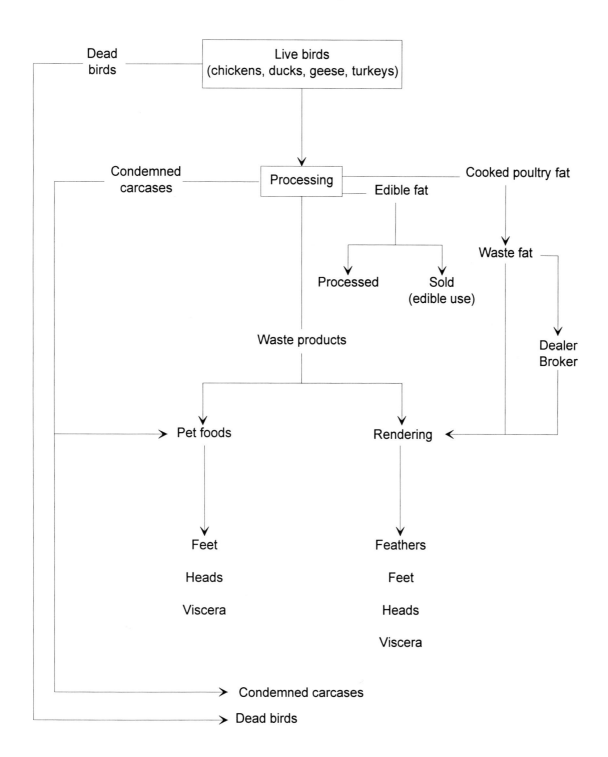

Source: UKRA.

2.6. The volume of animal waste arising from the meat industry in Great Britain largely reflects the number of animals and poultry slaughtered but there is not an exact correspondence. Table 2.1 shows the variation in the volume of animal waste over a ten-year period. Red meat waste volumes increased between 1982 to 1987 but fell by 9 per cent from then until 1992. The volume of waste arising from the poultry industry has been rising and is now at the highest point for the period.

TABLE 2.1 **Red meat waste arising from the meat industry in Great Britain**

				'000 tonnes
	Waste from slaughter	Blood	Knacker waste	Total
1982	1,229	90	100	1,419
1983	1,310	96	107	1,513
1984	1,327	97	108	1,532
1985	1,342	98	109	1,549
1986	1,299	95	105	1,499
1987	1,347	99	115	1,561
1988	1,247	90	120	1,457
1989	1,270	91	125	1,486
1990	1,279	92	126	1,497
1991	1,323	95	130	1,548
1992	1,221	88	120	1,429

Waste arising from the poultry industry in Great Britain

					'000 tonnes
	Waste from slaughter	Blood	Mortalities	Feathers	Total
1982	209	27	40	107	383
1983	214	28	41	110	393
1984	221	28	43	113	405
1985	233	30	45	119	427
1986	245	31	47	126	449
1987	263	34	51	135	483
1988	273	35	53	140	501
1989	263	34	51	135	483
1990	265	34	51	136	486
1991	274	35	53	141	503
1992	282	36	54	144	516

Source: MAFF, PDM and MMC.

2.7. Most but not all of the total supply of animal waste is used for rendering. Table 2.2 shows that in 1992 73 per cent of the combined total of red meat waste and poultry waste in Great Britain was rendered. The rest was accounted for by sales to pet food manufacturers (15 per cent); by disposal as waste, the main items disposed of being blood and feathers (8 per cent); and the remainder by sales of special items to manufacturers of particular types of food, pharmaceuticals and other specialist products. The total volume rendered has been fairly constant in the last five years at around 1.4 million tonnes. In the remainder of this chapter we shall focus on the animal waste supplied for rendering.

TABLE 2.2 **Total animal waste and proportion rendered in Great Britain**

					million tonnes
	Red meat	Poultry	Total	Total rendered	% rendered
1987	1.56	0.48	2.04	1.51	74
1988	1.46	0.50	1.96	1.39	71
1989	1.49	0.48	1.97	1.41	72
1990	1.50	0.49	1.99	1.37	69
1991	1.55	0.50	2.05	1.41	69
1992	1.43	0.52	1.95	1.42	73

Source: MAFF, PDM and MMC.

Abattoirs

2.8. The number of abattoirs has been declining for several decades, and in recent years the rate of closure has accelerated. Table 2.3, based on figures supplied by the Meat and Livestock Commission (MLC), shows that over 200 abattoirs ceased trading in the four years between 1987/88 and 1991/92 (years ending in March).

TABLE 2.3 **Abattoir numbers and throughputs, Great Britain, 1968/69 to 1991/92**

Year ending March	Abattoir numbers	Total throughput* '000	Average throughput per abattoir*
1968/69	2,062	11,352	5,505
1969/70	N/A	N/A	N/A
1970/71	N/A	N/A	N/A
1971/72	1,890	12,473	6,600
1972/73	1,766	11,941	6,761
1973/74	1,671	12,544	7,507
1974/75	1,601	13,500	8,432
1975/76	1,554	12,665	8,150
1976/77	N/A	N/A	N/A
1977/78	1,444	11,645	8,064
1978/79	1,392	11,939	8,576
1979/80	1,231	12,534	10,182
1980/81	1,135	13,159	11,594
1981/82	1,062	12,551	11,819
1982/83	1,046	13,340	12,754
1983/84	1,040	13,686	13,160
1984/85	1,022	13,606	13,313
1985/86	1,000	13,574	13,574
1986/87	980	13,702	13,982
1987/88	919	13,964	15,195
1988/89	852	13,231	15,529
1989/90	822	13,112	15,951
1990/91	779	13,620	17,483
1991/92	709	13,588	19,165

Source: MLC.

*Throughput is measured in cattle units. One cattle unit equals one adult cattle beast, or three calves, or five sheep, or two pigs.

2.9. In 1968/69 there were 2,062 abattoirs operating in Great Britain; at the time of the 1985 report there were around 1,000; and by 1991/92 the number had fallen to 709.

2.10. This reduction in the number of abattoirs disguises a growth in the number of animals slaughtered. In 1968/69 the total throughput of cattle units was 11.4 million; a peak was reached in 1987/88 of almost 14 million cattle units; although there has since been some decline, in 1991/92 throughput stood at 13.6 million. There has been a reduction in the number of smaller abattoirs and those that remain have been growing larger. Table 2.3 shows that the average number of cattle units processed annually per abattoir rose from 5,505 in 1968/69 to 19,165 in 1991/92. From 1977/78 when the annual average was 8,064, there has been an increase in the average every year.

2.11. The industry is becoming increasingly concentrated. In 1991/92 the 30 largest abattoirs, ie those processing over 100,000 cattle units a year, accounted for only 4 per cent of the total number of abattoirs but 37.5 per cent of the total throughput. The next 47 abattoirs, those processing between 50,000 and 100,000 cattle units a year, accounted for 7 per cent of the total number of abattoirs but 25 per cent of the total throughput. Thus 11 per cent of the abattoirs accounted for almost 63 per cent of the throughput. At the other end of the scale, abattoirs processing fewer than 1,000 cattle units a year accounted for almost 37 per cent of the total number of abattoirs but only 0.7 per cent of the total throughput; and those processing between 1,000 and 5,000 cattle units accounted for 18 per cent of abattoir numbers but only 2.3 per cent of the throughput. Thus almost 55 per cent of the total number of abattoirs accounted for only 3 per cent of the total throughput.

2.12. Animal waste arises as a low-value by-product from the supply of meat. Since the animals are reared mainly for their meat, the short-run price elasticity of supply of waste material is zero. In the long term, the price which an abattoir receives for animal waste will affect farmers but the long-run price elasticity of supply will also be very small. In addition, because there is a statutory requirement for animal waste to be cleared from abattoirs within 48 hours (and abattoirs in fact generally insist on a 24-hour removal service), the prices paid for waste do not affect the volumes of waste supplied by the abattoirs, even on a daily basis.

Gut-room contractors

2.13. Most of the larger abattoirs have a 'gut-room' where pet food materials, fats and other high-value by-products are segregated from the abdominal mass. Some operate their own gut-rooms whilst others contract them out to specialist contractors. Frequently, however, particularly at the smaller abattoirs, only a basic form of segregation of material takes place. In 1985 PDM was a major gut-room contractor with 20 gut-room contracts in England and Wales, but it now has only nine. Other gut-room contractors include Imperial Meat Company Ltd (IMC); Specialpack Ltd; and Nottingham Animal By-Products Ltd. All of the major gut-room contractors now operate fewer gut-rooms because of abattoir closures.

Knackers

2.14. The knacker trade, which deals with the carcases of fallen and diseased animals, has been in sharp decline since the introduction of charges to farmers for collection and disposal. Before 1990 knackermen used to pay farmers for dead carcases as they were able to make a profit from the sale of hides, pet food materials and animal waste to renderers. Since then, renderers have introduced charges for most knacker materials and the knackermen have responded by charging farmers. This led to a sharp decline in the number of animals being sent to knackermen as farmers have attempted to dispose of fallen stock in other ways. This has led to problems of unburied fallen stock. A recent study of the Scottish knacker trade estimated that knackermen were handling only 10 to 20 per cent of fallen stock. The trend is unlikely to be reversed in the near future because following the emergence of bovine spongiform encephalopathy (BSE) (see paragraph 2.46), processors of animal waste have been reluctant to use material from fallen stock either for pet food or animal feed.

The structure of the rendering industry

2.15. Until the 1950s the rendering industry operated on a small scale, and there were many plants generally servicing small local abattoirs. A restructuring of the industry came about as the result of five factors:

(a) the growing concentration of the abattoir sector;

(b) technological advances in the processing of waste material, including the development of continuous processing;

(c) a decline in the demand for edible gelatine and animal glue which led to increased supplies being available for rendering;

(d) the development of the motorway network; and

(e) the increased cost of re-equipment and the enhanced profit on the sale of the site for development.

By the 1970s a number of large-scale continuous rendering plants had been established.

2.16. The consolidation of the industry was rapid, reflecting the negligible entry by new firms and a number of family firms leaving the industry. In the 1970s the number of rendering plants in Great

Britain fell from 125 to 90 and by 1982 had fallen further to 74. Parallel to this decline was a reduction in the number of rendering companies. By 1983 there were 57. By the 1990s there were only 20 companies left within Great Britain and the number has continued to fall, the most recent closure being that of Beeson Bros (Crewe) Ltd (Beeson) at the end of 1992.

2.17. Until recently most renderers dealt with poultry waste as well as red meat waste. But since 1989 it has been necessary to process poultry waste separately from red meat waste (see paragraph 2.47), and this led to withdrawal from poultry waste processing by a number of smaller renderers. There are currently two companies in England and Wales which process only poultry waste, Wildriggs Proteins Ltd (Wildriggs), and Mid-Norfolk Proteins, but there are none in Scotland.

England and Wales

2.18. Table 2.4 shows the volumes processed and estimated market shares for renderers of red meat waste and renderers of poultry waste in England and Wales in 1992.

TABLE 2.4   **Estimated market shares of renderers in England and Wales in 1992***

Renderer	Red meat waste throughput† '000 tonnes	Share of market %	Poultry waste throughput† '000 tonnes	Share of market %	Total throughput† '000 tonnes	Share of market %
PDM	621†	64	246	81	867	69
Fats & Proteins (UK) Ltd	69	7	-	-	69	5
Smith Brothers (Hyde) Ltd	55	6	5	2	60	5
Gilberts Animal By-Products Ltd	45	5	-	-	45	4
A Hughes & Son (Skellingthorpe) Ltd	44	5	11	4	56	4
Peninsular Proteins Ltd	41	4	-	-	41	3
Wildriggs Proteins Ltd	-	-	22	7	22	2
Mid-Norfolk Proteins	-	-	15	5	15	1
Nine other renderers‡	87	9	2	1	89	7
Total	962	100	301	100	1,264	100

Source: MMC.

*The exact 12-month period varies from company to company.
†This figure includes a small volume of poultry blood.
‡Cheale Meats Ltd; Chetwynd Animal By-Products; P Waddington & Co Ltd; Blackburn Products Co Ltd; S Spavin; A H Taylor; Specialpack Ltd; A Burton; John W Green; J F Rockett; Leslie Sykes.

2.19. It can be seen from Table 2.4 that in 1992 PDM and its subsidiary and related companies dominated the market for red meat waste with a share of 64 per cent, a proportion similar to that estimated at the time of the merger with Croda International plc (Croda) in 1991. The other major renderers in England and Wales and their shares were:

— Fats & Proteins (UK) Ltd (Fats & Proteins) (7 per cent);

— Smith Brothers (Hyde) Ltd (Smith) (6 per cent);

— Gilberts Animal By-Products Ltd (Gilberts) (5 per cent);

— A Hughes & Son (Skellingthorpe) Ltd (Hughes) (5 per cent); and

— Peninsular Proteins Ltd (Peninsular), a subsidiary of Strong & Fisher plc, which is in turn a subsidiary of Hillsdown (4 per cent).

There were also a number of smaller operators, which between them had a market share of approximately 9 per cent. In addition a few abattoirs undertake their own rendering, but they account for less than 5 per cent of the total red meat processed and are excluded from the table.

236197   B

2.20. There are only five significant commercial poultry waste renderers, although some other red meat waste renderers in England undertake a small amount of poultry waste rendering. By far the largest poultry waste renderer is PDM, with an estimated share of 81 per cent of this market. The other significant operators are Wildriggs, Mid-Norfolk Proteins, Hughes and Smith. PDM and Wildriggs collect poultry waste from both England and Scotland. In addition, some poultry producers do their own rendering.

2.21. Figure 2.3 shows the location of animal waste rendering plants throughout Great Britain.

2.22. PDM operates differently from the rest of the rendering industry. All other renderers operate from one site but PDM has eight animal waste rendering plants, most of which specialize in different types of waste material. At present the high-grade rendering of fat and bones is undertaken at Widnes and Silvertown; clean offal with fat and bones are processed at Doncaster and Exeter; and 'dirty offal' (ie specified bovine offals (SBO) and knacker materials) together with fat and bones are rendered at Hartshill. The Widnes plant handles all blood and some poultry waste, but the bulk of the poultry waste is dealt with at Ditchford and Nottingham. The Market Harborough plant, acquired as a result of the merger with Croda, is currently 'moth-balled'.

2.23. Most other renderers process offal, bones and fat, but a few process SBO and poultry waste.

Scotland

2.24. There are only three commercial red meat waste renderers operating in Scotland, much the largest of which is Forrest, which last year processed around 102,000 tonnes of raw materials (including 15,000 tonnes of greaves and other materials not purchased in Scotland) or 71 per cent of all red meat waste rendered in Scotland. The other renderers are Dundas Brothers Ltd (Dundas Brothers) in the North-East of Scotland, which rendered around 25,000 tonnes (a share of 18 per cent) and Dundas Chemical Company (Mosspark) Ltd (Dundas Chemical) in the Borders, which processed around 16,000 tonnes (a share of 11 per cent). The two Dundas companies, although owned and operated by distant cousins, are totally independent of each other and have no financial relationship.

2.25. Each of these companies has one rendering plant, as shown in Figure 2.3.

2.26. Forrest has become increasingly dominant in Scotland: ten years ago it had around 50 per cent of the market compared with its current 71 per cent. Forrest is, however, a comparatively small producer, processing the equivalent of around 12 per cent of the total waste processed by PDM.

2.27. None of the three commercial red meat waste renderers in Scotland processes poultry waste. Poultry waste produced in Scotland is either rendered by the producers, sent to England for commercial rendering (see paragraph 2.20) or disposed of by on-farm burial or landfill.

Cross-border trade

2.28. At present PDM collects red meat waste only in England and Wales and Forrest only in Scotland. However, there is some minor cross-border trade among the other renderers.

2.29. In addition to poultry waste being transported from Scotland for processing by renderers in England, Dundas Chemical and Fats & Proteins have had an arrangement until recently whereby the latter sent all its SBO to Dundas Chemical in Dumfries, and in return Dundas Chemical sent its non-specified material to Fats & Proteins in Lancaster. Dundas Chemical is now resuming its own rendering of non-specified material.

2.30. We were told by Forrest that there were two main reasons why, although renderers in Scotland obtained supplies of raw materials in England and vice versa, the level of cross-border trade in red meat waste was low. First, the location of renderers in Southern Scotland and Northern England when taken with the volume of raw materials available to these renderers meant that the

FIGURE 2.3

Locations of rendering plants in Great Britain

Source: MMC.

13

English renderers could more economically collect and use the raw materials available in Northern England and the Scottish renderers could more economically do the same in Southern Scotland. Secondly, the renderers (including Forrest) did not have the necessary infrastructure to enable them to collect from further afield on a long-term and economically viable basis. We consider below (paragraph 2.42) whether Scotland should be regarded as a separate market from England and Wales.

Collection and transport

2.31. Transport of animal waste from abattoirs, meat preparation plants or butchers' shops to a rendering plant may be arranged in a number of ways. Most rendering companies collect the waste in their own vehicles driven by their own employees. A variant on this is the use of self-employed drivers who own the vehicle or, in the case of articulated trucks, the traction unit.

2.32. Some collections, principally fat and bone, are carried out by businesses independent of renderers, known as collectors or dealers. While there are few contracts between collectors and particular rendering companies, there is often a close working relationship and many collectors supply their waste exclusively to one particular renderer. Collectors mostly remove waste from butchers' shops and small abattoirs, often consolidating small collections of similar materials. Rendering companies differ widely in the proportion of their materials which they obtain from collectors.

2.33. Waste material may be transported direct to the rendering plant, or to a depot for consolidation and onward transport to the plant. The use of depots makes possible consolidation of small quantities of individual types of material and thus reduces transport costs. These benefits are only possible, however, when the volume of waste material purchased is high, and PDM and Forrest are the only renderers that operate in this way.

2.34. The most common vehicle used for transporting the waste is a 24-tonne articulated truck. Alternatively, and in particular for smaller loads, lorries collect skips that have been left overnight at the abattoir. The latter method is more expensive because of the greater handling time required, the limited loads that can be taken and the effect of the skip itself as a weight additional to the load. Different types of material cannot be carried in the same vehicle or skip except when the vehicle container has been custom-partitioned.

England and Wales

2.35. The size and nature of PDM's operations make its transport system quite different from those of other renderers. Because of the specialization between PDM's rendering plants (see paragraph 2.22) around one-third of the material collected is transported twice: after being taken to the nearest depot or plant some of the material is then redistributed to the plant specializing in that type of material. As a result the average distance over which material is transported is higher for PDM than for other renderers. For large abattoirs, PDM may make collections of different materials in separate lorries and take them to different plants.

2.36. We set out in Table 2.5 for each of the main renderers the proportion of its supplies which it obtains from within certain distance bands, excluding supplies delivered by collectors.

TABLE 2.5   Raw material supplies obtained from within certain distances in England and Wales

	Under 50 miles	50–100 miles	100–150 miles	Over 150 miles
				per cent
PDM:				
Doncaster	70	18	12	0
Exeter	42	37	12	9
Hartshill	47	15	29	9
Silvertown	38	23	26	13
Widnes	49	24	27	0
Nottingham	6	78	0	16
Ditchford	12	17	63	8
Fats & Proteins	42	57	1	0
Smith	60	40	0	0
Gilberts	15	35	30	20
Hughes	90	5	3	2
Peninsular	39	26	27	8

Source: The companies.

Note: The above distances include the redistribution of materials by PDM.

These figures show considerable variety in the trading patterns of PDM's different plants and of the smaller renderers.

2.37. PDM is also different from other renderers in mostly using self-employed owner-drivers to collect materials from the larger abattoirs. Company-owned vehicles with directly-employed drivers are used for collection rounds catering to smaller abattoirs and butchers' shops. Collection schedules are organized in the same way both for owner-drivers and for employees. For movement of materials between rendering plants, return loads are arranged, if possible, to minimize the times when lorries travel empty.

2.38. The other renderers use mainly their own drivers and vehicles for collecting waste, and transport it directly to their plant, but it may sometimes be necessary to hire additional vehicles from haulage companies.

Scotland

2.39. In Scotland, Forrest has different arrangements from the other two renderers. Although it has only one rendering plant, at Motherwell, it uses two depots, at Elgin, Grampian Region, and at Lochgelly, Highland Region (the latter owned by a subsidiary company), where waste collections are consolidated for onward shipment to Motherwell. The other renderers transport materials direct to their rendering plant. As Forrest has these depots, it can easily cover the whole of mainland Scotland, whereas the other renderers do not, and consequently the average distance it transports materials is higher for Forrest. Almost a quarter of its supplies come from more than 150 miles away. Table 2.6 sets out the proportion of supplies obtained by each of the renderers within certain distance bands (excluding supplies delivered by collectors).

TABLE 2.6   Raw material supplies obtained from within certain distances in Scotland

	Under 50 miles	50–100 miles	100–150 miles	Over 150 miles
				per cent
Forrest	60	10	7	23
Dundas Brothers	100	0	0	0
Dundas Chemical	10	70	10	10

Source: The companies.

2.40. Both Forrest and the other renderers use their own vehicles and drivers for collections, though the smaller renderers may also on occasion use outside haulage companies. Forrest also buys from collectors: four of them supply material direct to Motherwell and one collector brings material to each of the depots. The collectors do not deal with any other renderer.

2.41. Both Forrest and Dundas Brothers have recently modified some of their vehicles so that they can carry more than one type of waste. Some of the containers of Forrest's articulated trucks have been partitioned, while Dundas has acquired vehicles that can carry more than one skip.

2.42. As already described, very little red meat waste is transported across the English/Scottish border. This is reflected in the high proportion of waste (as shown in Tables 2.5 and 2.6) that is acquired by renderers within 100 miles of their processing plants both in England and Wales and in Scotland. Not only are most plants located at some distance from the border, but there are also few major abattoirs in the border areas. In practice, therefore, competition for supplies of red meat waste in England and Wales operates largely independently of competition in Scotland, and vice versa. So far as poultry waste is concerned, as already mentioned (paragraph 2.27), no commercial rendering of such waste is carried out in Scotland. We have found, therefore, that for most practical purposes England and Wales on the one hand and Scotland on the other may be regarded as two separate markets.

Production processes

Environmental and health and hygiene regulation

2.43. A number of the operations carried out in rendering plants were designated 'offensive trades' under the Public Health Act 1936, or in Scotland 'offensive businesses' under the Public Health (Scotland) Act 1897, and thereby came under the control of local authorities which were empowered to set operational standards. These controls are being superseded by new procedures established under the Environmental Protection Act 1990 (EPA). As before it is for local authorities to ensure that the prescribed standards are attained. Most of these standards cover the effluent and odours created by the main processes. With recent advances in technology it is now possible to treat effluent so successfully that discharge into a river can be accepted. As for odour control, the design of both process plant and the building housing it can bring about a substantial reduction of obnoxious output.

2.44. The EPA places a constant pressure on the rendering industry to improve standards as it incorporates the concept of Best Available Techniques Not Entailing Excessive Cost (BATNEEC). This concept is being given operational form by statutory guidance issued by the Secretary of State for the Environment; the rendering industry and local authorities participate in the development of this guidance. Renderers are expected to have until 1997 to implement the agreed standards. We were told that because of the growing environmental pressures and the costs they entailed for renderers some smaller businesses were reluctant to continue to operate in the industry. For those with a plant near a centre of population, the high value that may be obtained from selling their site for development can be more attractive than continuing as a renderer and having to make substantial investments in environmental control equipment.

2.45. The plant and facilities of a rendering factory are also affected by the Animal By-Products Order 1992, implementing a recent EC Directive, 90/667/EEC, which seeks to harmonize the arrangements for the processing and disposal of animal waste and came into force in the UK at the start of 1993. The main purpose of the Directive is to ensure that waste material is processed in such a way as to be unharmful to human or animal health.

2.46. EC member states are, however, able to take additional measures to those required by the Directive when there is a threat to human or animal health. In 1988 and 1989 the Government took such measures to contain the outbreaks of salmonella and BSE and these created considerable difficulties for the rendering industry.

2.47. The outbreak of salmonella in 1989 led to the slaughter of over 3 million poultry. Since that time, moreover, the output of meal from each rendering plant has been sampled and tested for salmonella; if a test is positive, meal supplies are stopped and remedial action is taken. In spite of this the major food retailers decided that they would require a guarantee from their poultry suppliers that none of their poultry and poultry products had been fed on diets containing proteins derived from poultry waste. As a result renderers began to process poultry waste separately from red meat waste, and there was less demand for meal made from poultry waste.

2.48. The outbreak of BSE led not merely to requirements that any animal suspected as suffering from the disease should be slaughtered and incinerated but also—and much more importantly from the viewpoint of the rendering industry—to the requirement that those parts of cattle that are most likely to contain the causative agent of BSE (ie the SBO) should not be used in food for human or animal consumption. SBO have therefore to be separated at the abattoir from other animal waste, transported to the rendering plant in a separate container, and processed separately at the plant. While the tallow can be used, the remaining output (greaves) has to be disposed of, usually by burial in a landfill site. A further Government regulation of 1988 prohibits the feeding to ruminants of meat-and-bone meal derived from ruminant animal waste, and this has had the effect of reducing the market for the meat-and-bone meal by around 15 per cent and blood meal by up to 80 per cent.

Production technology

2.49. The raw material inputs into the rendering process are the various types of animal waste; the principal outputs are tallow and meat-and-bone meal. The main elements of the rendering process are a feed system; the 'cooking' of the material; the extraction of tallow; and drying and milling. There may also be minor additions to the process, eg refining the tallow. A few very small renderers do not go as far as the drying and milling stage of the process but sell their part-processed output, known as 'greaves', to other renderers. All the main renderers, however, carry out the full process. In addition to the main process plant, storage facilities for end products are required, in particular tanks for tallow, silos for meal and, in the case of some renderers, storage facilities for greaves awaiting processing.

2.50. The chief distinction to be drawn in the first stage of processing is between 'continuous' and 'batch' plants. The former tend to be economic only for larger volumes of material. Batch plants tend to be relatively expensive in time and labour, as the quality of the output depends on the active management of the process by the operator and effective use of plant controls. Continuous plant by comparison needs little attention apart from monitoring to ensure that the process is going on within specified technical limits.

2.51. Another important factor is the trade-off between number and size of processing units. (Units are often referred to as 'cookers' although this is not an apt description of all types of plant, especially those that work through vacuum evaporation.) The larger the number of cookers the greater the flexibility, partly because the cookers themselves may have different operating ranges and partly because separate processing of different types of material can increase the value of output. On the other hand larger cookers are more cost-effective than smaller ones.

2.52. The final extraction of tallow is now usually carried out by using a press. The once popular alternative method of solvent extraction fell from favour, partly because it produces only a low grade of tallow and partly because the oil (and hence the energy) content of the residual bone meal output is much lower than when a press is used.

2.53. The outputs of a rendering plant depend not only on the way raw materials are processed but also on the types of raw material and the proportions in which they are combined. Broadly speaking, higher-quality outputs are produced by plants that process mainly fresh fat and bones while lower-quality outputs come from plants that in addition process offal and knacker material. A common manufacturing strategy is to produce as much high-grade product as possible from the inputs.

2.54. Plant maintenance is important for maintaining the efficiency of the process and is one of the largest single cost items. All renderers have programmes of preventive maintenance and hold substantial stocks of spare parts. Over the life of a cooker many of the moving parts will be replaced. It is normal practice in the industry to close down for at least one day a week to carry out maintenance with a minimum of assistance from manufacturers. With any rendering system the material being processed is not lost if there is a plant failure. In the event of major breakdown, renderers have arrangements for transferring material to another renderer, but PDM does not need to participate as the number of its plants makes transfer outside the company unnecessary.

2.55. Comparing the operational efficiency of different plants or sites is difficult as no two installations are identical. Assessments of efficiency for a single plant are usually based on the fuel consumption per tonne of material processed. In Chapter 3 we carry out a comparison between rendering companies based on overall costs per tonne.

2.56. Capacity utilization of rendering plants varies considerably over the year, as the total amount of raw material available is 30 per cent greater in the peak season (October) than in the low season (May). There is also a lesser variation between days of the week. There are two principal effects of this capacity requirement. First, it increases the capital cost required to enter the industry compared with what would be required were the supply of raw material stable. Secondly, it provides a substantial amount of spare capacity in the low season that gives renderers the incentive to bid for additional supplies at higher prices.

England and Wales

2.57. Three companies have installed continuous plant: PDM, Fats & Proteins, and Peninsular. All of PDM's eight rendering plants have continuous plant; four have only one unit (Doncaster, Silvertown, Exeter and Market Harborough), three have two units (Hartshill, Nottingham and Ditchford) and one has three units (Widnes). Peninsular has two units and Fats & Proteins has three. By comparison those renderers using the batch method tend to have a larger number of cookers, for example both Gilberts and Hughes have six. Generally speaking, the lesser flexibility that is provided by the choice of a smaller number of continuous units results in a greater degree of mixing of input materials and leads to a manufacturing strategy of producing types of meal and tallow that are at the bottom of the acceptable quality range but minimize costs.

2.58. Some renderers other than PDM buy greaves as a buffer against a shortage of raw material. Greaves may be stored without deterioration and processed further provided that they are later 'cooked' again like the raw material to remove any contamination. They are available for purchase, especially when the supply of raw material is at its seasonal high, either from sources in Northern Ireland or the Republic of Ireland or from the very small renderers who have no facility for producing meat-and-bone meal.

Scotland

2.59. Forrest is the only one of the three renderers to operate a continuous processing system. It has three units, one of which is normally used for low-grade material, one for high-grade material and one for SBO. Forrest closed its solvent extraction plant at the end of 1992. One of the reasons for this was that the animal feed produced had a lower oil content and there had been an increase in demand for higher oil content animal feed. Forrest has therefore replaced its solvent extraction plant with a high oil meal plant. Supplies of greaves for processing in the solvent extraction plant were also becoming more difficult. Dundas Brothers and Dundas Chemical both use the batch method, the former having seven cookers and the latter eight. Dundas Brothers still employs the solvent extraction process though it has plans to install a continuous press system in its place.

2.60. The Scottish renderers have differed in their approach to plant replacement and purchase. The first two of Forrest's cookers were installed in 1975 and 1978 and have remained in use since then; the third unit was added in 1990. Dundas Chemical has carried out a gradual process of replacement and change and in the last five years has installed a new boiler, storage tanks and a condenser. By contrast Dundas Brothers carried out comprehensive refurbishment in 1992.

Pricing of animal waste

2.61. Renderers pay abattoirs for high-grade materials such as fat and bone. Low-grade materials such as offal have a much higher moisture content and require longer processing, entailing higher fuel costs; they also have a lower yield of end products. Renderers therefore normally charge abattoirs for their removal. (In this section prices are to be taken to include charges, except when otherwise stated.)

2.62. Most contracts between animal waste suppliers and renderers are agreed orally; occasionally these are later confirmed in writing. Agreement on price may remain valid for many months but changes may readily be made at the request of either party.

2.63. In most cases contracts are between a renderer and an individual abattoir (or other supplier). But there are also cases where several abattoirs are under common ownership and prices are negotiated by a renderer with the group of abattoirs as a whole.

2.64. Over the last few years there has been considerable variation in prices of animal waste. Large changes have even sometimes occurred within a three-month period. A primary factor that influences prices in the medium to long term is the selling prices of the renderers' end products (principally tallow and meal), and these, as will be discussed later in this chapter, have also fluctuated considerably in recent times. Figure 2.4 shows that over the last five years major movements in end-product prices have been reflected in the raw material prices.

2.65. A second factor that has had an important impact on animal waste prices has been the need to comply with BSE and salmonella regulations, which led to additional separation of materials at the abattoir and rendering plant and additional costs for the renderers.

2.66. There are considerable differences between the prices of different categories of animal waste. While prices can be specified for a large number of different types of waste (for example, feet, skulls, stomach, pancreas), most sales relate to the broad categories which reflect the actual degree of physical separation which takes place in the abattoirs, namely best fat, other fats, bones, offal, blood and SBO in the case of red meat waste; and carcase, offal, blood and feathers for poultry waste.

2.67. The value of a particular category of waste to the renderer depends on the yield and quality of tallow and meal and the cost of processing. Raw materials from different suppliers may also differ in their transport costs. All of these factors, in addition to the degree of competition for a particular abattoir's supplies, are reflected in the prices. We shall discuss these various factors in turn.

2.68. The main categories of animal waste vary considerably in their yields of tallow and meal. At the one extreme 'best fat' can provide a high yield of the better quality of tallow in addition to a small amount of meal, while at the other extreme the greaves from the rendering of SBO may be taken to landfill. The main categories of bone and offal fall between these two extremes. Within each broad category there can also be considerable variation in terms of the value of the material to the renderer. One determinant of quality is the degree to which different types of material have been separated out. For example, the value of SBO will be much less if the fat around the large intestine (known in the industry as 'middles') has been removed. The value of material to the renderer will also depend on his own processing plant, as different plants are designed to yield different qualities of tallow.

2.69. Transport costs vary with the number of calls required to make up a full load. Larger volumes are attractive to renderers as they tend to mean greater separation of materials. Contracts with large abattoirs are much sought after because they offer the opportunity to make up a full load with one call and in one step supply a significant part of the materials required for a particular rendering plant.

2.70. The systems of collection and transport have been described in paragraphs 2.31 to 2.42. Collection costs vary considerably. At the most efficient end of the scale is a full load for a large vehicle; at the other end of the scale is the collection round servicing rural butchers' shops. Costs of transport vary mainly with the number of calls in a collection round, as distance by itself is relatively insignificant in cost terms. Renderers may in many cases offer the same prices irrespective of the distance that the material has to be transported to their rendering plant.

FIGURE 2.4

End-product prices received by PDM compared with its average raw material prices, 1975 to 1992

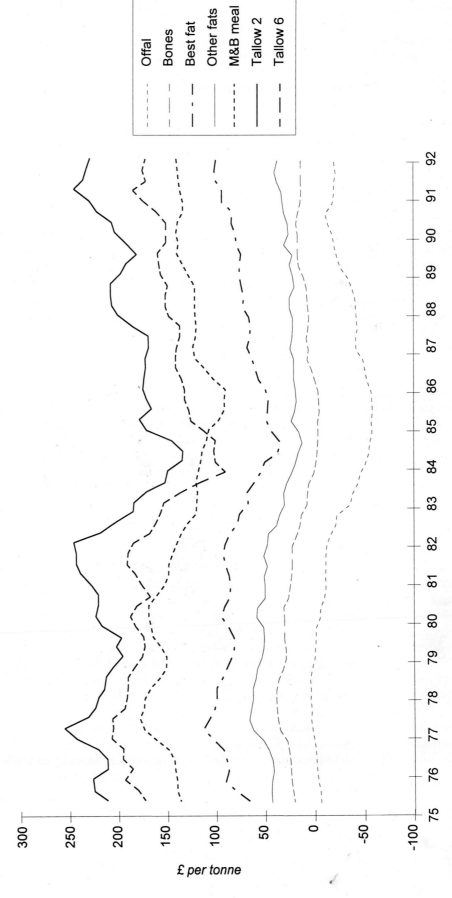

£ per tonne

Offal	
Bones	
Best fat	
Other fats	
M&B meal	
Tallow 2	
Tallow 6	

Source: PDM.

20

2.71. PDM sometimes agrees prices with abattoirs in the form of a 'package deal'. They vary depending on the individual circumstances. In a small proportion of cases, at the request of the supplier, a lower charge for offal may, for example, be offset by a lower price for fat. In particular, it may be more convenient to avoid the combination of charges for some materials and prices for others, and to agree that there should be zero charges for the lower-grade material accompanied by lower prices for the higher grades. PDM told us that such package deals were negotiated with around 2 per cent of its suppliers. More frequently PDM negotiated the purchase of a 'basket' of materials from the same source; this was the case with approximately 30 per cent of its suppliers. Smaller renderers told us that they negotiated few package deals.

2.72. Prices are also affected by the degree to which there is competition for the supplies of a particular abattoir. Competition is mainly focused on the large abattoirs as they entail lower transport costs as well as having a greater importance in supplying throughput for fixed processing capacity. The loss of a major supplier may have serious financial and commercial implications for a renderer, and we were told that the closure or loss of a major abattoir could cause a renderer to bid aggressively for alternative sources of raw materials.

2.73. One example of intense competition arising in such circumstances, generally referred to as a 'price war', lasted for a particularly protracted period from March to October 1992. Many abattoirs in central England and East Anglia were involved and there were also some effects in other regions. These events were triggered by the closure of two abattoirs that had been long-standing suppliers to Gilberts. For several months abattoirs in the areas affected were able to obtain significantly higher prices from renderers. As this was also the season when the volume of materials was low, renderers were under considerable pressure to offer high prices in order to obtain sufficient supplies to cover their fixed costs. In October 1992, with the seasonal increase in the availability of supplies, Gilberts and PDM, the protagonists in the price war, became less aggressive and the war came to an end. PDM's role is discussed further in paragraphs 6.14 and 6.15 and Appendix 6.2 provides a number of examples of much higher prices being offered by renderers during this price war.

The output of the rendering industry

2.74. The principal end products of the rendering process and their main uses are set out in Table 2.7.

TABLE 2.7 **End products of the rendering process and their uses**

End products	Uses
Tallow:	
Grade 1	Edible fats after further refining
Grade 2	Pet food ingredient
	Toilet soap making
Grade 4	Soap making
	Industrial uses
	Animal feed additive
Grade 6	Fatty chemicals
Meat-and-bone meal	Ingredient in compound animal feedstuffs and pet foods

Source: MMC.

There is also the semi-finished product greaves (see paragraph 2.49). Greaves are usually reprocessed by other renderers or by animal feed producers.

2.75. UKRA estimated that the volume of output of the UK rendering industry in 1992 was 195,000 tonnes of tallow (valued at £36 million) and 390,000 tonnes of meat-and-bone meal (valued at £53 million). Over the last ten years the annual production of tallow has varied between 189,000 and 205,000 tonnes, and that of meat-and-bone meal between 380,000 and 411,000 tonnes. Marketing arrangements for end products vary between companies and products. Renderers sell to final users both direct and through intermediaries who are known as brokers.

2.76. Despite their name, brokers act as independent buyers of the finished products. They enable renderers to make sales without a regular or long-term involvement in the market.

2.77. PDM as the major producer is active in the market for tallow and meat-and-bone meal. It employs Hi-Cal Proteins Ltd (Hi-Cal), a Jersey-based broker, for the sale of almost all of its meat-and-bone meal (representing over 40 per cent of PDM's total sales) to the UK animal feed compounding industry. This company acts as principal, and also provides a sales force through its UK agent, Thomas Mawer Ltd, in return for a fee of £3 per tonne sold, equivalent to about 2.2 per cent of product value sold through them. In addition PDM uses as brokers for some of its tallow the two largest UK tallow trading companies, which also act as principals and to which PDM pays £2 to £4 per tonne; and for some of its poultry-meat meal, a division of one of these two companies, at a fee of £3 per tonne. On the Continent PDM occasionally employs two continental-based brokers which act as agents between it and some export buyers in return for a 1 to 2 per cent commission.

2.78. PDM told us that in the domestic market usually between one-third and two-thirds of its contracts were arranged one month to six weeks forward; in the export markets all of its contracts were negotiated forward by three months but around 90 per cent of tallow was sold at a maximum of one month forward.

Prices of rendered products

2.79. Figure 2.4 shows for the period 1975 to 1992 the end-product prices received by PDM compared with its average raw material prices or charges. Tables 2.8 and 2.9 show the monthly ex-works prices in 1992 of the end products of PDM and Forrest.

TABLE 2.8 **1992 outputs: ex-works prices paid to PDM**

£ per tonne

	Blood meal	Meat-and-bone meal	Edible fats	Tallow 1 & 2	Tallow 6	Poultry meal	Poultry fat	Feather meal
Jan	285	125	350	210	155	194	167	152
Feb	268	125	350	212	155	200	169	157
Mar	288	125	370	211	154	183	166	144
Apr	274	131	370	202	160	205	169	138
May	269	137	370	195	162	190	168	134
Jun	274	143	370	186	163	189	170	130
Jul	270	142	370	196	155	188	170	131
Aug	262	144	370	207	155	187	169	133
Sep	261	143	370	212	156	191	173	137
Oct	259	137	370	226	165	191	174	143
Nov	270	138	370	234	179	204	175	148
Dec	268	140	370	250	189	191	183	145
Average	271	136	367	212	162	193	171	141

Source: PDM.

Note: Average prices are arithmetical monthly averages and are not weighted for tonnages sold.

TABLE 2.9 **1992 outputs: ex-works prices paid to Forrest**

£ per tonne

	Meat-and-bone meal	Tallow 1 & 2	Tallow 6
Jan	105	207	147
Feb	100	205	148
Mar	118	206	148
Apr	125	201	151
May	134	191	153
Jun	136	181	147
Jul	140	188	145
Aug	140	191	147
Sep	136	204	147
Oct	135	219	157
Nov	133	224	166
Dec	134	237	168
Average	128	204	152

Source: Forrest.

2.80. Prices of tallows depend on the prices of other oils (for example, soya bean oil or palm oil). If tallow prices rose substantially there would (other things being equal) be substitution for them by those other oils. In the last 20 years the prices of the main grades of tallow have maintained a stable relationship with the prices of other oils, as shown in Figure 2.5. Thus the tallow prices tend to reflect both increases and decreases in international edible oil prices. In the short term, where substitution is less easy, tallow prices can deviate from the long-term relationship with other international oil prices and reflect the balance of supply and demand for tallow itself, eg through a reduction in demand by UK soap manufacturers.

2.81. The price of meat-and-bone meal also tends to follow the prices of substitute products. Meat-and-bone meal is essentially a source of protein for animal feed, and its price reflects the cost of substitute proteins. The closest substitute for meat-and-bone meal is soya bean meal, the price of which is similar as it provides a comparable amount of protein. Figure 2.6 shows the path of meat-and-bone meal prices and soya bean meal prices over the period 1975 to 1992. Again there may be short-term fluctuations in the price of meat-and-bone meal as a result of changes in the balance of supply and demand. One cause of short-term fluctuations is the seasonal variation in animal slaughtering.

Barriers to entry into the rendering industry

2.82. In our questionnaire to renderers both in England and Wales and in Scotland we asked what they saw as the main barriers to entry into the industry.

2.83. There was little agreement between renderers as to the cost of becoming established in the industry, with estimates ranging from £0.5 million to £12 million for the minimum investment required. These estimates to a large extent reflected the different sizes of plant that the renderers operated, and among the very small renderers it reflected a lack of information about larger-scale production. If these small renderers were excluded, the range of estimates would be from £2.5 million to £10 million. PDM considered that the minimum would be around £10 million, but Forrest thought that it would be only half this sum if the entrant wished to operate a continuous processing line. Clearly the amount required would depend on the scale and type of operation envisaged and hence the capital equipment to be purchased. Peninsular, which has recent experience of re-equipping a plant with the latest technology, thought that the minimum cost would be £2.5 million to £3 million. As Table 2.4 shows, Peninsular processes in excess of 40,000 tonnes a year.

2.84. The high initial capital costs of entry were a factor mentioned by several renderers. PDM attributed the high initial capital costs in part to the extensive environmental control equipment required as part of any new processing plant. The difficulty of raising sufficient capital to set up in business was mentioned by some smaller renderers.

2.85. The problems of acquiring waste material were generally seen as a serious problem for a new entrant. As the supply of animal waste is finite, a new entrant could only gain raw materials at the expense of an existing renderer. PDM referred to the credibility problem for a new entrant since he would have no past record to reassure abattoirs of his ability to provide a high and reliable level of service.

2.86. PDM, Forrest and other renderers told us that it was difficult for a new entrant to obtain a site where suitable planning permission could be obtained of a similar size to theirs. Rendering plants, classed as an offensive trade, have always been unpopular for environmental reasons, and the increasingly stringent degree of environmental regulation, including the difficulties of complying with the EPA, has made it more difficult to find a site for which a licence could be obtained. Even gaining permission to make improvements to an existing site has approval problems.

2.87. Some knowledge of the industry was also seen by many renderers as vital. One told us that a new entrant would need to have experience in rendering, purchasing raw materials, processing material and marketing end products. Forrest referred to the need to obtain both experienced management and skilled employees.

FIGURE 2.5

Average prices of oils and tallows, 1975 to 1992

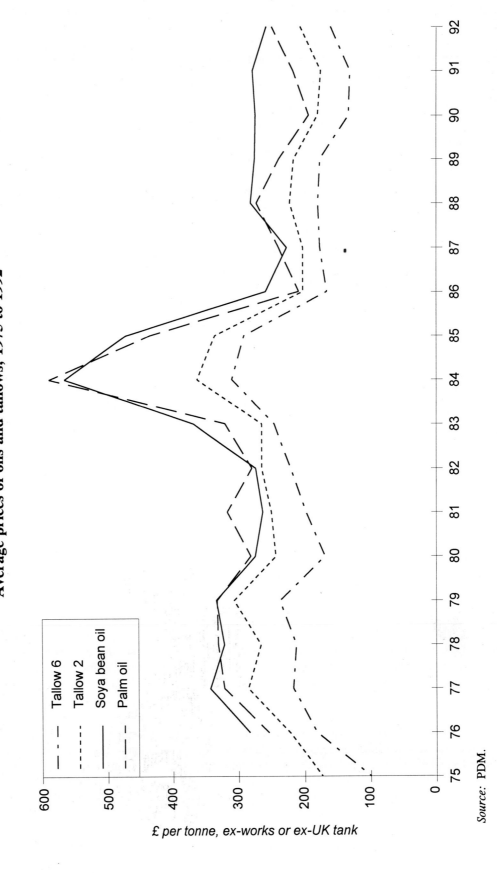

£ per tonne, ex-works or ex-UK tank

Tallow 6
Tallow 2
Soya bean oil
Palm oil

Source: PDM.

24

FIGURE 2.6

Average prices of soya bean meal and of meat-and-bone meal, 1975 to 1992

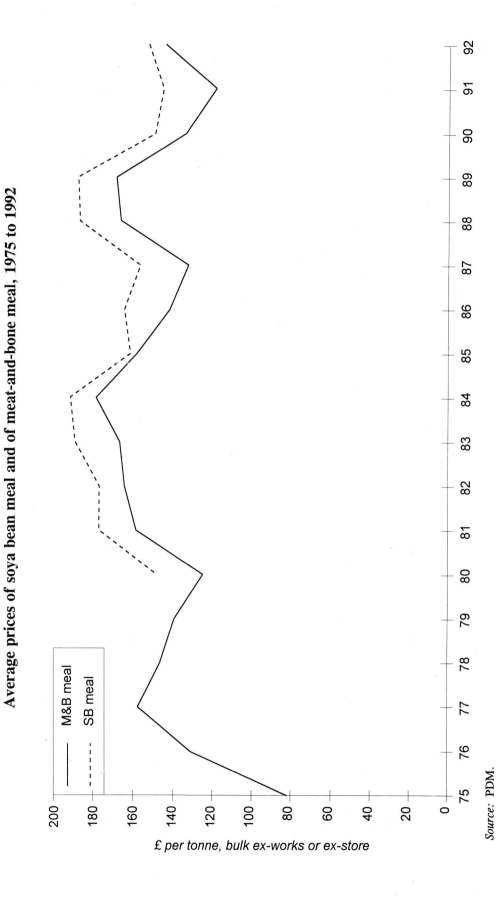

£ per tonne, bulk ex-works or ex-store

Source: PDM.

25

2.88. Another factor which was seen as an entry barrier was the need for alternative arrangements for the processing of raw material in the event of a major plant breakdown.

2.89. In our questionnaire to abattoirs we asked them whether they had considered undertaking their own rendering or forming a co-operative with other abattoirs to do so. Although a few had looked at the possibility, they had rejected it either because they lacked the expertise, or because they found it difficult to co-operate with competing abattoirs, or because they considered the processing of waste materials as marginal to their main business. Of more importance than all these factors at present was the low rate of profitability of the abattoir sector: even if they wished to become vertically integrated, financial resources were unavailable for investing in rendering capacity.

2.90. A further significant barrier to entry appears to be the reputation both of PDM and of Forrest. Their quality of service is perceived to be high and they have a reputation for retaliation when their interests are challenged by other renderers. This will be a disincentive to potential entrants.

2.91. The existing capacity of the rendering industry is a further deterrent. It is generally thought that there is surplus capacity within the industry and that even if there were further closures, the major operators would still have sufficient capacity to service the abattoirs. Other renderers are aware that PDM's plant at Market Harborough has been moth-balled, and that if needed it could quickly be brought into operation.

2.92. Despite the barriers we have just described we have been informed that there is a possible large-scale new entrant, which is considering establishing an integrated abattoir and rendering plant on the site of a former abattoir, either in Anglesey or in southern Scotland. In addition, European Organic Processing Ltd is seeking planning permission for a site to open a combined maggot breeding, rendering and organic waste disposal plant, and with the support of the Ministry of Agriculture, Fisheries and Food (MAFF) has applied for a grant from the EC. Consideration is also being given, we have been told, to the possibility of a co-operative venture by abattoirs in Scotland, supported by a regional council, should any of the existing renderers close.

3 The financial results of PDM, Forrest and other renderers

Scope of the chapter

3.1. In this chapter we discuss:

(a) measuring the financial results of the renderers—paragraphs 3.3 to 3.5;

(b) the financial results of PDM—paragraphs 3.6 to 3.30;

(c) the financial results of Forrest—paragraphs 3.31 to 3.45;

(d) the financial results of other renderers compared with PDM and Forrest—paragraphs 3.46 to 3.62; and

(e) the return on capital employed (ROCE) of PDM, Forrest and other renderers compared with those of food manufacturers and meat processors—paragraphs 3.63 to 3.66.

3.2. The information in this chapter was derived from published accounts, completed questionnaires, discussions with the companies and written submissions.

Measuring the financial results of the renderers

3.3. PDM, Forrest and most other renderers measure revenues and operating costs in £ per tonne of raw materials processed. They also use this measure for setting their profit targets. We have found that it is particularly useful for comparing the financial results of renderers of differing sizes. We have therefore used it to evaluate the revenues and costs of PDM and Forrest, as well as of a weighted average of the smaller renderers, although we are aware of its limitations when comparing renderers with differing mixes of raw materials. Results on this basis appear in tables throughout this chapter.

3.4. During the last five years most of the renderers have ceased to make payments to abattoirs for offal and have levied charges, particularly for BSE offal. These offal removal charges, as well as any sales of unprocessed raw materials, are included in turnover in their statutory accounts. For the purposes of our analysis of financial results, we have treated offal collection charges and sales of raw materials as deductions from the costs of raw materials, and have used end-product sales rather than turnover to measure the outputs of the renderers.

3.5. The renderers have different accounting year-end dates. Forrest's financial year ends on 31 December and that of PDM, as for many of the smaller renderers, on 31 March. In those tables where we show the results of several companies together, we have taken individual company information for the year-end nearest to 31 December (eg a company year ending on 31 March 1993 is shown as 1992).

PDM

3.6. The following companies and their subsidiaries comprise the whole of the PDM enterprise:

236197 C

(a) Prosper De Mulder Limited;

(b) Prosper De Mulder Transport;

(c) Prosper De Mulder Services;

(d) Frazer (Butchers) Limited;

(e) Francis Investments Limited; and

(f) Oracle Motors Limited.

A full list of the PDM companies and their subsidiaries is included at Appendix 3.1.

Statutory and management accounts

3.7. The statutory accounts of PDM's principal operating companies are prepared from financial records at the various plants. These records are subject to numerous adjustments before the preparation of the statutory accounts of each PDM company and the production of the audited consolidated accounts for the principal holding company, Prosper De Mulder Ltd, a process which necessarily lasts for at least six months.

3.8. Each month PDM prepares management accounts covering revenues and costs from the same financial records. By the time of the completion of the audit, PDM does not find it worthwhile formally to adjust its management accounts for the previous financial year so that they agree to the statutory accounts. The detailed information relating to costs and revenues supplied to us by PDM has been taken from its management accounts. Although there are unreconciled differences between these management accounts and the pro-forma consolidation of the statutory accounts, as shown in Table 3.7, we are satisfied that these differences are not in aggregate material for the purposes of our inquiry.

3.9. All the PDM companies and their subsidiaries file accounts with the Registrar of Companies, except for Prosper De Mulder Transport and Prosper De Mulder Services. These two companies were first used by PDM in 1985/86 to undertake transport and management services for other PDM companies and, as unlimited companies, are not required to file accounts. Although the PDM group is managed as a single entity, it has no legal obligation to prepare or file consolidated accounts for the combined enterprise, so that the financial position of PDM and the results of its operations cannot be obtained from publicly available sources.

3.10. We therefore asked PDM to supply us with a consolidated balance sheet and profit and loss account for the whole enterprise for the year ended 31 March 1992, together with most of the notes that would be required to meet the reporting requirements of the Companies Acts for a single parent company and its subsidiaries. The profit and loss account, balance sheet and the some of the accompanying notes that would be required are included at Appendix 3.2.

3.11. In Table 3.1 we set out summary financial information for each of the six companies which, with their subsidiaries, form the PDM enterprise. We have totalled the information for the four companies which do file accounts to give a disclosed total, and we have compared this disclosed total with the consolidated information from Appendix 3.2.

TABLE 3.1 **Summary financial information for PDM component companies: year ended 31 March 1992**

						£'000			per cent
	Turnover	Operating profit	Capital & reserves	Net borrowing	Trading assets		Operating margin	Debt: equity	Return on assets
Prosper De Mulder Ltd	97,344	4,359	12,177	12,270	24,447		4.5	100.8	17.8
Frazer (Butchers) Ltd	21,362	1,707	4,036	347	4,383		8.0	8.6	38.9
Francis Investments Ltd	24	0	21	153	174		0.0	728.6	0.0
Oracle Motors Ltd	8	6	143	(4)	139		75.0	-2.8	4.3
Disclosed	118,738	6,072	16,377	12,766	29,143		5.1	78.0	20.8
Prosper De Mulder Transport	11,098	1,147	4,896	0	4,896		10.3	0.0	23.4
Prosper De Mulder Services	681	63	365	0	365		9.3	0.0	17.3
	130,517	7,282	21,638	12,766	34,404		5.6	59.0	21.2
Eliminations	(31,390)	-	-	(6,489)	(6,489)				
Consolidated	99,127	7,282	21,638	6,277	27,915		7.3	29.0	26.1
Disclosed as a % of consolidated	119.8	83.4	75.7	203.4	104.4				

Source: MMC using audited accounts.

Note: Operating margin is operating profit as a percentage of turnover; debt:equity ratio is net borrowing as a percentage of capital and reserves; return on assets is operating profit as a percentage of trading assets.

The table shows how the retention of profits in the unlimited companies and the existence of loans between the various companies (which are not described in the accounts of the individual companies as being due to or from associates) give an incomplete picture of PDM's overall profitability and of its financial position to any person who has to rely on publicly available sources. It is evident from the table that anyone working from the available published accounts of the PDM companies would calculate overall margins of 5.1 per cent and a debt:equity ratio of 78.0 per cent. But the consolidated figures show margins of 7.3 per cent and a debt:equity ratio of 29.0 per cent. Anyone reading the accounts of Prosper De Mulder Ltd, not knowing that this company was part of a larger enterprise, might assume that the operating margin was only 4.5 per cent and the debt:equity ratio was 100.8 per cent. Indeed, we received a letter from one party expressing concern at PDM's low margins and high unsecured borrowings.

3.12. In addition to the consolidated figures for 1992, we also asked PDM to provide us with proforma consolidated accounts for each of the four years to 31 March 1991, with supporting cost information for all five years. This proved to be a lengthy task requiring for a time a substantial part of PDM's accounting resources, and PDM supplied us with the information requested for three years only. However, it did provide us with an estimate of profit before interest and tax (PBIT) and average capital employed, split between rendering and other businesses, for 1988 and 1989. Summarized financial results of the PDM enterprise for each of the five years ended 31 March 1992, extracted from this information, are set out in Table 3.2.

TABLE 3.2 **PDM: summary of consolidated financial results**

£'000

Year to 31 March

	1988	1989	1990	1991	1992
End-product sales:					
Rendering			64,713	53,733	63,599
Other businesses			15,938	16,258	22,686
			80,651	69,991	86,285
PBIT:					
Rendering	3,058	4,308	2,455	3,753	6,375
Other businesses	139	382	(274)	42	944
	3,197	4,690	2,181	3,795	7,319
Average capital employed:					
Rendering	19,064	20,299	20,696	21,123	21,062
Other businesses	4,100	4,500	5,687	6,302	6,668
	23,164	24,799	26,383	27,425	27,730
Employee numbers:					
Rendering			644	649	673
Other businesses			263	265	358
			907	914	1,031
					per cent
ROCE:					
Rendering	16.0	21.2	11.9	17.8	30.3
Other businesses	3.4	8.5	(4.8)	0.7	14.2
	13.8	18.9	8.3	13.8	26.4

Source: PDM.

Note: Rendering results include those from edible fats and gut-room contracts. Other businesses are mostly pet food materials and packaged pet food products.

Financial results of the rendering business

3.13. PDM's financial results for its rendering and associated businesses for the three financial years for which it was able to provide us with detailed information are set out in Table 3.3. Although PDM told us that it regarded its edible fat business as outside the scope of our inquiry, it has included the results from that business with those of its rendering operations. We do not believe that this has a material effect on the reported results of the rendering business. The results of the rendering business also include the processing of blood and feathers and the operation of gut-rooms.

TABLE 3.3 **PDM: financial results of rendering and associated businesses**

£'000

Year to 31 March

	1990	1991	1992
End-product sales	64,713	53,733	63,599
Cost of raw materials	18,778	24	3,719
Transport in	14,262	15,687	16,444
Transport out	1,827	2,661	3,916
Processing	20,998	24,646	26,658
Administration	6,104	6,810	7,329
Other operating costs	289	152	(842)
	43,480	49,956	53,505
PBIT	2,455	3,753	6,375
Tangible fixed assets	16,114	15,855	16,657
Net current assets	4,582	5,268	4,405
Average capital employed	20,696	21,123	21,062
			per cent
ROCE	11.9	17.8	30.3

Source: MMC using PDM data.

3.14. Equivalent information in terms of £ per tonne processed is set out in Table 3.4.

TABLE 3.4 **PDM: financial results of rendering and associated businesses per tonne processed**

£

	Year to 31 March		
	1990	*1991*	*1992*
End-product sales	78.55	63.80	72.26
Cost of raw materials	22.79	0.03	4.23
Transport in	17.31	18.62	18.68
Transport out	2.22	3.16	4.45
Processing	25.49	29.26	30.29
Administration	7.41	8.09	8.33
Other operating costs	0.35	0.18	(0.96)
	52.78	59.31	60.79
PBIT	2.98	4.46	7.24
Tangible fixed assets	19.56	18.83	18.92
Net current assets	5.56	6.25	5.01
Average capital employed	25.12	25.08	23.93
			'000
Tonnes processed	824	842	880

Source: MMC using PDM data.

End-product sales

3.15. An analysis of end-product sales and volumes processed for the three years to 31 March 1992 is set out in Table 3.5. From the table it can be seen that the tonnages of red meat materials processed by PDM in 1991/92 had grown by about 6 per cent compared with 1989/90, but for poultry material the increase was 23 per cent. End-product sales revenues have not grown in line with the tonnage of materials processed, because the selling prices of red-meat products declined in 1990/91 and did not fully recover in the following year.

TABLE 3.5 **PDM: end-product sales from rendering and volumes processed, 1990 to 1992**

	Year to 31 March			Average
	1990	*1991*	*1992*	*1990–92*
End-product sales (£'000)				
All products	64,713	53,733	63,599	60,682
Red meat	54,404	42,306	49,531	48,747
Poultry	9,961	10,684	13,548	11,398
Blood	348	743	520	537
Tonnes processed ('000)				
All products	824	842	880	849
Red meat	554	577	590	574
Poultry	200	206	246	217
Blood	70	59	44	57
Sales per tonne processed (£)				
All products	78.55	63.80	72.26	71.50
Red meat	98.20	73.32	83.95	84.92
Poultry	49.77	51.83	55.06	52.44
Blood	4.97	12.60	11.82	9.42

Source: MMC using PDM data.

PDM told us that for the year to 31 March 1993 it processed 620,535 tonnes of red meat waste (including blood) and 271,654 tonnes of poultry waste, a total of 892,189 tonnes.

Transport costs

3.16. Compared with other renderers, PDM's vehicles travel long distances to collect materials. The average length of journeys is increased by PDM's practice of having each plant specialize in processing different types of material. Some of the larger abattoirs will have separate collections by vehicles from up to three different PDM plants.

3.17. PDM analyzed its transport operations for us for September 1992, and found that about 35 per cent of its materials had been purchased by one plant, but were processed at another and usually more distant plant. The proportion of raw materials that was double-handled, in that the materials were unloaded from one lorry and then loaded onto another one, was estimated by PDM at less than 10 per cent. Many of the lorries have complicated rounds requiring collections from several abattoirs and deliveries to different plants before returning to their home plant. Organizing these rounds requires considerable efforts by the management of the individual plants and by PDM's head office.

3.18. PDM differs from all other renderers in its use of owner-drivers to collect waste. These are independent subcontractors who own the cab units. (PDM provides lease or hire purchase finance to the owner-driver for the purchase of his first cab unit.) The trailers are provided by PDM which arranges the drivers' rounds. Drivers at some plants receive a fixed payment per mile; at other plants they receive a payment based on standing charges, mileage and tonnage carried. PDM believes that the introduction of the owner-driver system led to a significant improvement in the efficiency of its transport operation. At the end of March 1993 PDM was using 83 owner-drivers, mostly for bulk collections from abattoirs and for the delivery of end products.

3.19. At the same time PDM had 116 employed drivers. PDM mostly uses them for its collection rounds covering butchers' shops, small abattoirs and boning-out plants. PDM collects butchers' waste from almost 6,000 shops, which represent nearly 80 per cent of PDM's suppliers, but supply only 7 to 8 per cent of its materials. It also told us that it had carried out a study of its collection costs for February 1993 and the average cost of collecting all raw material was £14.79 per tonne. The shop lorries collected 9,000 tonnes, about half of which came from butchers' shops and the rest from small abattoirs and boning-out plants. The average cost of collection by the shop lorries was £35.60 per tonne, compared with £14.79 per tonne for the owner-drivers and other forms of transport (mostly used for the larger abattoirs). The cheapest round by the shop lorries cost £13.82 per tonne and the most expensive £69.83.

3.20. We also asked PDM about the administration costs for butchers' shops. PDM said that the round sheets from the drivers were fed into the computer, and charges and payments were calculated as for any other supplier. It had not calculated the costs of having so many active accounts. However, it believed that overall the butchers' collections were profitable. There had been times when end-product prices were low and the small collections would have lost money, but PDM told us that it had taken the view consistently over the years that it should take the rough with the smooth and provide a service.

3.21. PDM also differs from other renderers by incurring a significant expense for outward transport. It has its own fleet of tankers for delivering tallow. PDM pointed out to us that it strictly segregated its transport between that engaged in raw material collection and that engaged in delivery of end products, to avoid cross-infection. PDM's growing export business had led to an increase in shipping charges.

Processing costs

3.22. Details of the capacity of the rendering machinery at each of PDM's seven plants currently operating are set out in Table 4.2 at paragraph 4.22. In the year to 31 March 1992 PDM's 880,000 tonnes processed represented about 85 per cent utilization of capacity.

3.23. PDM's processing lines have an average age of more than ten years, the newest dating from 1988. Plant and machinery is depreciated at 15 per cent per annum using the reducing balance method. The depreciation charge of assets related to processing was £1.9 million.

3.24. Expenditure on maintenance, at £7.4 million in 1991/92, far exceeds PDM's depreciation costs. PDM told us that maintenance included an element of upgrading and improvement. It is trying to reduce energy costs, and energy costs per tonne processed have indeed been reduced from £7.70 to £7.43 in the last two years. Spending on odour and effluent control was £2.6 million in 1991/92 and, in terms of £ per tonne of materials processed, this was more than any of the other renderers.

TABLE 3.6 **PDM rendering business: processing costs per tonne**

			£
		Year to 31 March	
	1990	1991	1992
Labour	5.76	5.94	6.30
Energy	7.70	7.69	7.43
Plant maintenance	6.00	8.05	8.44
Odour and effluent control	2.83	2.75	2.95
Depreciation	2.21	2.17	2.15
Other costs	1.00	2.66	3.01
	25.49	29.26	30.29

Source: MMC using PDM data.

Profits by business segment

3.25. The consolidated PBIT of all PDM's businesses has been shown in Table 3.2. In its management accounts PDM allocates a fixed charge based on tonnage processed to each of its activities to cover central overheads and interest. The management accounts therefore show the profit after interest for each business segment. Table 3.7 shows the PBIT for all PDM's businesses, reconciled to the profit after interest of each business segment.

TABLE 3.7 **PDM: profit after interest by business segment**

			£'000
		Year to 31 March	
	1990	1991	1992
PBIT	2,181	3,795	7,319
Interest payable	(1,077)	(1,065)	(779)
Exceptional repairs	-	700	-
Differences*	393	257	(987)
Profit after interest	1,497	3,687	5,553
Red meat waste rendering	677	2,682	2,725
Poultry waste rendering	1,191	686	1,537
Dripping and fat	242	414	264
Blood	(399)	(179)	210
Gut-rooms	132	103	163
Rendering businesses	1,843	3,706	4,899
Other businesses	(346)	(19)	654
	1,497	3,687	5,553

Source: MMC using PDM data.

*Differences are those arising between the statutory and management accounts referred to in paragraph 3.8. The differences relating to the rendering and associated businesses are shown separately in Tables 3.3 and 3.4 as 'other operating costs'.

3.26. The three-year period to 31 March 1992 shows a recovery in the profit after interest of red meat waste rendering from the effects of BSE, and an improved performance from blood and from the pet food businesses. The exceptional repairs in 1991 were the replacement of rotors in three of the large cookers, which have been treated as exceptional expenses for management accounting purposes only. We received management accounts and other information from PDM for 1992/93. They showed a sharp fall in profits from red meat waste rendering compared with the previous year, reflecting the effects of the price war. Since there were few changes in PDM's operations and assets, there would have been a similar fall in ROCE.

Gut-room operations

3.27. Under the terms of its 1986 undertaking 1.(iv)(c) (see Appendix 1.2), PDM is required to submit to the DGFT an audited annual statement of the profit and loss of its gut-room business together with reconcilable management accounts of each gut-room contract separately. PDM has not submitted management accounts for each gut-room, but has instead supplied to the DGFT a list showing the profit or loss of each gut-room together with a summary profit and loss account for its gut-room operations as a whole. These summary profit and loss accounts for the five years to 31 March 1992 are set out in Table 3.8.

TABLE 3.8 **PDM: gut-room profit and loss**

			Year to 31 March		£'000
	1988	1989	1990	1991	1992
Sales*	987	1,427	1,282	1,161	1,300
Less: Offal collection charges	-	-	-	326	443
Net sales	987	1,427	1,281	835	857
Purchases	380	576	448	50	4
Wages and National Insurance	323	418	514	437	428
Haulage	102	106	123	157	196
Rent	1	2	2	0	1
Repairs and other expenses	10	24	37	30	38
Administration charges	31	39	44	38	36
	847	1,165	1,168	712	703
Profit	140	262	113	123	154

Source: PDM.

*Sales include sales of rendering materials to PDM, sales of pet food materials to PDM and third parties and kill charges payable by abattoirs.

3.28. Many of the items in the above profit and loss account involve transactions with other parts of PDM's business. These inter-company transactions include all the sales of rendering materials, some of the sales of pet food materials, all of the offal collection charges, most of the haulage and all the administration charges. Inter-company transactions have not been shown separately from transactions with third parties in PDM's returns to the DGFT.

3.29. We describe PDM's administration charges to its gut-room operation and its transfer prices between its gut-room operation and its rendering business at paragraph 6.16, where we deal with a complaint from Imperial Meat Company Ltd (IMC).

3.30. PDM pointed out to us that gut-room contracting formed a relatively insignificant part of its total activities and that the profits in Table 3.8 were only a small proportion of its overall profit. However, PDM derives further profits from rendering the waste and processing the pet food materials from its gut-rooms, which are not reflected in its gut-room accounts.

Forrest

Financial results

3.31. Forrest supplied us with financial information for each of the five years to 31 December 1992, based on the statutory accounts of William Forrest & Son (Paisley) Ltd, and excluding inter-company transactions and balance sheet items which were not related to the rendering operation. The financial results of Forrest's rendering operation are summarized in Table 3.9. Forrest proposed an alternative calculation of ROCE to that shown in the table, which is considered in paragraph 3.42.

TABLE 3.9 **Forrest: summary of financial results**

£'000

| | | Year to 31 December | | | |
	1988	1989	1990	1991	1992
End-product sales	9,652	8,764	7,926	7,317	8,414
Cost of raw materials	4,626	3,680	1,609	561	2,442
Transport in	1,181	1,257	1,758	1,958	1,915
Processing	2,353	2,726	3,195	3,289	2,989
Other operating costs	434	402	446	520	562
	3,968	4,385	5,399	5,767	5,466
PBIT	1,058	699	918	989	506
Tangible fixed assets	2,335	1,922	2,046	1,898	1,830
Less: Investment grants	461	404	358	320	261
	1,874	1,518	1,688	1,578	1,569
Net current assets	371	391	406	373	300
Average capital employed	2,245	1,909	2,094	1,951	1,869

per cent

ROCE	47.1	36.6	43.8	50.7	27.1

Source: Forrest.

3.32. Equivalent information in terms of £ per tonne processed is set out in Table 3.10.

TABLE 3.10 **Forrest: summary of financial results per tonne processed**

£

| | | Year to 31 December | | | |
	1988	1989	1990	1991	1992
End-product sales	104.27	101.61	79.18	69.92	83.93
Cost of raw materials	49.98	42.66	16.07	5.37	24.35
Transport in	12.76	14.57	17.56	18.70	19.11
Processing	25.41	31.61	31.92	31.43	29.81
Other operating costs	4.69	4.67	4.46	4.97	5.61
	42.86	50.85	53.94	55.10	54.53
PBIT	11.43	8.10	9.17	9.45	5.05
Tangible fixed assets	25.22	22.28	20.44	18.13	18.26
Less: Investment grants	4.98	4.68	3.58	3.06	2.61
	20.24	17.60	16.86	15.07	15.65
Net current assets	4.01	4.54	4.05	3.57	2.99
Average capital employed	24.25	22.14	20.91	18.64	18.64
Tonnes processed	92,572	86,259	100,104	104,660	100,246

Source: MMC using Forrest data.

Cost of raw materials

3.33.   Forrest uses a much higher proportion of greaves than most other renderers. By processing bought-in greaves when the kill is at its seasonal low, Forrest is able to use its plant nearer to capacity. Greaves are more expensive than other materials but yield on average 70 per cent meal and 26 per cent grade 6 tallow. In Table 3.11 we show the value and weight of greaves and of other raw materials acquired by Forrest for rendering.

TABLE 3.11   **Forrest: value and weight of raw material purchases**

£

Year to 31 December

	1988	1989	1990	1991	1992
£'000					
Cost of materials	4,626	3,680	1,609	561	2,442
Less: Greaves	2,577	1,782	1,187	1,052	1,290
Cost of other materials	2,049	1,898	422	(491)	1,152
Tonnes					
Materials processed	92,572	86,259	100,104	104,660	100,246
Less: Greaves	18,928	14,099	16,201	12,479	11,507
Materials collected	73,644	72,160	83,903	92,181	88,739
£ per tonne					
Greaves	136.18	126.39	73.29	84.30	112.11
Other materials	27.82	26.30	5.02	(5.32)	12.98

Source: MMC using Forrest data.

Forrest attributed the decline in prices paid to abattoirs and other suppliers in 1990 and 1991 to the effects of BSE, and the subsequent increase in 1992 to the effects of the price war in England (because of the shortage of raw materials available for processing) on the Scottish market.

Transport costs

3.34. Transport costs are more appropriately measured in terms of tonnes collected rather than tonnes processed. In Table 3.12 the tonnages of greaves, which are usually delivered by the supplier, have been deducted from tonnes processed to give tonnes collected.

TABLE 3.12   **Forrest: transport costs per tonne collected**

Year to 31 December

	1988	1989	1990	1991	1992
Transport costs (£'000)	1,181	1,257	1,758	1,958	1,915
Tonnes collected	73,644	72,160	83,903	92,181	88,739
Cost per tonne (£)	16.04	17.42	20.95	21.24	21.58

Source: MMC using Forrest data.

Forrest has to collect material over longer distances than renderers in England. Forrest told us that the acquisition of Elgin Animal By-Products Ltd in 1990 brought new sources of materials in north-east Scotland, which was the main cause for the increase in transport costs in that year. Because of the long distance, some materials from small collections were consolidated at depots in Elgin and Lochgelly for onward shipment to Newarthill. Unlike PDM, Forrest only employs its own drivers for collections from abattoirs. Due to its production of edible tallow, fat and bone have to be collected separately from offal which, as for some of the other renderers, increases the cost of transport.

3.35.   Forrest collects waste from about 600 butchers' shops. Accounting costs are reduced by neither charging nor paying for butchers' waste. Forrest told us that the direct cost of transport resulting from its shop collections amounted to an additional £15 per tonne. It also drew our attention to a gradual shift in the intake of raw materials from butchers' shops to larger establishments, which had enabled it to reduce its transport fleet and contain costs. Forrest estimated that in 1992 it made a profit of about £14 per tonne on the materials from its butchers' collections in spite of the higher transport costs.

Processing costs

3.36. Forrest's processing capacity is almost 4,300 tonnes per week (224,000 tonnes for a full year), which is significantly higher than the total of all animal waste arising in Scotland. In 1992 Forrest processed 100,246 tonnes of raw materials and greaves, operating at less than 45 per cent of capacity.

3.37. In 1990 Forrest installed a third cooker, although tonnage was not increasing. Forrest told us that this additional machine was installed to provide sufficient capacity to meet peak requirements, to provide a reserve in case of breakdown and to enable BSE material to be processed separately. In 1991 the new cooker was upgraded with a consequent reduction in energy costs. In 1992 a new milling plant was installed to replace the solvent extraction plant and a milling plant which had both been in use since 1978. Forrest told us that this investment would lead to reductions in processing costs, particularly further savings in energy costs in addition to those shown in Table 3.13.

3.38. Forrest's processing costs per tonne of material processed are set out in Table 3.13. Forrest told us that its processing costs were higher than they might have been because of the use of its solvent extraction plant until the end of 1992, and because of its production of edible tallow. Forrest, unlike most of the English renderers, has received investment grants on some of its capital expenditure. These grants, which are also included in Table 3.13, are amortized at the same rate as the related assets are depreciated.

TABLE 3.13 **Forrest: processing costs per tonne**

£

Year to 31 December

	1988	*1989*	*1990*	*1991*	*1992*
Labour	4.56	5.33	5.02	4.97	5.10
Energy	7.88	10.48	10.49	8.71	8.30
Plant maintenance	7.97	9.43	8.85	8.82	8.59
Odour and effluent control	0.02	0.00	0.71	2.01	1.74
Depreciation	3.10	3.29	2.86	2.72	2.26
Investment grants	(0.70)	(0.57)	(0.41)	(0.35)	(0.80)
Other costs	2.59	3.64	4.40	4.54	4.62
	25.41	31.60	31.92	31.43	29.81

Source: MMC using Forrest data.

3.39. Forrest explained to us that although its use of the only remaining solvent extraction plant in Great Britain led to higher processing costs, this was justified by the resulting higher end-product sales value. Solvent extraction enabled Forrest to obtain a higher yield of tallow, which more than compensated for the fact that the meat-and-bone meal had a lower oil content and so attracted a lower price. An increase in the demand for higher oil animal feed was one of the reasons given by Forrest for its decision to close the solvent extraction plant.

Operating cash flow, profitability and ROCE

3.40. Forrest's financial results and capital employed in terms of £ per tonne processed are set out in Table 3.10. Forrest's capital employed has changed little over the last five years, apart from the write-down of leasehold property described in paragraph 3.46. One reason for this is that its purchases of new fixed assets have been only slightly greater than its annual depreciation charge. Another reason has been Forrest's use of second-hand equipment.

3.41. Forrest has been able to fund its fixed asset purchases from its operating cash flow, as is shown in Table 3.14.

TABLE 3.14 **Forrest: operating cash flow and purchases of fixed assets**

£'000

Year to 31 December

	1988	1989	1990	1991	1992
PBIT	1,058	699	918	989	506
Depreciation	408	456	498	524	460
Investment grants	(65)	(49)	(41)	(36)	(80)
Fixed asset disposals	29	-	7	1	14
Change in working capital	144	(185)	154	(88)	235
Operating cash flow	1,574	921	1,536	1,390	1,136
Purchases of fixed assets	441	626	584	636	716

per cent

% of operating cash flow	28.0	67.9	38.0	45.7	63.0

Source: MMC.

3.42. In January 1988 Forrest had its leasehold land and buildings revalued by independent valuers, and this resulted in a write-down of £999,980 which was recorded in the accounts for that year. Forrest argued that for the purposes of our inquiry ROCE should be calculated on the basis of historical cost rather than on the amounts shown in the statutory accounts. The effects on ROCE of reversing the revaluation of the leasehold properties, including the resulting increase in the annual depreciation charge, are shown in Table 3.15 for each year to 31 December. In each year there is a reduction in ROCE, for example in 1992 from 27.1 to 17.3 per cent.

TABLE 3.15 **Forrest's proposed adjustment to ROCE**

							£'000	per cent	
Year	PBIT	Additional depreciation	Adjusted PBIT	Average capital employed	Leasehold revaluation	Adjusted capital	Adjusted ROCE	Unadjusted ROCE*
1988	1,058	(40)	1,018	2,245	480	2,725	37.3	47.1
1989	699	(40)	659	1,909	940	2,849	23.1	36.6
1990	918	(40)	878	2,094	900	2,994	29.3	43.8
1991	989	(40)	949	1,951	860	2,811	33.8	50.7
1992	506	(40)	466	1,869	820	2,689	17.3	27.1

Sources: MMC and Forrest.

*ROCE in Table 3.9.

Capital expenditure and cost projections

3.43. At our request Forrest supplied capital expenditure and cost projections for the three years to 1995, and tables setting out its projected financial results, cash flow and capital expenditure are included at Appendix 3.3. Forrest told us that it expected an increase in capital expenditure in the next three years. One of its cookers was 18 years old and would need to be replaced, and the requirements of the EPA would lead to expenditure of £650,000, principally for the installation of a bio-filter to handle foul air. Forrest's cash flow will continue to be sufficient to fund its projected capital expenditure.

3.44. Forrest's projections show a small decline in materials processed compared to 1992, and a substantial decrease in greaves processed from 11,000 tonnes to 5,000 tonnes. Forrest explained to us that the reason for the projected decrease in greaves purchases was the reduction in available supplies.

If Forrest's purchases of greaves do continue at the same levels as in 1992, there would be an immediate improvement in projected PBIT and cash flow, with ROCE increasing to levels similar to those experienced in recent years.

3.45. Forrest pointed out to us that, unlike a batch processor whose costs did not vary significantly with tonnages processed, a continuous processing system had lower costs per tonne the greater the volume it achieved. Forrest's projections indicate that its fixed costs will continue to grow in line with inflation.

Other renderers

3.46. The operations and financial results of three of the other renderers are described in detail in Appendix 3.4. Their results are compared with those of PDM and Forrest in Appendix 3.5.

3.47. Summaries of the tables in Appendix 3.5 are included below. In these summary tables 'Other renderers' refers to an average of the results of the three smaller renderers, weighted by tonnes of materials processed. Because the renderers have varying year-ends, which may tend to invalidate comparisons when there are changes in selling prices or costs, we have also calculated totals for the three years 1989 to 1991, again weighted by tonnes of materials processed. As explained in paragraph 3.5, we have taken individual company information for the year-end nearest 31 December (eg PDM's results for the year ended on 31 March 1992 are shown as 1991).

Comparative performance of the renderers, 1989 to 1991

Operating costs, revenues and profitability

3.48. In Table 3.16 we have set out the inward transport costs of PDM, Forrest and the smaller renderers for 1989 to 1991 in £ per tonne. Some of the renderers buy significant quantities of greaves, which are normally delivered by the supplier. In most of the other tables we have used £ per tonne processed as the basis of measurement, but in this table we have eliminated greaves tonnages so that transport costs are measured in terms of £ per tonne collected.

TABLE 3.16 **Comparative inward transport costs per tonne of materials collected**

				£
	1989	*1990*	*1991*	*1989–91*
PDM	17.46	18.79	18.92	18.40
Forrest	17.42	20.95	21.24	20.03
Other renderers	10.33	10.67	11.60	10.88

Source: MMC from data supplied by companies.

The smaller renderers obtain almost 25 per cent of their materials from collectors, with the transport costs included in the price of materials. The proportions of materials delivered to PDM and Forrest in this way are much lower at 10 to 15 per cent. Adjusting the relative inward transport costs for delivered materials would reduce the differences in Table 3.16, but PDM and Forrest would still have costs about 50 per cent higher than those of the smaller renderers. PDM and Forrest have the additional expense of their collections from butchers' shops, and PDM incurs significant costs in moving materials between its plants. PDM also incurs a significant expense, not shown in Table 3.16, for outward transport on some of its end-products sales. Forrest with its long distances, its butchers' shop collection service and two depots also has relatively high transport costs.

3.49. In Table 3.17 we have set out the processing costs of these renderers in £ per tonne for 1991. The basis of allocation of costs to items such as odour and effluent control and other costs follows the accounting practices of each renderer, and this has resulted in some inconsistencies in the presentation of these costs between one renderer and another.

39

TABLE 3.17 **Processing costs per tonne, 1991**

£

	PDM	Forrest	Other renderers
Labour	6.30	4.97	5.68
Energy	7.43	8.71	7.26
Repairs and maintenance	8.44	8.82	4.14
Odour and effluent control	2.95	2.01	1.33
Depreciation	2.15	2.37	4.73
Other costs	3.02	4.54	3.48
	30.29	31.43	26.62

Source: MMC from data supplied by companies.

Capacity utilization varies widely between the renderers. As already noted PDM's utilization in 1991 was about 85 per cent; that of the three smaller renderers varied from 56 to 69 per cent with an average of 62 per cent; but Forrest's was about 45 per cent. We noted that the smaller renderers who had newer machinery than PDM or Forrest also had lower costs for energy and repairs, but a higher charge for depreciation.

3.50. In Table 3.18 the renderers' operating costs for 1989, 1990 and 1991 are shown. We show three components of cost in the table: transport (both inward and outward); processing; and other operating costs (mostly administration). In Table 3.18 transport costs are calculated on the basis of £ per tonne processed, not per tonne collected as in Table 3.16.

TABLE 3.18 **Comparative operating costs per tonne of materials processed**

£

	1989	1990	1991	1989–91
Transport costs:				
PDM	19.53	21.78	23.13	21.52
Forrest	14.57	17.56	18.70	17.09
Other renderers	10.11	10.43	12.10	10.88
Processing costs:				
PDM	25.49	29.26	30.29	28.40
Forrest	31.61	31.92	31.43	31.65
Other renderers	22.42	24.00	26.62	24.33
Other operating costs:*				
PDM	7.76	8.27	7.37	7.79
Forrest	4.67	4.46	4.97	4.70
Other renderers	4.64	5.36	5.63	5.20
Total operating costs:				
PDM	52.78	59.31	60.79	57.71
Forrest	50.85	53.94	55.10	53.44
Other renderers	37.17	39.79	44.35	40.41

Source: MMC from data supplied by companies.

*Including administration costs.

PDM and Forrest have significantly higher transport and processing costs, as well as total operating costs, than the three smaller renderers. (About £4.45 of PDM's transport costs relates to outward transport on sales of end products.) PDM also has significantly higher administration costs than the other renderers.

3.51. Forrest told us that it did not consider that it was appropriate or sustainable to compare it with smaller renderers and simply to apply a weighting in terms of tonnes processed. Its business operations differed from those of other renderers, and so it had a different cost structure. As already stated, it attributes its higher transport costs to its butchers' shop collections, its use of two depots and to its need to keep materials separated for the production of edible tallow. Until the end of 1992 its processing costs were increased by its use of solvent extraction. However, Forrest believed that these higher costs were more than justified by the higher prices it had achieved for end products and by its higher profit per tonne.

3.52. In PDM's view, 'the business of PDM cannot be compared with those of other renderers on pure financial grounds because they are different in so many fundamental respects from those of other single plant renderers in England and Wales'. PDM told us that comparative measurements of overall revenues and operating costs in £ per tonne were simplistic, and therefore misleading. It was virtually the only processor of feathers and blood. It said that the particular costs of these raw materials, the special costs of such materials and the value of the end products produced from them (feather and blood meal) were only reflected in PDM's financial results and not in those of any other renderer. More generally, PDM's proportion of low-yielding, high moisture-content material was significantly higher than that of any other single renderer or of all the other renderers taken together.

3.53. PDM also gave us a number of reasons for its higher operating costs. These included the costs of its shop collections, the movement of materials between its plants, and the shipping costs on its export sales. While some of these expenses are incurred as a result of the obligation which PDM feels to provide a comprehensive service, other expenses are incurred in pursuit of increased sales revenues. For example, the movement of materials between plants allows clean fat and bones to be processed separately, with improved yields of high-grade tallows.

3.54. We have therefore calculated the 'processing margin' for PDM, Forrest and the other companies. This margin is the difference between total operating costs and end-product sales and is available to cover the costs of raw materials and profit. In Table 3.19 we show our calculation of processing margin, and its division between purchases of materials and PBIT.

TABLE 3.19 **Comparative profits per tonne of materials processed**

£

	1989	1990	1991	1989–91
Total operating costs:				
PDM	52.78	59.31	60.79	57.71
Forrest	50.85	53.94	55.10	53.44
Other renderers	37.17	39.79	44.35	40.41
End-product sales:				
PDM	78.55	63.80	72.26	71.49
Forrest	101.61	79.18	69.92	82.50
Other renderers	86.59	63.27	60.90	70.46
Processing margin:				
PDM	25.77	4.49	11.47	13.78
Forrest	50.76	25.24	14.82	29.06
Other renderers	49.42	23.48	16.55	30.55
Cost of raw materials:				
PDM	22.79	0.03	4.23	8.84
Forrest	42.66	16.07	5.37	20.10
Other renderers	39.32	17.64	13.07	23.54
PBIT:				
PDM	2.98	4.45	7.24	4.94
Forrest	8.10	9.17	9.45	8.96
Other renderers	10.10	5.84	3.48	6.51

Source: MMC from data supplied by companies.

3.55. The processing margins of all the renderers have fallen after 1989 because of the adverse effects of BSE on both end-product prices and operating costs, although these were partially offset by collection charges for SBO and other offal. In 1989 and 1990 Forrest's use of solvent extraction gave it higher end-product sales for every tonne of raw materials, offsetting its relatively high processing costs. PDM had a noticeably lower processing margin in all three years than any of the other renderers, all of which mainly processed red meat materials. Table 3.7 shows that PDM's poultry waste rendering was profitable in all three years, and suggests that its inclusion with its other operations in Table 3.19 should not have materially affected its PBIT compared with that of other renderers. The inclusion of edible fats would increase PBIT slightly, while the inclusion of blood would decrease it; and the overall effect on PBIT would not be material.

3.56. PDM told us that in Table 3.19 its end-product sales, which included products derived from poultry waste, feathers and blood, were compared with those of renderers whose products were derived almost completely from red meat materials. It also told us that some of its end products included additives bought in for blending with its own products. In Table 3.20 we have taken PDM's sales of red meat products (as shown in Table 3.5) and deducted the cost of additives before calculating revised figures for sales per tonne processed, which we compare with the sales of Forrest and the other renderers. The table shows that PDM's end-product sales from red meat materials were higher than those of the other renderers, but below those of Forrest in 1989 and 1990.

TABLE 3.20 **Comparative end-product sales from red meat waste rendering per tonne of materials processed**

	1989	1990	1991	Average 1989–91
End-product sales (£'000)	54,404	42,306	49,531	48,747
Less additives	3,213	2,981	3,643	3,279
	51,191	39,325	45,888	45,468
Tonnes processed ('000)	554	577	590	574
Sales per tonne processed (£)				
PDM (1)	92.40	68.15	77.77	79.21
Forrest (2)	101.61	79.18	69.92	82.50
Other renderers (2)	86.59	63.27	60.90	70.46

Source: (1) PDM; (2) MMC using data supplied by companies.

3.57. The costs of raw materials included in Table 3.19 include purchases of greaves and additives by PDM, and of greaves by Forrest and some of the other renderers. The average price per tonne purchased, eliminating these items to leave rendering materials only, is set out in Table 3.21. PDM's purchases still include poultry waste, blood and feathers, but more than 65 per cent are for red meat waste.

TABLE 3.21 **Comparative costs of rendering materials per tonne purchased**

				£
	1989	1990	1991	1989–91
PDM	20.55	-2.17	0.57	6.14
Forrest	26.30	5.02	-5.32	7.37
Other renderers	30.39	13.60	9.66	17.90

Source: MMC from data supplied by companies.

As explained in paragraph 3.48, the smaller renderers obtain almost 25 per cent of their materials from collectors, while PDM and Forrest obtain 10 to 15 per cent. Some of the higher prices paid by the smaller renderers reflect the higher element of the collectors' transport costs included in their purchases.

Capital employed and profitability

3.58. In Table 3.22 we set out an analysis of average capital employed. Rendering is characterized by a high level of fixed assets: the rendering machinery itself; odour and effluent control equipment; buildings; and lorries with their trailers. Current assets, mostly stock and debtors, are low. Stocks of end products are usually held for only a few days and raw materials cannot be held in stock at all. Debtors are low because brokers generally pay within 14 days for end products. Some of the smaller renderers have net current liabilities, partly as a result of postponing payment for materials and other purchases.

42

£

	1989	*1990*	*1991*	*1989–91*
Plant and machinery:				
PDM	11.23	10.71	10.29	10.74
Forrest	15.15	13.97	11.86	13.66
Other renderers	24.90	27.95	28.76	27.20
Other fixed assets:				
PDM	8.33	8.12	8.63	8.36
Forrest	7.13	6.47	6.27	6.62
Other renderers	24.91	26.63	28.45	26.66
Tangible fixed assets:				
PDM	19.56	18.83	18.92	19.10
Forrest	22.28	20.44	18.13	20.28
Other renderers	49.81	54.58	57.21	53.87
Capital employed:				
PDM	25.12	25.08	23.93	24.71
Forrest	22.14	20.91	18.64	20.56
Other renderers	44.56	50.28	53.54	49.46
				per cent
ROCE:				
PDM	11.9	17.8	30.3	20.0
Forrest	36.6	43.8	50.7	43.5
Other renderers	22.7	11.6	6.5	13.2

Source: MMC from data supplied by companies.

3.59. Fixed assets in Table 3.22 are shown after deducting accumulated depreciation but, in the case of Forrest, before deducting investment grants. PDM and Forrest have older machinery which is further depreciated than that of the other renderers.

3.60. Some of the smaller renderers have much higher values for land and buildings than PDM and Forrest. This may reflect the effects of using the historical cost convention in businesses which have been established for many years. In the case of Forrest the write-down of leasehold properties, already referred to in paragraph 3.42, reduces fixed assets by some £10 per tonne processed.

3.61. PDM differs from the other renderers in having significant net current assets, equivalent to more than £5 per tonne processed. At 31 March 1992 it held stocks of almost £2.9 million, equivalent to about three weeks' production. It had trade debtors of £9.9 million, which exceeded trade creditors of £7.2 million. This may be partly due to the longer credit it gives on its export sales, while it has a reputation for prompt payments to abattoirs (as have some of the smaller renderers). Forrest has low net current assets, while the smaller renderers have net current liabilities.

3.62. Within the weighted average of the results of the three smaller renderers, the best perform-ance of an individual renderer was considerably better than this average. The same renderer had significantly lower operating costs and a ROCE which was consistently higher than that of PDM, but lower than that of Forrest.

Comparative returns on capital employed

3.63. In this section we compare the performance of the renderers with other sectors of UK industry. We recognize that there are a number of measures available and in this case we have taken the percentage of profit before interest and tax to tangible capital employed (ROCE). Tangible capital employed includes tangible fixed assets, stocks and debtors, less creditors. Cash balances, borrowings, proposed dividends and tax due after more than one year are excluded from tangible capital employed.

3.64. The MMC have in recent years taken comparative data on sectors of UK industry from an annual article in the Bank of England's Quarterly Review on the *Profitability of Large Companies*. However, in November 1991 the Bank ceased to publish this article. The UK industry information used for comparison in this report has been calculated by the MMC using the MicroEXSTAT corporate financial database, the same database used by the Bank for its 1990 and 1991 articles. These aggregate sector results are drawn up on a basis consistent with that used for computing ROCE for the companies involved in this inquiry.

3.65. In Table 3.23 the ROCE of PDM, Forrest and the weighted average of the three other renderers are compared with those from the database for 56 food manufacturers and ten meat processors.

TABLE 3.23   **ROCE of renderers compared with food manufacturers and meat processors, 1988 to 1992**

					per cent
	1988	*1989*	*1990*	*1991*	*1992*
PDM (1)	21.2	11.9	17.8	30.3	-
Forrest (1)					
Unadjusted	47.1	36.6	43.8	50.7	27.1
Adjusted	37.3	23.1	29.3	33.8	17.3
Other renderers (1)	-	22.7	11.6	6.5	-
Food manufacturers (2)	19.1	21.3	23.3	22.6	23.3
Meat processors (2)*	13.9	16.9	18.5	17.6	9.8

Sources: (1) MMC from company data; (2) MMC from MicroEXSTAT.

*The two principal meat processors included here are Hillsdown Holdings plc and Union International plc.

3.66. The ROCE of PDM is generally higher than that of the meat processors, but only in 1991 is it significantly higher than that of the food manufacturers. The ROCE of Forrest, adjusted or unadjusted, is consistently higher than that of PDM, the three other renderers, the food manufacturers or the meat processors.

4 PDM

Introduction

4.1. In this chapter we look first at PDM's present structure, management and activities, and its development and diversification (paragraphs 4.2 to 4.23). Secondly, we describe PDM's compliance with the relevant legislation for the protection of public health and the safeguarding of the environment (paragraphs 4.24 to 4.32). Thirdly, we consider the 1985 report and its aftermath, including the continued growth of PDM (paragraphs 4.33 to 4.39), and the Croda report and its aftermath (paragraphs 4.40 to 4.48). Lastly, we examine PDM's links with certain other companies in the rendering industry (paragraphs 4.49 to 4.70).

Structure, management and activities

4.2. PDM is a family-owned group of private companies which was founded in 1926 by the parents of the present Chairman, as a knackery and exporter of horse meat. Its principal activity today is the production of tallow and meat-and-bone meal by rendering animal waste. Its other activities include the manufacture of pet foods and frozen raw material for the pet food industry; and the sale of oils, fats and sundries for the catering trade.

4.3. Those companies which comprise the PDM enterprise are listed in paragraph 3.6 and Appendix 3.1. For the purposes of the present inquiry the PDM companies of principal interest are:

Name	Location	Activity
Prosper De Mulder Ltd (parent company)	Doncaster	Manufacturer of meat-and-bone meal, tallow and pet food
John Knight (Animal By Products) Ltd	Silvertown, London	Manufacturer of meat-and-bone meal, tallow and frozen pet food
Granox Ltd	Widnes	Manufacturer of meat-and-bone meal, poultry meal, poultry fat, tallow, blood meal and pet food
De Mulder & Son Ltd	Hartshill, Nuneaton	Manufacturer of meat-and-bone meal and tallow
J L Thomas & Co Ltd	Exeter	Manufacturer of meat-and-bone meal and tallow
De Mulder (Mkt Harborough) Ltd	Market Harborough	Manufacturer of meat-and-bone meal and tallow
Webster Craven Ltd	Leeds	Manufacturer of dripping, sale of catering supplies and collection of animal by-products
G E & H Mitchell Ltd	Bridlington	Sale of dripping and catering supplies and collection of animal by-products
Chettles Ltd	Ditchford near Rushden and Nottingham	Manufacturer of feather and poultry meal, poultry fat and pet food
Prosper De Mulder Transport	Doncaster	Provision of transport services by owner-drivers to PDM and Frazer Group companies
Prosper De Mulder Services	Doncaster	Provision of management services to PDM and Frazer Group companies

236197 D2

4.4. As already mentioned, in this report we refer to Prosper De Mulder Ltd and its subsidiary and related companies as PDM.

4.5. The various companies comprising PDM are owned by the present Chairman and his family and managed as a single entity. The shareholders of these companies (excluding subsidiaries) are summarized in Table 4.1.

TABLE 4.1 **Shareholders of PDM companies**

per cent

	P F De Mulder	Mrs J F De Mulder	P N De Mulder		A J De Mulder		Other trusts
			Beneficial	Trusts	Beneficial	Trusts	
Prosper De Mulder Ltd	-	-	20	15	20	15	30
Prosper De Mulder Transport	-	-	20	15	20	15	30
Prosper De Mulder Services	-	-	20	15	20	15	30
Frazer (Butchers) Ltd	1	1	49	-	49	-	-
Francis Investments Ltd	1	99	-	-	-	-	-
Oracle Motors Ltd	2	-	49	-	49	-	-

Source: PDM.

4.6. Because the PDM group of companies does not have a single ultimate holding company, we addressed questions about the ownership of other companies to all the above shareholders and to the trustees of the two PDM pension schemes. In reply they stated that they did not have any other interests in companies or firms engaged in the animal waste or ancillary industries.

4.7. PDM is managed by the Board of Prosper De Mulder Ltd, which consisted in June 1993 of the following members:

Mr P F De Mulder: Chairman
Mrs J F De Mulder (wife of Mr P F De Mulder)
Mr A J De Mulder (son of Mr P F De Mulder): Managing Director
Mr P N De Mulder (son of Mr P F De Mulder): Managing Director, De Mulder & Sons Ltd
Mr D J Page: Non-executive director
Mr H F Hales: Raw Materials Director
Mr W G Braide: Finance Director
Mr P D Foxcroft: Sales Director
Mr P R Bacon: Joint Managing Director, John Knight (Animal By-Products) Ltd
Mr D Bacon: Joint Managing Director, John Knight (Animal By-Products) Ltd
Mr R Handisides: Group Technical Director
Mr C Reynolds: Edible Products Director
Mr R G McLennan: Secretary.

4.8. PDM's management style has traditionally been somewhat informal. For example, it has not been the practice to keep Board minutes, PDM taking the view that, as most directors were in close contact with each other at its Doncaster Head Office, informal, albeit unrecorded, meetings of the directors covering both policy decisions and the day-to-day running of the business were in effect held almost daily. Formal minutes of AGMs, however, have been maintained since 1985. We have considered PDM's financial accounting and reporting systems in Chapter 3.

4.9. While the local managers are responsible for the routine running of PDM's operating plants, decisions to buy new equipment, or entailing major maintenance expenditure, are referred to Head Office. The procurement of raw materials (see paragraph 8.25) and the sale of end products (see paragraph 2.77) are also controlled from the centre.

Development and diversification

4.10. PDM's first rendering plant was installed at Doncaster in 1938. Prosper De Mulder Ltd was incorporated in 1955 to continue and develop the rendering business and its associated activities. A process of expansion began to take place some 25 years ago, as detailed in the 1985 report. During the period 1970 to 1981 PDM acquired around 50 businesses engaged in the rendering trade or associated activities. Most were subsequently closed but among those that are still part of PDM are Chettles, acquired in 1979, and Granox Ltd (Granox) (at Widnes), acquired in 1980.

4.11. In Scotland, the PDM Pension Fund Trustees acquired in 1977, and subsequently sold in 1981 to Forrest, the rendering and collection business of Frank Gysels Ltd (Frank Gysels), serving an area in Fife to the north, south and east of Edinburgh.

4.12. Also in 1981, PDM began to undertake the operation of gut-rooms on behalf of abattoirs (see paragraph 2.13).

4.13. PDM told us that its corporate strategy had been based on the establishment of a country-wide network of rendering plants having sufficient capacity to process, in the most technically efficient way available, all the varying quantities and qualities of raw material obtained from its suppliers. This strategy had begun to be put in place with the purchase of the Silvertown and Exeter rendering plants from Unilever Plc in 1969. The attainment of PDM's present position in the red meat waste sector followed its substantial acquisition of the Springfield Group of Companies in 1978, and the purchase in 1980 from S & W Berisford Ltd of Granox, which operated the rendering factory at Widnes.

4.14. So far as the processing of poultry waste is concerned, PDM acquired in 1979 from Hypromel Products Ltd (Hypromel) a feather meal manufacturing plant at Ditchford, and in 1986 from Midland Cattle Products Ltd (MCP), a traditional rendering plant at Stoke Bardolph near Nottingham; PDM immediately converted the former MCP plant to process exclusively poultry waste material and by 1991 had increased the capacity of the plant nearly threefold.

4.15. Also purchased by PDM from Hypromel in 1979 was the business of the collection of red offals for freezing and supply to pet food manufacturers. This freezer plant business was eventually moved into new plants established first at Silvertown in 1984, and at Doncaster in 1985. The plate freezing plant at Doncaster was extended in 1987.

4.16. PDM itself has been a manufacturer of canned pet food, principally from its plant in Doncaster, since 1969.

4.17. PDM's existing edible fat (beef dripping) manufacturing business known as James Jennings & Son Ltd of Darlington was expanded by the acquisition of the business of P Webster Ltd in Leeds in May 1981 and the dripping and refining business of Craven Calvert Ltd in December 1990. The latter has since been moved on to the same site as, and consolidated with, the business of P Webster Ltd and is called Webster Craven Ltd. These businesses also supply frying fats and catering sundries to the catering trade.

4.18. In recent years PDM has concentrated on its strategy to diversify away from the 'commodity'-related constraints of the traditional markets for its finished products by seeking ways in which to add value to its raw materials, whilst at the same time maintaining its core business. Two significant areas of diversification, pet foods and food products, are continually being developed and each has been strengthened by acquisitions as described in paragraphs 4.19 to 4.21.

Pet foods

4.19. The acquisition of Wells By-Products at Newark in 1991 extended and strengthened PDM's position in the supply of ingredients to the major multinational pet food companies (eg Pedigree, Spillers, Quaker, BP Nutrition and Nestlé) and has resulted in PDM becoming a leading processor and supplier to this sector. PDM also supplies blended ingredients to customers' specifications. Waste which formerly went into the rendering process is now supplied in frozen and chilled slurry form from both Newark and Doncaster, where special digests are also produced. Frozen ingredients, in addition, are produced at Silvertown.

4.20. Doncaster is also the site of the pet food canning plant which supplies supermarket groups and other multiples with both PDM's and own-label pet foods. At Widnes other products are produced for sale to pet food wholesalers and retailers. The Nottingham factory produces cooked pet foods and a 'complete' dry dog food. At Ditchford a small but growing cooked pet meat production unit is in operation, whilst the Silvertown factory also produces frozen retail packs of pet food.

Food products

4.21. Prior to its acquisition of Nortech Foods Ltd (Nortech) in April 1992, PDM's involvement in food products was restricted to the beef dripping businesses referred to in paragraph 4.17. Following this acquisition, PDM formed a Food Products Division with its own management structure. Nortech now produces speciality edible animal and poultry fats for incorporation in the recipes of UK and other EC food manufacturers. PDM is developing the Nortech site to increase production capacity, and told us that it was determined to invest heavily in research and development and capital equipment in the food products sector.

Plant capacity

4.22. Table 4.2 summarizes the maximum capacity of PDM's seven (currently operational) rendering plants.

TABLE 4.2 **Maximum capacity of PDM's operational rendering plants**

Location	Type	Tonnes/wk	Total
Doncaster	Low-grade	2,800	
Hartshill	Low-grade	3,700	
Exeter	Low-grade	2,000	8,500
Silvertown	High-grade	3,000	
Widnes	High-grade	1,500	4,500
Widnes	Poultry	1,700	
Nottingham	Poultry	2,450	4,150
Widnes	Blood	1,200	1,200
Ditchford	Feather	1,650	1,650
Total			20,000

Source: PDM.

4.23. Table 4.3 summarizes the changes in capacity made by PDM between 1986 and 1993.

TABLE 4.3 **Changes in capacity made by PDM, 1986 to 1993**

tonnes per week

Date	Location	High-grade non-poultry	Low-grade non-poultry	Blood	Poultry offals	Feathers
1986	Nottingham		-1,000		+900	
1987	Nottingham				+600	
1987	Hartshill		+1,000			
1988	Silvertown	+2,000	-2,500			
1989	Widnes		-1,700			
1990	Widnes			+1,000		
1990	Widnes				+1,700	
1991	Nottingham				+950	
1991	Gloucester			-1,000		
1991	Widnes			+500		
1991	Ditchford					+600
1991	M/Harborough	+1,000				
1992	M/Harborough	-1,000				
1993	Ditchford					+400
Overall changes		+2,000	-4,200	+500	+4,150	+1,000

Source: PDM.

Public health and the environment

4.24. PDM told us that its advantage in having separate plants at Ditchford and Nottingham dedicated to the separate processing of poultry waste was offset by the successive problems of salmonella and BSE. The decision by the major feed compounders not to feed poultry-based material back to poultry caused the sales of PDM's recently launched high-value feed, Lipromel, based on liquid blood, offal and feathers, to fall by 75 per cent within a few weeks. In 1990 PDM closed its specially commissioned Lipromel production plant at Widnes, subsequently adapting and reopening the plant for processing blood.

4.25. PDM said that the principal purpose of the Processed Animal Proteins Order 1989 was to prevent salmonella recontamination from occurring to already sterile end products. Conventionally, recontamination had been minimized by means of biocidal organic acid. Alternatively, PDM had adapted the food industry system known as Hazard Analysis Critical Control Points (HACCP). In 1990 PDM commenced HACCP implementation programmes at Doncaster, Silvertown and Widnes. Those at Silvertown and Widnes had been completed, eliminating there both the high cost of organic acid and the incidence of salmonella isolations. PDM also considered that the HACCP approach had led to improved overall standards in other operational areas, such as quality assurance and environmental control.

4.26. PDM estimated that the ruminant-to-ruminant feed ban cost the rendering industry some 15 per cent of the markets for its meat-and-bone meal and up to 80 per cent of its blood meal market. As the largest force in UKRA, PDM, as was widely recognized, had led the industry-wide campaign which persuaded the compounders to continue using meal in their non-ruminant feeds. PDM had also helped persuade the rendering industry itself to adopt a responsible attitude to the collection and processing of SBO following the ban on the use of SBO in any feed.

4.27. PDM, for its part, had dedicated processing facilities at Hartshill, where SBO was stored in a separate bay and then processed as a single batch, usually once a day. A post-processing cleaning operation ensured no possible contamination of 'uncontaminated' material; and the SBO greaves were loaded directly on to a vehicle and delivered to a registered landfill site in accordance with the statutory requirements. PDM pointed out that it was also involved in EC-commissioned research into BSE deactivation by rendering methods.

4.28. As regards PDM's compliance with the increasingly stringent legislation for the protection of the environment, PDM told us that it had submitted its applications under the provisions of Part I of the EPA in respect of each of its plants, as required, between 1 April and 30 September 1992. To date, the Widnes factory had been issued with authorization by its local authority. PDM expected each of its other sites to receive authorization under the EPA by September 1993.

4.29. So far as the application of Part II of the EPA was concerned, and in particular the duty of care imposed under section 34, PDM was playing a major role in discussions through UKRA, and with support from MAFF, to try and gain exemption for animal by-products. Presently proposed exemptions still left outstanding matters of concern, in that animal by-products would continue to be regarded as 'waste' by the Department of the Environment (DoE), and PDM's owner-drivers, and other contracted hauliers, would not be exempt from the need to register as carriers of controlled waste. However, the situation was currently under review by DoE.

4.30. Similar discussions were taking place on the appropriateness of renderers' raw materials falling within the ambit of the Controlled Waste (Registration of Carriers and Seizure of Vehicles) Regulations 1991 issued under the Control of Pollution (Amendment) Act 1989, subject to which PDM might be required to register separately its whole transport fleet.

4.31. PDM told us that between 1983 and 1992 it had spent some £1.2 million at its various plants on odour control and as much again on capital effluent treatment measures. £1.2 million was also the expected cost of the effluent treatment improvements currently being carried out to National Rivers Authority guidelines at the Widnes factory, which stands on gallygoo.

4.32. In addition, for the three years to 31 March 1992 revenue expenditure on odour control and effluent disposal in relation to PDM's reference businesses amounted to £2.1 million, £2.3 million and £2.6 million respectively. These costs would increase after completion of the Widnes project.

The 1985 report and aftermath

4.33. The MMC's first report on PDM and the rendering industry, published in 1985, concerned the supply of red meat waste in Great Britain as a whole. The conclusions and recommendations of the 1985 report are summarized in Appendix 4.1.

4.34. While a monopoly situation was found to exist in favour of PDM, this did not, and was not to be expected to, operate against the public interest. The implementation of PDM's pricing policy, however, both for raw materials and for gut-room contracts, was a step taken for the purpose of exploiting or maintaining the monopoly situation, and was the subject of an adverse public interest finding. The MMC recommended that the DGFT should obtain an undertaking from PDM in relation to its gut-room activities.

4.35. In 1986 PDM gave three undertakings to the DGFT, relating to profitable and self-standing operation of its gut-room activities; unconditional purchasing of lower-grade raw material; and prior notification by at least one month of any further acquisitions of renderers or collectors of animal waste (the 1986 undertakings, reproduced at Appendix 1.2).

4.36. Between 1986 and 1991, PDM pre-notified the following seven acquisitions:

Date of acquisition	Business acquired
2 June 1986	Collection business of H Prescott & Sons Ltd
8 September 1986	Collection business of MCP and factory at Stoke Bardolph near Nottingham
20 February 1987	Collection business of Stoke Mandeville Animal Products Ltd
14 December 1987	Rendering business of Norfolk Fat and Bone Company Ltd
30 November 1990	Collection business of Ashworths Products Ltd
3 December 1990	Fat refining and dripping manufacturing business of Craven Calvert Ltd
7 January 1991	Rendering business of Croda International plc

4.37. In addition, PDM told us that it was involved in the possible purchase of a number of businesses which it did not, in the event, acquire. In 1986, for example, the purchase of the business of Forrest was agreed but broke down because the then family owner did not wish to become involved in a merger reference, as seemed likely at the time. PDM had also been offered the business of Gilberts on 'numerous occasions' in recent years, but each time the vendor had chosen not to proceed. In 1989 PDM entered into negotiations to buy the rendering business of Chetwynd, but that matter did not proceed to completion for a variety of reasons. In 1990 PDM opened negotiations to buy the business of Faversham Animal By-Products Ltd (FAP) and S J Chandler Ltd (S J Chandler), but withdrew after it transpired that the proprietors had already agreed a partial sale to Cheale, which obtained an injunction in the High Court against the proprietors (see paragraph 4.58).

4.38. PDM told us that, while it followed a policy of expansion through acquisition, it did not actively seek companies to acquire. Generally vendors approached PDM in the belief that it was likely to be a willing purchaser. Nevertheless we learned both from PDM and from other sources that PDM had made a number of approaches in recent years with a view to the possible purchase of existing businesses.

4.39. In December 1990 PDM requested the DGFT to release it from the 1986 gut-room undertakings. A month later it withdrew this request because, it explained, it had just acquired Croda and expected that merger to be referred to the MMC. The PDM/Croda merger was referred to the MMC on 13 March 1991.

The Croda report and aftermath

4.40. Rendering was a small and unprofitable part of the activities of Croda, a broadly-based group of chemical companies. Under the merger with Croda, PDM had acquired the plant and equipment, stocks and goodwill of the business carried on at Market Harborough (which processed high-grade waste collected mainly from shops) and taken a ten-year lease on the site. The MMC's second report on PDM was published in August 1991 (see Appendix 4.2).

4.41. The Croda report found that the rendering industry had been experiencing difficult and turbulent trading conditions. First the prices of tallow and meat-and-bone meal, which had been at peak levels in 1984, had fallen back sharply by 1986, and after stabilizing for a time had dropped even further in 1990. These price movements were initially due to reductions in the prices of competing commodities such as palm oil and soya bean meal which were in world-wide surplus. Secondly, the industry had been hit by the salmonella and BSE crises.

4.42. As a result of these developments, renderers had had to cut the prices they paid for high-grade waste and introduce progressively higher charges for collecting low-grade waste, and to implement a high charge for collecting SBO. At the same time the growing public awareness of environmental issues had put pressure on the rendering industry to achieve higher standards of odour and effluent controls. For those renderers who wished to remain in business this had led to a need for capital investment on a scale which was substantial in relation to the turnover and profits which they could reasonably expect to achieve.

4.43. The report also found that concentration in the rendering industry had continued. Whereas the 1985 report had calculated that the number of rendering companies in Great Britain in 1983 was 57 (down from about 160 in the 1950s), the number trading early in 1991 was down to around 30, of which three operated only in Scotland and four processed edible fats only. Only two cases of new firms entering the market since 1985 had come to the MMC's attention: B & E (Rassau) Ltd which had opened a rendering plant in South Wales in 1988 (since closed), and Cheale (see paragraph 4.37).

4.44. Over the same period PDM had further developed its strategy of concentrating production on a few large plants which specialized in processing particular types of waste. This specialization had caused PDM's transport costs to rise as material had to be hauled longer distances to the appropriate plant; SBO, in particular, were brought to Hartshill, Nuneaton, from all parts of England and Wales.

4.45. A summary of the conclusions of the Croda report is provided at Appendix 4.2. The report found that the merger had an adverse effect on competition in the collection of high-grade waste in the South-West and South-East of England, and had modestly enhanced PDM's position in the overall waste collection market in England and Wales. But these effects were marginal in relation to the structural defects in competition which existed before the merger. Moreover, Croda was no longer an effective competitive force. The report considered that the merger was likely to improve PDM's efficiency and bring wider public health and environmental benefits. These effects, though also modest, would assist PDM in carrying out functions which represented an important public service as well as a commercial activity. Having taken account of the limited adverse effects on competition on the one hand, and the important public issues of health and the environment as well as efficiency gains on the other hand, the MMC concluded that the merger did not and might be expected not to operate against the public interest.

4.46. PDM ceased production at Market Harborough in February 1992 and moth-balled the plant (see paragraph 8.8).

4.47. On 6 April 1992 PDM acquired that part of Nortech that specialized in the processing of high-grade fats, having pre-notified the DGFT as a matter of courtesy: PDM did not consider this a rendering business (see paragraph 8.19).

4.48. PDM has also purchased several small animal waste collection businesses, some without pre-notifying the DGFT, and including a number subsequent to its acquisition of Croda. Appendix 4.3 lists all of PDM's acquisitions between 1986 and 1992, identifying those not pre-notified together with their approximate weekly tonnage acquired and the related goodwill recorded in PDM's accounts.

Links with other companies

4.49. During the course of our inquiry it was alleged to us that PDM also had links with certain other animal waste enterprises, and we put these allegations to PDM (see paragraphs 19 and 20 of Appendix 7.1). The following paragraphs provide factual accounts of PDM's links with E Clutton & Sons (Marchwiel) Ltd (Clutton); the Klein family and G H Klein & Son Ltd (G H Klein); Specialpack; and Tyneside Butchers By-Products Ltd (Tyneside Butchers).

Clutton

4.50. Clutton is owned by Mr E Clutton and his wife, and carries on a business as a licensed knacker and animal waste collector from Marchwiel, near Wrexham in North Wales. Mr Clutton told us that PDM had formerly acquired his rendering business in 1972 and changed its name to Clutton Animal By-Products Ltd. He had continued as a director until December 1992, although the company had already become a non-trading subsidiary of PDM some years before. Mr Clutton told us that his own business collected animal waste from abattoirs and butchers' shops in Wales, and that most of this was collected from its yard by PDM.

4.51. When Beeson closed in 1992, because the local authority was buying its site, Mr Clutton made a payment to Beeson for the goodwill and some of the vehicles. He told us that his principal interest in Beeson had been the knacker business, although he was now collecting some rendering materials from abattoirs which had formerly been supplying Beeson. Mr Clutton estimated that more than half the additional materials he received were sold to customers other than PDM.

4.52. Mr Clutton and his family own a further company which operates an incinerator for cattle infected with BSE. Mr Clutton stated that this business was completely independent from PDM.

The Klein family and G H Klein & Son Ltd

4.53. The Klein family first came to our attention as the 50 per cent owners with PDM of Stannard & Co (1969) Ltd (Stannard) (see Appendix 3.1), of which G H Klein & Son Ltd (G H Klein) was formerly a dormant subsidiary. Stannard was a collector and also operated a rendering plant from a site in Stapleford Abbotts, Essex. The Klein family also acquired a 50 per cent interest in J P Redfearn & Sons (Wakefield) Ltd (Redfearn), a dripping and tallow manufacturer.

4.54. In 1983 a fire destroyed the rendering plant at Stapleford Abbotts. Mr S Klein told us that the insurance claim from the fire was not settled for almost five years, and Stannard was unable to rebuild its plant. In 1989, following the death of his father, there was an extensive reorganization of the Klein businesses. Stannard ceased to trade and became a holding company. Its collection business was transferred to G H Klein, leaving Stannard with the Stapleford Abbotts site, which has planning permission for 20 houses and has since been valued at more than £1 million.

4.55. The Kleins came to an agreement with PDM that G H Klein could operate from a temporary building on PDM's Silvertown site. In addition, G H Klein is able to make general use of administrative and other facilities at Silvertown. PDM supplies fuel for its vehicles from the pump at Silvertown and undertakes the maintenance of its vehicle fleet. It is invoiced by PDM for all these items. PDM became G H Klein's largest customer and pays it the highest price for bone of any of PDM's collectors, because, we were told, its material contains a large proportion of mixed butchers' waste which has a high fat content and is therefore worth more (taking this into account, the price paid by PDM equated to prices paid for bone to other collectors).

4.56. In 1990 Redfearn went into receivership and the goodwill and certain motor vehicles were sold to PDM.

Acquisition of G H Klein by the Klein family

4.57. In February 1991 the two PDM directors of Stannard resigned and on 8 March 1991 the Klein family acquired G H Klein from Stannard for a nil consideration, which reflected its net worth. All the Klein businesses were financially weak at that time. Portalot Ltd had a large deficit following the collapse of its associate, Redfearn. Palmer and Klein Ltd, a refiner of recovered vegetable oil, had incurred trading losses. At 31 March 1991 only Stannard had a surplus of assets over liabilities, mostly represented by its building site, an illiquid asset. [*Details omitted.* *See note on page iv.*]

S J Chandler and FAP

4.58. As mentioned in paragraph 4.37, during 1990 PDM negotiated with the Chandler family to buy S J Chandler, a collection business, and two rendering plants near Faversham and Canterbury. Cheale, however, was also interested in buying the Canterbury rendering plant, and in the event Mr J Chandler signed an informal document which was subsequently held to be a legally binding contract for the sale of that plant to Cheale. PDM withdrew from the negotiations entirely and told us that its last contact with the Chandlers was in October 1990.

4.59. In January 1991 G H Klein began negotiations to acquire the separate waste collection business of S J Chandler and the rendering assets (excluding the land and buildings) of FAP. These negotiations were successfully concluded on 5 March 1991. S J Chandler and its directors agreed not to compete with the business they were selling for three years, while S J Chandler, its directors and FAP also undertook that they would procure that FAP's premises would not be used for rendering for a period of ten years. The second of these restrictive covenants, it was submitted to us, would not have been imposed had G H Klein not been acting on behalf of PDM.

4.60. G H Klein paid £40,000 for S J Chandler, and £219,000 for the rendering assets of FAP, which it immediately arranged to be resold. On 15 May 1991, during the MMC's PDM/Croda inquiry, G H Klein submitted written details of its disposals. Of proceeds amounting to £155,000, only £65,000 related to the rendering assets. On the face of it there was a large loss on the sale of the rendering assets but, in the absence of G H Klein's accounts for the year to 31 March 1992 (which were not available at the end of May 1993), we cannot be certain of this. G H Klein told us that these asset disposals, together with a bank loan, new hire purchase finance and deferral of £80,000 of the purchase consideration, enabled it to finance the two acquisitions. It also told us that there had not been a loss on the asset disposals.

4.61. Although Mr Klein could not provide accounts for G H Klein for the year ended 31 March 1992, he was able to tell us that at that date G H Klein owed PDM £200,000 and that his mother owed PDM £41,512.

4.62. PDM told us that it had not in any way supported G H Klein's acquisition of S J Chandler and FAP. Because it would have had to pre-notify to the DGFT any acquisitions by a company in which it had a 50 per cent holding, G H Klein was hived off from Stannard and put firmly into the Klein family's ownership. During 1991/92 G H Klein had not been able to meet all its repayments for the businesses it had bought and was gradually building a debt with PDM. PDM had decided to support G H Klein for two reasons. First, PDM had had a connection with the Klein family for more than 20 years. Secondly, and more important, it was concerned to protect its investment in Stannard. If G H Klein were to go into liquidation, Stannard might be forced to sell the Stapleford Abbotts site on unfavourable terms. Both the loans to G H Klein and that to Mrs Klein, made after the death of her husband, were interest-free, and there was an understanding that, if not repaid earlier, they would be repaid when Stannard's building site was finally sold.

Specialpack

4.63. Specialpack is a gut-room contractor established in 1976 by Mr P Carrigan. It is one of the larger independent gut-room contractors, and has a factory in Sheffield where some of the materials from its gut-rooms are processed. In 1983, because of serious trading problems in another commercial venture, Sharneyford Supplies Ltd, Mr Carrigan needed to raise funds to honour his obligations to that company's creditors.

4.64. Mr Carrigan told us that when he was considering selling Specialpack, his accountant showed him an advertisement, seeking to buy a specialist animal or food processing company on behalf of an international investor. Mr Carrigan sent us a copy of the advertisement which had been placed in the 14 July 1983 edition of *Accountancy Age*.

4.65. Mr Carrigan told us that he replied to the advertisement and was contacted by Mr J M Smith of Itcos SA, Geneva (Itcos), acting on behalf of Champel Investments SA (Champel). Champel then bought all of the issued ordinary and preference shares of Specialpack. Mr Carrigan continued as the sole director of Specialpack and ran the business in much the same way as before the sale, with very little supervision from Mr Smith, who continued to act as the representative of Champel.

4.66. We wrote to Itcos and received a reply from Mr Smith. He explained that the ordinary shares of Specialpack were held by Champel, which was incorporated in Panama but administered from Itcos' office in Geneva. The preference shares were held by Cendrier Services SA (Cendrier Services), which was incorporated in Liberia. Champel was owned by an offshore trust. Cendrier Services was beneficially owned by Itcos, but was acting in a nominee capacity to the order of the trustees.

4.67. Mr Smith told us that he was not authorized to reveal the names of the beneficiaries of the offshore trust, but he was able to confirm that to the best of his knowledge and belief none of them was or ever had been resident in the UK.

4.68. Mr Carrigan told us that he had no reason to believe that Specialpack was owned or controlled by PDM, and expressed strongly the contrary view. Further, he supplied written evidence showing that Specialpack did not receive preferential prices from PDM. He did not know the identity of the ultimate owners of the company.

4.69. PDM told us that it did not own or control Specialpack. As already mentioned (paragraph 4.6), we obtained assurances from the shareholders of PDM and from the trustees of its two pension schemes that they did not hold any interests in the animal waste or ancillary industries apart from shareholdings in PDM.

Tyneside Butchers

4.70. Tyneside Butchers was a small renderer which closed in 1990. The liquidator told us that Mr Spires, the owner of the company, was old and unwell; and that he had received payments from PDM. PDM told us that Mr Spires was taken on as a part-time employee at a salary of £10,000 per annum to help out in the North-East and to look after the general administration of the collection business in that region.

5 Forrest

Introduction

5.1. In this chapter we first outline the historical background leading to Forrest becoming a part of Strong & Fisher (Holdings) plc (Strong & Fisher), which, in turn, is predominantly owned by Hillsdown (paragraphs 5.1 to 5.5). We then describe Forrest's structure and activities, and its compliance with environmental and public health requirements (paragraphs 5.6 to 5.13). Finally, we set the company in the context of its ultimate ownership by Hillsdown, and refer to its recent acquisitions (paragraphs 5.14 to 5.19).

Historical background

5.2. Forrest was established by Mr William Forrest, in Paisley, in 1865. In 1917 it was incorporated in Scotland as a limited company. The company moved to its present, more isolated location at Newarthill, Motherwell in 1975.

5.3. In 1985 the present Managing Director of Forrest, who had been with the company for 20 years, was part of an attempted management buy-out of the company from the Forrest family. The shareholders, through Mr R Forrest, who was about to retire, had earlier been in negotiation with PDM, from which they had bought Frank Gysels in 1981 (see paragraph 4.11 and Appendix 5.1). In the event, however, they chose, in 1986, to sell their business to Hillsdown. Hillsdown told us that it had been seeking to acquire a rendering business and in its view Forrest was the best available.

5.4. Hillsdown acquired in England, at about the same time, North Devon Meat Ltd (NDM), of which Peninsular, then a co-operative first established in 1978, formed a division. The co-operative's main *raison d'être* was to process NDM's (and two or three other abattoirs') animal waste, which still today accounts for around one-quarter of Peninsular's throughput.

5.5. In November 1990 both Forrest and Peninsular became subsidiaries of Strong & Fisher, as part of a capital reconstruction whereby Hillsdown took a 70.3 per cent shareholding in that company in order to rescue it from financial difficulty. Peninsular took on its present name in January 1991, having first been incorporated as a limited company six months earlier. Appendix 5.1 illustrates the relationship of Forrest (and Peninsular) with Hillsdown and Strong & Fisher.

Structure and activities

5.6. Forrest renders, through three continuous cookers, fats, bones, offal, and SBO collected from abattoirs, boning-out plants, knackers and butchers' shops (see Chapter 2). The disposal of blood, as fertilizer, is carried out by Transorganics Ltd, which rents facilities at the Newarthill site. Forrest's end products are grade 2 tallow, feed-grade tallow, grade 6 tallow and meat-and-bone meal. A small pet food operation was begun experimentally in September 1992 but ceased a few months later.

5.7. In addition to Forrest's activities at Newarthill, as indicated in Appendix 5.1 Forrest's subsidiary R McCulloch Ltd (R McCulloch), and W C Hodgkinson (Cleland) Ltd (W C Hodgkinson), are engaged in the collection of deadstock from farms. W C Hodgkinson owns the Newarthill site, while R McCulloch operates its collection service from a depot in Lochgelly. John Moran Ltd, owned as to 80 per cent by Forrest, is engaged in gut-room operations and the production of natural sausage casings from a separate site in Ayrshire. Forrest also has a depot in Elgin, Morayshire in the far north of Scotland and uses the depot owned by R McCulloch in Lochgelly, between Dundee and Edinburgh.

5.8. Forrest's raw materials are sourced principally in Scotland. Greaves are brought in from both the Republic of Ireland and from Northern Ireland and, to a lesser extent, England, but no longer in the former quantities, mainly as Forrest closed down its 15-year old solvent extraction operation in 1992 and thus no longer has the same requirement for greaves. Also in 1992, Peninsular supplied Forrest with 2,300 tonnes of raw material which Peninsular was unable to process when installing its new plant (see paragraph 2.83). (Forrest supplied Peninsular with some 600 tonnes of meat-and-bone meal in return.) Another Hillsdown-owned company, Daylay Foods Ltd (Daylay) (see paragraph 5.17), has for many years bought meat-and-bone meal from Forrest on an arm's length basis.

5.9. Forrest's procurement prices and charges and its end-product sales prices are determined in the manner described in Chapter 6 and are subject to agreement by the Managing Director. Profitability is monitored principally by reference to profit per tonne of raw material purchased, with monthly and accumulative management accounts produced to a strict timetable. Production yields and energy usage per tonne processed are monitored weekly, and on a monthly basis using additional figures of purchases, sales and stocks.

Environmental and public health

5.10. Forrest told us that compliance with the EPA and other environmental and public health controls necessitated considerable capital expenditure and raised running costs. Complaints about the plant were not yet a problem, though housing was beginning to encroach on the surrounding buffer land, but in the late 1980s Forrest had been obliged to cease using an old mine shaft to dispose of effluent. The installation of a new effluent treatment plant complying with the environmental protection requirements cost over £140,000 and that of a sewage disposal pipeline a further £113,000. Odour control capital expenditure was doubled. A further £93,000 on air pollution control was currently contemplated as part of Forrest's review of ways of improving its environmental controls and reducing processing and waste disposal costs (see Chapter 3).

5.11. Forrest said that it enjoyed good relations with its local regulatory authorities, which now visited its site frequently and were in regular contact with Forrest; it was conscious, however, that the stringent requirements of the EPA might make such relations for the rendering industry generally more difficult. Forrest expressed confidence that it would be granted the necessary authorization under the EPA. It had been requested to delay its application until 31 March 1992 because of the authorities' volume of work. Indications were that it would be required to enhance its quality control system and put in a bio-filter. Capital expenditure of some £750,000 over three years was in prospect.

5.12. As regards the Directive 90/667/EEC, Forrest's plant was already capable of complying with its requirements, though it expected that further and more stringent directives would be introduced which might require totally segregated processing lines in separate buildings for high- and low-grade materials. Forrest had invested approximately £30,000 in conveyors for the processing of SBO, which was carried out separately at the end of the day in cooker no 2. Forrest would, ideally, like to have a complete line dedicated to SBO but the investment was difficult to justify. Forrest disposes of its SBO greaves at a landfill site under licence from MAFF and the local environmental health department. Forrest told us also that it had worked with MAFF on research into the testing of BSE-infected cattle.

5.13. Forrest does not otherwise undertake specific research projects, though it does seek to keep abreast of the latest developments and technology relating, in particular, to processing plant and energy-saving equipment. For this purpose it has access through Hillsdown to the work done by its sister renderer in Canada (see paragraph 5.15).

Hillsdown

5.14. In the year to 31 December 1992, Hillsdown had a turnover of £4.37 billion and profits before tax of £154 million. Hillsdown's business is primarily in the food sector in the UK, continental Europe and North America; its main areas of activities are organized in the following divisions:

(a) food processing and distribution;

(b) fresh meat and bacon;

(c) poultry and eggs;

(d) furniture; and

(e) house building, property and specialist operations.

5.15. The Fresh Meat and Bacon Division accounted for approximately £880 million of Hillsdown's turnover in 1992. It comprises FMC plc (FMC), the holding company for the red meat slaughtering and processing activities of FMC (Meat) Ltd and for the bacon and ham curers, C & T Harris (Calne) Ltd; the Harris Pork and Bacon group, specializing in value-added ham and bacon products; and Strong & Fisher. In 1992 FMC was the UK's largest processor of beef, lamb and pork. In Canada, where Maple Leaf Foods is one of the largest pork producers, the Fresh Meat and Bacon Division has further significant rendering operations, processing 10 to 15 times more tonnes than Forrest.

5.16. Apart from its interests in rendering through Forrest and Peninsular, Strong & Fisher is also the UK's leading hide and skin trader, fellmonger and tanner. It is organized into a separate By-Products Division (the Forrest Group) and Leather Division, each linked by a common dependence on raw material emanating from the red meat slaughtering industry, the decline of which has affected the performance both of Strong & Fisher and of the Fresh Meat and Bacon Division as a whole in recent years. Strong & Fisher has announced its wish to add a third division over time and also told us of its interest in expanding its rendering business both organically and by acquisition, should a suitable opportunity arise. The Chairman of Strong & Fisher is a main Board Director of Hillsdown.

5.17. Hillsdown's Poultry and Eggs Division turned over approximately £870 million in 1992. It is the largest chicken processor in the UK, including such names as Buxted Chickens Ltd and Premier Poultry Ltd, while Moorland Foods Ltd is the second largest turkey-processing operation. In addition, Daylay is the leading supplier to the UK's major retailers of a total range of egg products, and Ross Breeders Ltd is Europe's largest poultry-breeding company. Maple Leaf Foods is also a significant poultry processor in Canada. The division's UK processing operations are currently near the end of a complete reorganization initiated following Hillsdown's acquisition from Unigate Plc, early in 1992, of the then second largest UK chicken producer, J P Wood. Processing capacity has been cut from over 3 million to under 2 million birds a week and older facilities replaced with more advanced and more efficient ones in order to enhance competitiveness on a European basis.

5.18. We were told that in accordance with Hillsdown's established management philosophy, trading between Forrest and Peninsular and other group companies took place on an arm's length basis. As a consequence each business sought to obtain its raw materials at the best price available; each business was free to supply the competitors of Hillsdown subsidiaries; and each business was free to compete for customers. It was Hillsdown's policy to devolve the maximum possible autonomy to its subsidiaries with the minimum involvement in the running of their operations. Hillsdown also had a record of well-directed and committed capital expenditure, which was of particular importance in the rendering industry and which in Forrest's case had enabled its operations to continue while other companies had been forced to close.

Forrest's recent acquisitions

5.19. Forrest told us that since becoming part of Hillsdown it had acquired the goodwill and certain assets of the following loss-making or unviable businesses:

Date of acquisition	Businesses acquired	Approximate tonnes/week
December 1987	*Grant Brothers Ltd* was an old established business run by three elderly brothers. Unable to continue with its management, and with no one in the family interested in so doing, the family offered it for sale to Forrest.	70
December 1987	*Strathmore Meat Co Ltd* was losing money. Forrest was approached and asked if it would be interested in acquiring it.	135
April 1990	*Elgin Animal By-Products Ltd* (Elgin)—Following the loss of the Elgin processing plant through fire in early 1989, the owners decided that replacement was not justified. The owners tried to negotiate the merger of their business with that of Dundas Brothers. Dundas Brothers was not interested in merging the businesses and Elgin approached, and was subsequently acquired by, Forrest.	450
November 1990	*Alexander Haddow & Sons Ltd* was a family-run business which was acquired from the family by one of the directors. Three years later the company was suffering unacceptable and ongoing losses and was offered to Forrest.	30

Much the most significant, as well as the largest, of these acquisitions by Forrest was that of Elgin, a rendering company which had operated on two sites (not acquired by Forrest), at Elgin and at Conon Bridge near Inverness. Thereby Forrest established a strong presence north of its traditional area and became a collector throughout the Scottish mainland.

6 The pricing practices of PDM and Forrest

6.1. The way in which prices for animal waste are set is described in paragraphs 2.61 to 2.73. In brief, agreements are generally made orally between abattoir and renderer and can be renegotiated at short notice. The prices of animal waste reflect major changes in the prices of the renderers' own products. Abattoirs generally agree prices with renderers for each of the main categories of waste they supply, and the prices reflect not only the quality and quantity of material and the costs of transportation and collection, but also the degree of competition for the abattoir's supplies.

6.2. In this chapter we shall consider the pricing practices of PDM and then of Forrest and describe the analysis we have carried out of their prices, both overall and in specific cases. We shall in this chapter use 'prices' to refer to both prices and charges, except when otherwise indicated.

The pricing practices of PDM

6.3. PDM told us that of its own contracts about 10 per cent were for more than one month, 60 per cent were for one month, and the remainder operated on a day-to-day basis. In most cases it agreed contracts with individual abattoirs but there were also some 14 cases, covering 80 abattoirs, where PDM negotiated with companies that owned more than one abattoir and reached a single agreement for the abattoir group. In such cases prices might be agreed that did not vary between the abattoirs in the group on account of quality or cost of collection, and an overrider discount was occasionally agreed that applied to the group as a whole.

6.4. PDM told us that the operators of abattoirs were aware of changes in its output prices and that this formed part of the basis of the negotiation. When output prices changed substantially the prices for animal waste followed suit, and usually more rapidly in the case of increases than with decreases. In a few cases involving major suppliers PDM had agreed a formula with the abattoir linking the price to be paid for animal waste to the prices for tallow and meat-and-bone meal.

6.5. PDM told us that the main factors determining its prices were the end-product prices, the quality and quantity of the supplies, the nature of the arrangements for collection and transportation, and competition. The factor that had the largest impact on prices was the quality of material. Quality was measured mainly by the yield of the material in terms of tallow and meat-and-bone meal and the water content. We discussed in detail with PDM the way in which the various factors affected the prices of each category of raw material, and this is reflected in our analysis of PDM's prices set out in Appendix 6.1 (and discussed further in paragraphs 6.8 to 6.11).

6.6. PDM said that its buyers assessed the quality of the material by inspection and on that basis offered a price to the abattoir. The buyer was also familiar in most cases with the inputs and processing methods of the abattoirs which provided some indication of the quality of each of the categories of material available. PDM did not, however, normally test the quality of material it acquired either at the abattoir or at its processing plant. PDM told us that it would be logistically and administratively impossible to separate, weigh, test and price all the different types of material bought from each abattoir. The only precise data available to PDM on the yields that could be expected from the material acquired were the yields actually achieved by each processing plant. These yields reflected the mix of raw material processed. PDM said that these actual yields varied by only 2 or 3 per cent compared with estimated yields, ie it was able to estimate overall yields for a given plant fairly exactly. The only circumstances in which PDM currently tested the quality of materials purchased was when

236197 E

the actual yields of a plant diverged significantly from those expected. Using its information on average yields, expected end-product prices and expected total costs, PDM was able to provide its buyers every month with average target prices for each category of material. A more detailed account of this and other aspects of PDM's pricing and costing system is set out in paragraphs 8.24 to 8.67.

6.7. As regards competition, PDM accepted that its intensity could vary on a geographical basis. In reference to the period in 1992 when competition was more intense (often referred to as the 'price war' and described in paragraph 2.73), PDM agreed that higher prices were paid to those suppliers affected by the price war whereas unaffected suppliers continued to be paid prices at previously prevailing levels. Thus, certain abattoirs in the Midlands were cited to us by PDM in order to show that prices had increased where an abattoir had been approached by Gilberts but had not increased where an abattoir was not considering a change of renderer. PDM also said that prices were influenced not only by the continuing competition between renderers for particular abattoirs' supplies but also by the bargaining strength of large suppliers.

6.8. We considered whether PDM, given its market share and lack of competitors of comparable size, might be able to discriminate between suppliers in its prices and charges in the sense of charging suppliers different prices for material of comparable quality and similar cost of collection. If this were so, we would expect to find that prices were dispersed over a range much wider than what might be considered the natural competitive range. In order to investigate this possibility we analysed PDM's prices and charges for the months of May and October 1992. We attempted to estimate the range of prices arising from physical factors (principally the quality and quantity of material and the arrangements for collection and transportation) and to compare these ranges with actual prices. We also considered the relationship between actual prices and PDM's target prices. All the information we have used, both as to prices and yields, was supplied by PDM and relates to its own operations. PDM was not, however, able to provide us with information on the quality or expected yields of materials supplied by individual abattoirs (as explained in paragraph 6.6), and hence the need for the more extended analysis we have carried out.

6.9. The details of our investigation are set out in Appendix 6.1. We found that while the range of prices actually paid was very wide indeed, the price differences that might in theory be attributable to the physical factors were also large when they are added together. In particular, the differences in quality within a particular category of material could, because of their effects on output yields, lead to a wide variance in the value of the material to PDM. However, our investigations showed that many individual prices could not be explained by differences in physical factors combined with a reasonable price range to account for competition. The analysis of price ranges revealed an unexplained residual of price differences of £23 per tonne for SBO and of at least £36 for other offal in May 1992 and of £29 per tonne for best fat in October 1992. We also found that the majority of best fat and SBO bought in May and October 1992 and of bone in October 1992 was priced well above PDM's target prices. In addition there were many cases where the prices paid were far higher than could be accounted for by variation in output yields, even if yields were used that maximized end-product sales. For example, the prices of most of the tonnage of bone collected in May 1992 were in the range £20 to £30 per tonne, whereas the target price based on yields that maximized end-product sales would be £16 per tonne.

6.10. Some of PDM's prices that do not wholly reflect physical factors may be the result of its negotiations with abattoir groups (as described in paragraph 6.3). We found that the highest prices paid in May and October 1992 to abattoir groups for best fat were £17 and £19 higher respectively than the highest prices paid to other abattoirs.

6.11. In order to check whether the range of prices paid by PDM was different during the price war that took place during the middle part of 1992 than at other times we examined the range of PDM's prices in April 1993 and compared them with those of May and October 1992. We found that there was no significant difference (see also paragraphs 14 and 15 of Appendix 6.1) between April 1993 on the one hand and May and October 1992 on the other.

6.12. As a result of a number of complaints, we also considered whether there was any evidence that PDM's pricing had been predatory. The approach that we adopted for predatory pricing involved a twofold test: first, that the prices paid should mean that average total costs were not fully covered by the increase in sales revenue; and secondly, that there should be an intention on the part of PDM to prejudice the survival of its competitor in the market.

6.13. We looked at a number of cases. Most related to acquisitions of material direct from abattoirs and arose during the price war of 1992; they are described in Appendix 6.2. We also looked at a case involving a gut-room operated by PDM. It is dealt with in paragraph 6.16.

6.14. The cases described in Appendix 6.2 do not provide evidence that PDM's prices were predatory in the full sense of that term as defined in paragraph 6.12. It could not be demonstrated in any of the cases that it was PDM's intention to eliminate or undermine a competitor. It is clear nevertheless that during the price war PDM was offering prices that were too high to allow recovery of average total costs—and the case of the Anglo-Dutch Meats abattoir at Charing is an example of this. PDM accepts that some of the contracts that it undertook in the middle months of 1992 were not profitable, and those contracts meant overall losses for PDM in each of the months of May to August, as shown in its management accounts.

6.15. PDM emphasized to us its determination to retain its supplies of raw material. It has been able to sustain considerable losses in the course of carrying out that strategy—PDM estimated at around £2 million the cost to it of the 1992 price war, and this meant a considerable reduction in its profits on rendering in that financial year. In some of the cases where contracts were loss-making it may be the case, as PDM indicated, that it was only after prices were agreed that it was realized that the prices paid would mean a loss on the contract. PDM has, however, a system of average target prices for each of the main categories of raw materials and this, combined with its considerable experience of the business, provided an indication of the extent of losses being incurred during the middle months of 1992. PDM told us that the losses incurred at that time were greater than the losses often incurred in the middle months of the year when supplies were at their lowest.

6.16. The gut-room case we examined occurred before the 1992 price war. IMC, a specialist gut-room operator, complained to the DGFT that in September 1991 PDM had taken on a contract at West Devon Meats, Hatherleigh, at uneconomic prices in breach of its 1986 undertakings. We found that PDM's administration charge of £50 per week to each of its gut-rooms, while sufficient to cover its direct administration costs, did not cover indirect costs. PDM uses a system of inter-company transfer prices for materials transferred from its gut-room operation to its rendering operation and, when these were used, PDM appeared to have taken on the contract on a profitable basis. However, when we costed the contract using the prices actually paid at that time by PDM to IMC and the charges for the removal of offal and SBO made by PDM to the abattoirs where IMC operated the gut-room, we found that the Hatherleigh contract had been taken on at a loss. There was no evidence that PDM had intended to damage IMC. A full account of our investigation of IMC's complaint is set out in Appendix 6.3.

The pricing practices of Forrest

6.17. Forrest told us that the prices and charges it offered were determined by the quantity and quality of material, the economics of collection and particular features of each individual contract. However, it also said that in order to gain sufficient throughput to cover its costs and gain a reasonable profit margin it would on occasion have to offer higher prices as required in order to obtain supplies. Forrest stated that in determining the maximum prices it would offer when competing for an abattoir's business with another renderer it would be looking for at least some contribution to overheads in addition to covering incremental costs. A fuller account of Forrest's pricing system is set out in paragraphs 9.24 to 9.40.

6.18. As in the case of PDM, we considered whether Forrest might be carrying out a discriminatory pricing policy in the sense of charging suppliers differently for material that was comparable in quality and similar in cost of collection. We carried out a similar investigation to that mentioned in paragraph 6.8 and this is described in detail in Appendix 6.4. We found that Forrest's prices varied substantially in a way that was not always attributable to physical factors.

236197 E2

6.19. Adopting the same approach as set out in paragraph 6.12 we also looked at a number of cases in which Forrest offered high prices for its supplies. These cases are described in Appendix 6.5. We were not able to identify any instances where it could be demonstrated that Forrest's intention was to eliminate or undermine a competitor. We did, however, identify two cases, those of abattoirs at Turriff and Biggar, where prices were such that revenues were insufficient to cover average total costs. This would tally with Forrest's policy of paying whatever prices were necessary to gain the required throughput consistent with making some contribution to overheads.

6.20. The cases we examined (involving both Dundas Brothers and Dundas Chemical—see Appendix 6.5) showed that Forrest, where it thought it necessary to obtain supplies, had offered prices that reflected competition as well as other factors and had on occasion been prepared to pay prices that, while they meant that incremental costs were covered, did not cover average total costs, ie they made only a partial contribution to overheads. While we do not have any evidence that it was Forrest's intention to undermine the position of its competitor, Dundas Chemical, the effect of Forrest's pricing practices is to have deprived Dundas Chemical of a significant portion of its supplies.

7 Evidence of third parties

7.1. We invited views and information from animal waste suppliers, renderers and collectors of animal by-products, customers of renderers, trade associations, Government departments and other interested parties. The evidence we received is summarized principally in this chapter. Summaries of the complaints and allegations made against PDM and Forrest, together with PDM's and Forrest's responses, are provided in Appendix 7.1.

Suppliers of animal waste

Biggar Quality Meats Ltd

7.2. Biggar Quality Meats Ltd (Biggar), which said that it was one of the top three abattoirs in Scotland in terms of the number of sheep it slaughtered, told us at a hearing that the slaughtering industry was very competitive, particularly since the introduction of the Fresh Meat (Hygiene and Inspection) Regulations 1991. It regarded England and Wales as having a separate animal waste market from Scotland because of the distances involved.

7.3. Biggar had not experienced any problems with Forrest as it always provided an excellent service, but it said that it would be concerned if Forrest's competitors, Dundas Brothers and Dundas Chemical, went out of business as this would eliminate any bargaining power.

7.4. Up until July 1992 Biggar had sold its waste to Forrest. Then Dundas Chemical approached Biggar and made a bid for its rendering material. The offer was approximately £800 a week more than Biggar had been receiving from Forrest. Biggar consulted Forrest and it made a slightly better offer and a back payment of about £4,000. Biggar felt that it had benefited from the price war and it was now receiving about £1,000 per week more for its material. However, others in the industry had also moved their prices, and ultimately this had worked into the trading price. Biggar said that Forrest had told it that it could not afford to lose its volume of material and was prepared to work at a loss.

7.5. Biggar said that since this incident it had wondered if perhaps Forrest had not always paid the best price and was worried about what would happen if Dundas Chemical ever went out of business. It was concerned to the extent that it said it would be prepared to make a marginal financial sacrifice to keep Forrest's competitors in business.

7.6. Biggar told us that smaller abattoirs in the industry received less payment than itself, based on the fact that they had less volume of material. In areas with little or no competition between renderers, Biggar believed that abattoirs were not getting paid at all for their waste.

F A Gill Ltd

7.7. F A Gill Ltd (F A Gill), a medium-sized pig abattoir, told us that it had a long-established relationship with its local waste collector, Rick Strain. It hoped that there would be no further concentration of ownership, which it felt had been caused by economic pressures on processing plants. It would be concerned if concentrated ownership forced higher charges on the abattoir sector.

Edward Hamer International Ltd

7.8. Edward Hamer International Ltd (Edward Hamer), a Welsh operator of an abattoir and meat processing facility, told us that it felt particularly vulnerable to the rendering trade in Wales since during the past 12 to 18 months it was unable to get any other company besides PDM to collect its material. It felt that it had to pay PDM whatever it requested for the removal of its material. It had approached other companies but was told that they 'dare not even consider' collecting its material. It was evident that PDM monopolized the industry.

John Manson Ltd

7.9. John Manson Ltd (John Manson), a supplier of meat and poultry,[1] told us that it originally had its own by-products department but, because of poor returns for tallow and bonemeal, it had closed the department. Waste from its 36 shops was collected by John Knight (Animal By Products) Ltd. The butcher trade had suffered from the encroachment of supermarkets and the number of its own shops had reduced from 80 to 36.

7.10. John Manson said that the disposal of its waste was only a minor irritant and that it had not considered using an alternative renderer if its present one started to charge for collections. It would, however, be concerned if charges were introduced and commented that most small independent butchers already paid a collection charge.

Saxby Bros Ltd

7.11. Saxby Bros Ltd (Saxby), a producer of pork products, thought that there were only two substantial companies which handled animal waste. However, it felt that even if a monopoly situation existed there was no alternative as local authorities did not wish to handle this problem. Saxby told us that it no longer slaughtered, but that when it was dealing with PDM, it found the company to be efficient and reliable.

E Simpson Ltd

7.12. E Simpson Ltd, a pork butcher and sausage manufacturer, told us that on balance it had been well served by its animal waste removers although at times prices received fell short of expectation.

Tesco PLC

7.13. Speaking on behalf of its suppliers, Tesco PLC (Tesco) told us that at present approximately 70 per cent of all animal waste was collected and subsequently sold through PDM. It said that PDM had grown significantly over the last five years, mainly through its acquisitions. In many areas PDM was now the only company offering a collection service.

7.14. Tesco said that although the value of this waste was relatively small, it still formed an integral part of an abattoir's return. It therefore felt that it would be unhealthy for the meat industry and commercially damaging to its suppliers if PDM continued to grow.

Mr John Warman

7.15. Mr John Warman, a knackerman, gave us written evidence and attended a hearing. He told us that before PDM entered the market in East Anglia, he was paid £15 per tonne for knacker offal

---

[1] During the course of our inquiry John Manson went into voluntary liquidation.

by local renderers. When PDM came into the market, it offered a guaranteed price of no less than £30 per tonne. Asked how it could pay so much more, PDM said that it had installed a new cooker at its John Knight plant which took only two hours' cooking time, at a lower temperature than the orthodox method of dry cooking, and destroyed all bacteria.

7.16. To Mr Warman's concern, and to that of others like himself, PDM gradually began buying out the local renderers. The knackermen were assured by PDM that it would not take advantage of the situation. Mr Warman found, however, that gradually the price of his knacker offal fell to £2 per tonne. In time, he was told he would have to *pay* £20 per tonne for the removal of his waste material, a charge which eventually rose to £90 per tonne. Mr Warman told us that the payment knackermen used to receive for their offal was a large part of their income and such a loss had resulted in the closure of some knacker yards. Mr Warman believed that this situation had arisen as a result of PDM monopolizing the rendering industry and he therefore opposed any further take-overs by PDM.

An abattoir group

7.17. In written and oral evidence, an abattoir group which owns a chain of slaughterhouses told us that although PDM and its subsidiaries dealt with the majority of animal waste in England, this in itself did not present a problem. There was concern, however, that the rest of the rendering trade generally accepted PDM's price as the market price, although PDM's price was based on its own trading results and not on general trading conditions. This price structure therefore:

(a) insulated PDM against the possibility of poor trading by allowing a purchase price movement to balance a low sales price;

(b) made it possible for PDM to cover its production by future sales, and any discount suffered was recovered by a purchase price adjustment; and

(c) did not always give suppliers of animal waste a true market price or a fair return against the end-product price.

7.18. The abattoir group told us that the situation in Scotland was similar, although operated by Forrest. There the market was restricted by imposed prices based on the fact that there was no competition from PDM. It felt that the lack of free enterprise penalized the suppliers of animal waste unreasonably and it was inevitable that higher costs would be passed on to the public as part of the cost of meat production.

7.19. Although at present there were about 800 abattoirs, the abattoir group was concerned that this number would reduce drastically as a result of the Government's implementation of the new EC regulations. It told us that this view was in line with the Meat & Livestock Commission's expectation.

A Yorkshire abattoir

7.20. A small- to medium-sized Yorkshire abattoir told us that, as there was no competition for the disposal of animal waste in the area where it operated, it had to pay the high charges fixed by PDM. Negotiation with PDM was difficult and rarely achieved. Apart from the rendering industry the chances of finding other means of disposal were remote and would be uneconomical.

A manufacturer of canned meat

7.21. A manufacturer of canned meat was concerned about the monopoly situation which PDM had gained over the last five years by its acquisition of rendering plants and supplying agents. There was now a virtual stranglehold on the outlets available for manufacturers and abattoirs to dispose of their animal waste.

7.22. It told us that until recently it had to dispose of its waste material via one of PDM's agents at a cost of £60 per tonne. It had now found another company, Gilberts, which would dispose of the same waste material for £35 per tonne. It felt that such a difference in price was due to PDM's virtual monopoly in the market which restricted free and fair competition and consequently forced producers to pay unrealistic prices.

A butcher

7.23. A butcher told us that the number of companies licensed to collect and process inedible waste had vastly declined during the last five years. Because of this abattoirs and butchers had to pay for collection of their by-products rather than receiving payment for what was after all a valuable source of protein, minerals and oils. It was currently paying £6 per drum, for the collection of its chicken by-products, and this was in an area where there were other abattoirs on the same road.

Competitors of PDM and Forrest

Competitors of PDM

Beeson Brothers (Crewe) Ltd

7.24. Beeson was a knacker yard which manufactured pet food and carried out some rendering until 1992. It told us that the local council made a handsome offer for its site although at the time Beeson was looking towards expanding. It said that PDM had benefited from its closure only in so far as Clutton now collected its raw material and supplied it to PDM. PDM only acquired a very limited amount of its equipment as the bulk of it went to Wykes Engineering.

7.25. Beeson told us that rendering was not a lucrative business at present, with particular problems for small companies caused by the new environmental requirements. The industry was becoming more and more concentrated because slaughterhouses were either closing down or cutting back.

E Clutton & Sons (Marchwiel) Ltd

7.26. Clutton, a collector and knacker yard, told us that its business had previously been owned by PDM. Clutton collected offal, bones and fats from abattoirs and supplied them to PDM. The number of abattoirs had declined over the years, but the remaining ones had expanded. About two years ago, PDM had offered Clutton the knacker side of its business because it did not want to handle BSE waste. Clutton was now completely independent of PDM but still collected for it on occasion in return for payment.

7.27. Clutton had recently started an incineration business which was also independent of PDM. There were about six incinerators in the country. Although at present the business was profitable, the future for incineration was uncertain because BSE would not last indefinitely. Clutton was contracted by MAFF to kill diseased animals and was paid £100 per cow.

7.28. When Beeson closed down, Clutton took over some of its collection business. It paid Beeson £150,000 for the business, including lorries. PDM was not involved financially or in an advisory capacity. Clutton's offal collection had doubled and its knacker trade trebled as a result of the closure of Beeson. All the material for rendering was supplied to PDM, and in addition material was supplied to maggot farms, pet food businesses and mink farms.

European Organic Processing Ltd

7.29. European Organic Processing Ltd (EUROP) told us that it was a potential new entrant to the rendering market in the UK. It said that although the market had been dominated by PDM and Hillsdown, it still had an opportunity. EUROP planned to offer customers a better service than PDM, particularly in respect of its attitude towards customers. This could give EUROP an edge long enough for it to establish itself as a force within the industry.

7.30. EUROP believed that when it entered the market, the price paid for disposal would fall, although it was not its intention to force the prices down. It had made allowances in its strategy to withstand any price cutting by PDM and welcomed competition. It would be using the very latest technology and methods and it believed that its operating costs would probably be better than the industry had enjoyed to date.

7.31. One of the major difficulties EUROP had faced was finding a site, particularly because of resistance from local residents. It had asked local authorities to identify possible sites and this approach had provided a good response.

7.32. EUROP had the feeling that MAFF considered PDM an important force in the industry and that the entry of a new player could destabilize PDM's business. EUROP had, however, been accepted for an EC grant, for which it had needed MAFF's support.

Fats & Proteins (UK) Ltd

7.33. Fats & Proteins, a renderer, felt that PDM could not in reality influence the market for meat-and-bone meal because of the competition from vegetable products such as soya. Fats & Proteins competed with Forrest in Scotland. With an articulated trailer, there was no reason for Forrest not to travel south of the border. Fats & Proteins was prepared to travel beyond a 100-mile radius to collect material if it was available.

7.34. Fats & Proteins told us that on occasion PDM had telephoned to talk about its prices and how it wanted to keep them at certain levels, suggesting that Fats & Proteins should do the same. Fats & Proteins had always maintained an independent pricing policy.

7.35. Fats & Proteins felt that some abattoirs and boning-out plants were becoming concerned about the long-term survival of the smaller renderers, as indicated by their reluctance to trade with PDM.

7.36. Fats & Proteins said that because, on the face of it, PDM's accounts showed it to be weak, it would not be in the national or public interest for PDM to take over yet more rendering operations or increase its market share. However, there was concern of possible connections with a trading company, Hi-Cal in Jersey, which, if it had big reserves, could be used to influence the UK rendering industry significantly.

Gilberts Animal By-Products Ltd

7.37. At a hearing, Gilberts, a renderer, accused PDM of purchasing materials through acquired companies such as Stannard and Klein. Gilberts had one collector which supplied it with material. It would have liked more but PDM had most of the collectors. Collectors were unlikely to change customers because they feared intimidation by PDM. Abattoirs also tended to deal with people they were used to, perhaps because they feared the consequences.

7.38. In 1992 Gilberts had been engaged in a price war with PDM. In February 1992 two abattoirs which supplied Gilberts closed. They had provided 25 per cent of Gilberts' throughput (about 300 tonnes per week). Before this, PDM had started 'pinching' material and was determined to encroach on Gilberts' customer, Barratt & Baird (see Appendix 6.2). PDM began to take Barratt & Baird's offal at a considerably lower price at a time when charges on offal were high. Gilberts had no doubt that PDM was losing money on this contract; PDM also began syphoning-off other materials which were traditionally Gilberts'. When Gilberts approached PDM, it denied all knowledge of the incident. This was the beginning of a confrontation with PDM: Gilberts began to encroach on PDM's customers in return. Unfortunately other competitors were also drawn into the price war.

7.39. Owing to the massive loss of material, Gilberts placed an advertisement for suppliers in the *Meat Trades Journal*. It found that those which responded were from the north of England where there was no competition to PDM.

7.40. Gilberts said that at present, offal charges should be about £30 per tonne. PDM, however, was charging £35 in some places and nil in places where competition was keenest. The reality of the market was that PDM set the prices, because of its dominance, and others tended to follow. PDM set its prices in a way which was intended to exploit and reinforce its monopoly position. It charged high prices where there was no competition, such as in East Anglia, and loss-making prices where there was competition. This made it very difficult for competitors to make a living. The fact that PDM deployed these tactics on an intermittent rather than on a continuous basis made life uncomfortable for competitors over a long period, as the history of the industry indicated.

7.41. Gilberts accepted that PDM was entitled to compete with it just as it was entitled to compete with PDM; what it objected to was PDM competing in an unfair and predatory manner.

7.42. Gilberts told us that the main barriers to entry into the animal waste market were finance and planning, and that the cost of plant would be a minimum of £6 million. Potential new entrants were faced with a 'David and Goliath' situation as PDM could exploit its dominance by intimidation. PDM could also influence the market by undercutting its competitors. PDM was known to have given out false information whereby it claimed that it was putting up the prices of meat-and-bone meal so that competitors would do likewise. Competitors then found that PDM had not in fact put up its prices. Gilberts also said that there was not a realistic market for second-hand machinery because PDM was able to acquire 70 per cent of it, which left little for anyone else.

Imperial Meat Company Ltd

7.43. IMC's business consists principally of the operation and management of gut-rooms. It also collects certain animal waste products, in particular glands, from abattoirs where it is not engaged as a contractor. It currently operates nine gut-rooms and in addition has two staff at Barratt & Baird's abattoir in Birmingham recovering glands and pigs' stomachs. IMC told us that the number of gut-room contracts it operated had considerably diminished since the time of the 1985 report. This was due largely to the reduction in the numbers of abattoirs, and to competition from abattoirs' in-house operations, from PDM and from other gut-room contractors.

7.44. IMC believed that PDM had a strong economic interest in obtaining as much rendering material as possible from gut-room operators. The control of these materials reinforced PDM's position as the dominant producer and improved the economics of its collection operations because of the saving in collecting fats from both abattoir and gut-room operator in the same location. It also helped to foreclose the market for the purchase of materials against its competitors.

7.45. IMC told us that in its submission to the MMC's previous inquiry, it had complained that PDM offered to take over gut-room contracts at prices which were uneconomically high. The 1985 report had led to PDM being required to give undertakings about the operation of its gut-rooms (see Appendix 1.2). Gut-room contracting was not considered to be PDM's mainstream business and therefore its participation was only as a means of reinforcing its dominant market position and not for making a profit.

7.46. Following the take-overs of competing rendering businesses such as MCP and Croda there was now little competition in the rendering sector. (Until its take-over, Croda had purchased fats from IMC's gut-rooms.) IMC also drew attention to the cumulative effect of the take-over of smaller 'niche' businesses such as Nortech.

7.47. IMC had complained to the OFT about the actions of PDM in obtaining a contract to operate the gut-room at the abattoir owned by West Devon Meats Ltd at Hatherleigh, Devon, at prices which were unlikely to be economic on the basis of prices prevailing when PDM agreed to take over the gut-room (see Appendix 6.3). IMC understood that the OFT was unable to form a definite conclusion as to whether PDM's conduct constituted a breach of undertakings. IMC believed that PDM's conduct arose out of concern that the materials from Hatherleigh might be offered to Peninsular's rendering plant in Devon, which would adversely affect the economics of PDM's rendering plant in Exeter.

7.48. IMC was concerned that PDM's involvement in the industry as a gut-room operator as well as a renderer gave rise to the possibility of distortion of competition which would be very difficult to detect. Where PDM transacted business with an abattoir as collector of rendering materials, as gut-room operator and in removal of waste materials it could be very difficult to unravel exactly how much PDM was paying for rendering materials, how much it was paying for the gut-room concession, and how much it was charging for the removal of waste materials. This problem made it difficult for the OFT to monitor PDM's undertakings or to come to any rapid conclusion upon complaints that gut-rooms were being operated by PDM on an uneconomic basis.

7.49. IMC suggested that there was difficulty in investigating complaints of predatory behaviour, and that justice delayed could very easily be justice denied. IMC put forward a number of possible remedies for what it considered to be the weaknesses of the 1986 undertakings, including substituting new undertakings with amended wording (which would be enforceable by civil action as a result of changes to the law made in the Companies Act 1989), substituting the undertakings by order, or requiring PDM not to take on new gut-room contracts. IMC said that the difficulties of enforcement were so great that the last remedy merited serious consideration.

7.50. IMC said that prices of rendering materials would fluctuate strongly if the market was subject to normal competitive disciplines. This was because such materials were supplied as a by-product, their supply being determined by market forces affecting the meat industry and not by the market for the products themselves. Supply was therefore totally unresponsive to changes in the demand for, or the price of, rendering end products. Since the take-over of MCP and Croda, normal competitive forces in the market had ceased to apply and PDM had in effect been able to impose its own prices on the market. The result was that the price of rendering materials had become much more stable. Only two independent rendering companies were now left to compete nationally with PDM. These were Hillsdown and Gilberts. Hillsdown, however, did not compete on a systematic basis with PDM.

7.51. PDM's dominance of the rendering market prevented the proper operation of competitive pricing mechanisms. PDM was able to act independently of competitive market disciplines and to engage in discriminatory or predatory pricing practices. IMC felt that the present monopoly situation could only be resolved by structural remedies.

G H Klein & Son Ltd

7.52. G H Klein, a collector, told us that until March 1991 it was 50 per cent owned by PDM. Now it was wholly-owned by the Klein family. Two-thirds of its supplies went to PDM, although it was not under pressure to supply PDM.

7.53. After a fire at its plant in 1983, G H Klein continued its rendering business at rented premises and at Redfearn (see paragraph 4.53). It acknowledged that the numbers of collectors and dealers were declining but did not feel that there was a limited choice of renderers to supply. It told us that it had well-established rounds for collecting materials, but that this would not stop it collecting from PDM's or any other collector's customers if the opportunity arose. Other collectors and dealers would have the same attitude.

7.54. G H Klein said that if a rendering plant was for sale in the future, it would like to re-enter the rendering business even though there would be active competition for the business amongst existing renderers. It would also like to extend its collection business if the opportunity arose.

J G Pears Ltd

7.55. J G Pears Ltd (Pears) is a by-products collector and a pig farmer. Pears told us that it recently gained a new source of material from a company called Oakland Turkeys. Both Pears and PDM had made an offer for the material but Pears managed to secure the contract. In 1992, however, it lost a big source of material from Castlefield Foods to PDM and had also recently lost its material from Housleys Poultry although it did not know to whom.

7.56. In 1991, Pears acquired Dalehead Foods' material from PDM. PDM's reaction to this was to spy on Hughes (which Pears was supplying) to find out where the material was coming from and to pressurize Hughes not to take the material. PDM threatened to price Hughes out of the market if it did not comply. Hughes, however, did not submit to PDM's pressure. Pears blamed PDM for the reduction in the number of renderers. It said that PDM's tactic over the years had been to target a particular renderer and put it under financial pressure until it finally went out of business.

7.57. Pears told us that since the 1985 report, PDM had been building up the poultry side of its business. It had acquired a number of companies under the name of Chettles. Pears commented that there was very little competition in feather rendering as there were only Pimlotts (Mid-Norfolk Proteins), Hughes and Chettles. Pimlotts was too far away and Pears would not deal with Chettles because it was owned by PDM. Landfill sites for tipping feathers were rare and Pears knew of only one in Scunthorpe. Pears accused PDM of deliberately delivering large quantities of feathers to Hughes to fill up any spare capacity so that Hughes would not be able to render Pears' or anyone else's feathers.

7.58. Pears said that obtaining planning permission for a rendering plant from the local authority was difficult. If sites were available, many others would be attracted to rendering. If Hughes were to close, its tonnage would more than likely to go to PDM because of its ability to pay a good price. Pears said that in order for any collection business to be a viable one, there was a need for new renderers which would not be intimidated by PDM.

Smith Brothers (Hyde) Ltd

7.59. At a hearing, Smith, a renderer, said that it was unlikely that PDM's large output allowed it to influence the market prices of tallow and meat-and-bone meal as others had suggested, because it had to compete with other proteins, oils and fats.

7.60. Smith had five collectors delivering to its plant. It said that there was a tendency for collectors to become tied to one renderer because they now had less choice.

7.61. Regarding its relationship with PDM, Smith said that they had a mutual respect for each other even though they collected in the same area. It told us that inducements such as back-dating payments were generally accepted in the trade. During the price war between PDM and Gilberts (see paragraph 7.38) PDM had induced a customer, Cold Choice Meats Ltd, back from Smith by back-dating payments.

7.62. Abattoirs were reluctant to change renderers, because they tended to take a short-sighted view about long-term competition. Their main concern was receiving a good service and dealing with a professional outfit and PDM satisfied both requirements. However, Smith felt that it would be difficult for PDM to increase its market share any further because abattoirs, especially the bigger ones, were becoming concerned that competition between renderers was disappearing.

7.63. Smith felt that PDM was obsessed with tonnage and volume, and retaining that volume. If a customer was poached from it, PDM always tried to replace that lost tonnage, even if it did not need to. Smith said that competition was restrained because competitors had very little effect on PDM's total tonnage because of their own lack of capacity.

7.64. When Beeson, Smith's nearest competitor, was withdrawing from the industry, Smith had approached it with a view to an offer, but the response was negative. Smith then approached one of

Beeson's collectors. Again the response was a negative one. Smith could not say whether this was because the collector was satisfied with PDM or because Beeson had arranged for the collector to transfer its material to PDM. Smith also believed that PDM had bought Beeson's machinery even though it did not need it.

7.65. Smith told us that the barriers to entry into the animal waste market were environmental problems, the reluctance of local authorities to give planning permission, capital expenditure requirements and the availability of raw material.

Specialpack Ltd

7.66. In written and oral evidence, Specialpack told us that it was a gut-room contractor and a renderer making grade 2 tallow. Its business was owned by Champel Investments, a Swiss company, and it robustly refuted the rumours in the industry that Specialpack was owned by PDM.

7.67. Specialpack told us that its material now came from seven abattoirs. It had lost several abattoir suppliers through closures in recent years. It believed that the small number of companies remaining was a result of unreasonable price demands of the red meat industry. The average abattoir wanted to handle its by-products for absolute minimum costs in terms of investment and labour. In return, however, it expected the top price for its product, irrespective of quality. Specialpack drew attention to the fact that gut-room contractors incurred the expense of the operation and in some cases were even made to pay for water, effluent and electricity.

7.68. Some abattoirs were now starting to install their own rendering plants to handle their own materials. Specialpack told us of two examples of such diversification. Abattoirs were adopting in-house rendering because of the basic lack of profitability in the red meat industry. The abattoirs were left with a restricted market for red meat sales. Whereas formerly an abattoir traded perhaps with 400 small butcher shops, it might now be trading with five supermarkets. These could dictate prices, leaving the abattoirs with little bargaining power with regard to a realistic achievement of red meat values.

7.69. Specialpack said that the UK meat industry had a throw-away attitude to its by-products. In-house operations could be one solution to this problem. Specialpack thought that the idea of rendering plants being attached to slaughterhouses could be an as yet unexplored feature of the industry. The best guess of Specialpack's consultancy arm was that abattoirs would need to slaughter a minimum of about 1,000 cattle per week for any such scheme to be viable, though many other features would need to be fully taken into account.

7.70. The industry had shrunk drastically since Specialpack entered in 1976. Then, there were about 1,800 abattoirs, most of which were small family businesses glad to have a service. Now, because the business was in so few hands, abattoirs were demanding top prices for their material, with no room for the renderers to negotiate. Problems arose because the red meat industry and the by-products industry lacked co-ordination and co-operation.

Wildriggs Proteins Ltd

7.71. Wildriggs, a renderer, told us that it had lost an important supplier of chicken waste, North Country Poultry (NCP), to PDM. NCP's other products were blood and feathers. NCP could no longer dispose of its feathers at its local landfill site. PDM had a plant about 50 miles from NCP which could dispose of feathers, so NCP switched all of its business to PDM. Wildriggs was concerned that there was a strategic risk that PDM could make it a condition that if it took a company's feathers it should also take the rest of the material.

7.72. Wildriggs was emphatic that PDM paid less for poultry waste in areas of the country where there was no competition. For example, in the Norfolk area PDM was paying zero, in some cases, for viscera.

7.73. Wildriggs said that it was aware that PDM had a long-term agreement with the Premier Group, part of Hillsdown, to service its chicken plants, but that it was not concerned about this. However, Hillsdown was also interested in going into pet foods because it had a significant amount of raw material available. Wildriggs was particularly concerned about this because it would lose contracts with its pet food companies.

7.74. Wildriggs said that the MMC should restrict any further aggression in the market and prevent further mergers. Although this would not necessarily help any company that was in difficulty, it would delay closure.

7.75. Wildriggs said that if PDM or Forrest were prevented from pricing discriminatorily, the consequence would be a move towards regional collection arrangements. Plants that were based regionally would be able to offer the best prices to the abattoirs. At the moment PDM could justify from a strategic point of view paying over the odds and transporting materials a significant distance to disadvantage competitors. PDM could be deterred from that kind of behaviour if, when it offered a very high price in one part of the market to drive out a competitor, it was made to offer the same price throughout the UK.

7.76. Wildriggs felt that poultry processors should be encouraged to get involved in the rendering business, thereby opening up the animal waste industry to more options. Wildriggs believed that the threat of environmental problems held them back. The rendering industry was treated unfairly by the EPA, as it was impossible to render without producing an odour, though it was a requirement that in the next five years there should be no smell around the boundary of the plant. The industry had always argued for some form of subsidy from the Government, otherwise only the stronger companies such as PDM and Hillsdown would survive.

Other competitors of PDM

7.77. A collector told us that it had witnessed a systematic take-over of smaller firms by PDM, followed in many cases by closure. The result was that PDM had a monopoly in the market which it believed could only be to the detriment of customers, fair competition and the growth of new enterprise. PDM used unfair measures, such as predatory pricing, to try to force it out of business. PDM used this tactic in areas where there was competition. In areas with no competition, PDM paid very little, or in many cases nothing, for material. PDM also used a partner in a firm called Stannard & Klein to obtain animal waste at inflated prices from customers who would not knowingly deal with PDM.

7.78. A manufacturer of pet food was concerned that any distortion in the animal waste by-product market would prejudice farmers. Lower prices would be paid to farmers, and consumers of these products would also suffer. It was particularly concerned that PDM and/or its subsidiary companies might have breached some of its 1986 undertakings.

7.79. A pet food manufacturer noted that the MMC inquiry was directed towards animal by-products required for rendering. It pointed out that PDM, Hillsdown and their subsidiary companies appeared to be operating in the market for edible (pet food) offal, which was inextricably linked with the market for inedible (rendering) offal, because all this material was derived from abattoirs. It believed that the MMC questionnaire sent to abattoirs did not fully address the issues, and in particular that PDM might be rendering edible offal. The questionnaire did not request any information regarding prices for the various categories of edible and inedible offal.

7.80. During 1992, a PDM subsidiary told a pet food manufacturer that it would no longer supply it with edible green offal. It believed, however, that PDM and/or its subsidiaries were selling red and green offal into the pet food industry. PDM's motives could be to deprive the market of this raw material in the short term, with a view to moving further into the pet food supply market and aiming to control prices in the long term (see paragraph 18(a) of Appendix 7.1). PDM's subsidiaries were purchasing red and green (pet food) offal from abattoirs in which other subsidiaries of PDM operated the gut-rooms at prices far in excess of market prices. In the long term this would prejudice the interest of the ultimate consumer of products which incorporated such raw materials.

7.81. The manufacturer told us that it had heard through the industry that PDM and Hillsdown had entered into an agreement/arrangement whereby Hillsdown would supply PDM for five years with all the waste products, both edible and inedible, from its poultry plants in England and Wales. This included items which were required by this manufacturer and other pet food manufacturers. They were concerned that this material might be rendered in future, and about the effect this might have on the supply of this material.

Competitors of Forrest

Dundas Brothers Ltd

7.82. Dundas Brothers, a Scottish renderer, told us that it obtained materials from four local abattoirs and two boning operations. It had gained one account from Grampian Country Pork but had lost two substantial ones, Buchan Meat and ISM, to Forrest (see Appendix 6.5). In February 1992 it had approached Buchan Meat for its material, offering a reduction in charges per tonne for the removal of offal from £50 to £30. In September, however, Forrest had regained the Buchan Meat account. Dundas Brothers was certain that Forrest had offered prices which involved a loss. It felt that the only reason Buchan Meat had accepted Forrest's offer was because at that time it was in a parlous trading position. It would not have otherwise done so, as it realised the implications of losing Forrest's competitors.

7.83. Dundas Brothers told us of Grampian Regional Council's proposal to set up a new rendering plant in the area. It knew that the reason for this was because Grampian Regional Council was worried about the viability of Dundas Brothers, which could leave Forrest as the only renderer in the area. Dundas Brothers felt that to build such a plant would put extra capacity into a market that was already suffering with overcapacity. Furthermore, such a large investment would require commitment from suppliers to back it, but they were already struggling with their own margins. Dundas Brothers commented that it was now complying with all relevant regulations and was running its operation to general satisfaction.

7.84. Dundas Brothers was confident that it still had a future in the rendering business because there was enough material in the market and Scotland was large enough for competition. Also the company was looking at ways of diversifying. It felt that if it was located in the north of England rather than in Scotland, it would find competition from PDM very tough.

Dundas Chemical Company (Mosspark) Ltd

7.85. Dundas Chemical told us that about three years ago it changed its business from knackery to rendering. This was due mainly to feed compounders rejecting material from fallen stock after the BSE scare. Its sole business until recently was processing SBO (see paragraph 2.29).

7.86. Dundas Chemical said that companies going out of business tended to sell to PDM as it was the only likely buyer, and one that offered a fair deal. Competitors had no chance in bidding against PDM because they could not match its offers. The sale of Beeson was an example. Effectively, there-fore, PDM was considered a pension fund for the industry.

7.87. PDM was a more formidable competitor than Forrest because PDM had the financial power to see competitors out of the market. Forrest, on the other hand, was financially inefficient because it had excessive overheads. Dundas Chemical made comparisons between Forrest and Fats & Proteins, stating that Forrest, with a turnover above £9 million, employed 120 people while Fats and Proteins, with a turnover of £7.5 million, employed just 30 people.

7.88. Since Dundas Chemical had competed with Forrest in 1992 (see Appendix 6.5), Scotland's prices were now on a par with England's. In one incident, Sandyford Foods in Ayr had been receiving £5 per tonne from Forrest for its bones. Dundas Chemical offered it £20 a tonne, to which Forrest made a counter-offer of about £30. This remained the current price. Dundas Chemical complained that Forrest had on a number of occasions taken its potential suppliers such as Biggar and Bryson

Meats by predatory pricing. It felt that suppliers feared repercussions from Forrest if they dealt with another renderer, although some were receptive to the argument that they would be left at the mercy of Forrest if its competition was driven out.

7.89. Dundas Chemical believed that there was an understanding between PDM and Forrest not to encroach on each other's territory, as it would not be uneconomic for Forrest to obtain supplies of animal waste from England. Indeed Dundas Chemical collected in areas near Liverpool.

7.90. Over the next ten years it was unlikely that some of the existing renderers would survive, particularly with the EPA coming into force: this necessitated heavy investment.

Customers of renderers

Cussons UK Ltd

7.91. Cussons UK Ltd (Cussons), a soap manufacturer, told us that tallow was traded on a world-wide basis so it was subject to world commodity pricing and fluctuation. Competing vegetable oils kept the price of tallow competitive.

Oakleigh Manufacturing

7.92. Oakleigh Manufacturing (Oakleigh), a pet food manufacturer, told us that it collected animal by-products from abattoirs and poultry stations and used them in pet foods. It regarded its business as providing a high degree of service in clearing by-products. It told us that the materials had to be dealt with very quickly in order to retain their value, and that it generally found a healthy balance between competitive forces and the need to provide a service. Oakleigh did not believe that a monopoly existed as there was a certain amount of trading between companies operating in this sector.

Pedigree Petfoods

7.93. Pedigree Petfoods (Pedigree), a manufacturer of pet foods, told us that it used 2,500 tonnes of poultry meal and about 1,200 tonnes of tallow in dry pet food products. Most of the poultry meal and much of the tallow was purchased from PDM (although tallow was also bought from a number of other suppliers). It estimated that these purchases accounted for approximately 1 to 2 per cent of PDM's output of rendered materials.

7.94. Pedigree rated PDM very highly as a supplier as it provided an excellent service which was flexible, responsive, of high quality and competitively-priced. It praised PDM for the efficiency and responsibility with which it conducted its rendering operations.

Pointer Products (Eastwood) Ltd

7.95. Pointer Products (Eastwood) Ltd (Pointer) wrote that it manufactured dry dog food and used meat greaves in its product. Most of the meat greaves were obtained from a supplier in Ireland. Pointer had experienced severe problems with suppliers of meat greaves. The supply of meat greaves was cyclical, and was dependent on the 'kill'. Pointer still experienced some difficulty in obtaining supplies and was concerned that the supply of dried meat greaves was in relatively few hands, which could, and perhaps did, leave room for manipulation.

Quaker Oats Ltd

7.96. Quaker Oats Ltd (Quaker), a producer of pet foods, said that it was a major purchaser and user of animal waste. As red meat waste was available from a number of different suppliers it had no concerns that a monopoly existed in this area. It was, however, concerned that a monopoly situation existed in the market for poultry waste, which was mainly dominated by PDM. Quaker said that it would be impossible to obtain all of its poultry waste requirements from sources in the UK other than those controlled by PDM.

7.97. Quaker believed that PDM's domination had come about because a major cost of processing poultry waste was the disposal of feathers. As there were very few companies capable of rendering feathers, PDM was able to exert a purchasing power greater than any of its rivals. Furthermore, PDM consistently drove competition out of the market, either by purchasing or paying for competitors' facilities (particularly those with feather-processing capabilities) to be closed down. Quaker also commented on PDM's access to a further 25 to 30 per cent of the UK poultry waste market through the conclusion of a deal with Hillsdown.

7.98. Quaker's concern was that PDM would use its market strength to drive out smaller competitors. The absence of competition could lead to higher prices for consumers or lower efficiency on the part of PDM. Quaker told us that it would support any sensible measures to ensure continued competition within this market. PDM should be prevented from acquiring any further rendering businesses, particularly Mid-Norfolk Proteins, one of the few independent businesses with the ability to process feathers. Furthermore, if PDM entered into transactions similar to the Hillsdown contract, it should be obliged to guarantee to make a certain amount of poultry waste available to third parties for processing at reasonable prices, thus ensuring true competition within the pet food supply industry.

Mr Anthony Sterne

7.99. Mr Anthony Sterne, a broker, told us that he sold tallow, and that under the name T S By-Products Ltd he sold meat-and-bone meal. He told us that the production of tallow was determined by the number of cattle slaughtered. He also exported materials from the Republic of Ireland because the number of suppliers in England had declined, either because they had gone out of business or because PDM had taken them over; by comparison, there were 13 renderers in the southern part of the Republic alone. His main suppliers in the UK were the Hillsdown group and Gilberts for meat-and-bone meal, and his most important customers for tallow were Unilever PLC (Unilever) and Croda.

7.100. Mr Sterne felt that it was unlikely that a new entrant would come into the rendering market.

Unilever PLC

7.101. Unilever told us that it had two subsidiary UK companies, Unichema Chemicals Ltd (Unichema) and Lever Brothers Ltd (Lever Brothers), with particular interests in the supply of tallow. Unichema processed tallow into a range of oleochemicals and Lever Brothers used it for the manufacture of toilet soap. Neither company was concerned about the present structure or behaviour of the market for the supply of tallow. However, Lever Brothers said that it would be concerned if any dominant supplier sought to use its market power to increase prices unreasonably.

7.102. Unilever said that if the price of tallow for soap-making became too high, Lever Brothers might have to import tallow or discontinue the manufacture of soap in the UK and import soap chips for local finishing. The manufacture of soap bars in Europe was declining in favour of liquid products which did not require tallow. If this trend continued it would probably impose restraint upon tallow suppliers' pricing.

7.103. Unichema told us that the oleochemical industry in Europe suffered from substantial overcapacity and that competition in the market was intense. Manufacturers on the Continent enjoyed economies of scale not available to Unichema.

7.104. Unichema told us that quantities of grade 6 tallow which were not utilized within the UK and Republic of Ireland were shipped by rendering companies to outlets on the Continent. The UK price for grade 6 tallow had fallen below the continental price because of the transport costs incurred by renderers. This price differential was vital to its continuing success because without it continental manufacturers would fill unused production capacity and destroy the UK market with marginally-priced goods. This situation could arise if a single supplier of low-grade tallow became too dominant. However, Unichema was satisfied that this was not the case but said that it would be concerned if the balance changed significantly.

John Wyatt Ltd

7.105. John Wyatt Ltd (Wyatt), a tallow trader, told us that it bought fats from renderers to sell to the animal feed industry and to other customers such as soap manufacturers. It also sold a small amount of meat greaves. It said that PDM and Hillsdown were significant suppliers of tallow. It had a fairly close working relationship with PDM since they had worked together developing fat into feed.

7.106. There were about six tallow traders in the market, and some other brokers for proteins (meat-and-bone meal, fish meal etc and soya meal). There was strong competition between brokers because they could be vying for the same customers and suppliers. Wyatt said that there was a certain amount of loyalty from renderers in terms of the years of working together and the business that the broker had brought to the renderer.

7.107. Unilever, one of Wyatt's biggest customers, had a substantial influence on the price for tallow simply due to the strength of its purchasing power. Unilever could (and had been known to) import tallow with the result that the UK market had a surplus and therefore prices were drastically reduced.

7.108. Wyatt told us that renderers also provided competition to some brokers in that they sometimes sold their tallow directly to customers. PDM sold its tallow directly through its trading arm, Thomas Mawer Ltd. Wyatt also acted as a middleman between PDM and customers. It introduced PDM to customers and in return PDM continued to supply Wyatt in the knowledge that the material was going to those customers. Suppliers relied on middlemen for information on the market. Obtaining supplies from middlemen gave customers flexibility should their main source of supply be lost or interrupted.

7.109. In Wyatt's opinion it was unlikely that existing renderers would go out of business unless it was because of environmental pressures. Other renderers had the same opportunities as PDM to take over any business that was closing down.

A manufacturer of leather care products

7.110. A manufacturer of leather care products told us that, as a purchaser of products obtained from animal waste, it would be concerned about any exercise of monopoly power which increased the cost or reduced the quality of such products.

A pet food manufacturer

7.111. A pet food manufacturer told us that animal waste could only be obtained from three companies in the UK which were controlled by at most two parent companies. There were a number of agents which dealt in animal waste but since they all had the same sources, their prices were similar. It had obtained quotes from Europe which were cheaper but, with the added cost of haulage, the price worked out the same.

Trade associations

Highland Venison Market Ltd

7.112. Highland Venison Market Ltd (Highland Venison), a game and venison dealer, told us that there was undoubtedly a case for a monopoly inquiry, if only to reassure the trade of an outlet for its waste at an affordable price. It felt that the build-up of animal waste in any processing plant would not only be in contravention of the EPA, but would stop production overnight. There was a need for processors of animal waste to be licensed and to make collection mandatory at an acceptable price.

Licensed Animal Slaughterers and Salvage Association

7.113. In a written submission, the Licensed Animal Slaughterers and Salvage Association (LASSA) told us that the collection of waste was still a predominant element in the continuation of the knacker trade and that failure to collect would mean the closure of knacker yards by the local Health Department. LASSA was concerned that although the service provided by PDM in England and Wales and by Forrest in Scotland had always been satisfactory, the escalating cost of the service was seriously threatening the knacker trade.

7.114. LASSA strongly believed that PDM and Forrest had firm control over the by-products processing industry, with an arrangement not to encroach upon each other's territory. An example of PDM's dominance in England and Wales was that when another renderer competed with PDM (in the East Midlands), prices of waste fell from £60 per tonne to nil. However, it later appeared that the two renderers had come to an 'arrangement' under which prices rose to £25 per tonne.

7.115. LASSA felt that the situation in the market was unlikely to change, owing to lack of competition. It also felt that the high capital and running costs of setting up discouraged new entrants.

Masters of Foxhounds Association

7.116. The Masters of Foxhounds Association (MFHA) told us that PDM held a monopoly in England, and similarly Forrest in Scotland. A monopoly certainly existed in the disposal of green and proscribed offal even if other outlets were available for the disposal of good quality waste.

7.117. The MFHA said that the services of PDM and Forrest were excellent, but criticized the costs of the services. It was against the public interest for trade prices to be dictated by the sales performance of PDM rather than by the real market price of the commodity.

National Cattle Breeders Association

7.118. The National Cattle Breeders Association (NCBA) told us that the methods of disposal of waste from slaughterhouses and fallen stock from farms were covered by European Directives. Until recent legislation, slaughterhouse waste provided the largest part of total animal waste.

7.119. After the outbreak of BSE, new legislation was introduced which prohibited the use of specified offals. This caused the industry to introduce new procedures to segregate and identify material. There was an increase of waste material, which resulted in a charge being made for removal, whereas before the material had had some value. The NCBA was doubtful about the justification for such charges.

7.120. Initially the pressure of poor returns and the investment required to implement new procedures encouraged companies to withdraw from the rendering market. The market was now dominated by one company. Waste disposal had a high capital requirement and for a long period the industry made poor returns. However, the NCBA believed that this situation no longer existed.

236197 F2

7.121. The NCBA also told us that, in the knacker industry, margins had not been sufficient to encourage new investment. Many existing knackeries were maintained in old property with poor facilities and it would be difficult (due to local opposition) and expensive to establish new businesses. Although the disposal of fallen stock had developed locally with hunt kennels, there was still a knacker service available in some parts of the country. This was run mainly by small one-man businesses serving agriculture, with the minimum of regulation, as had been true for over a century.

7.122. The NCBA told us that the collapse of the offal and hide markets had caused the demise of a number of knackery businesses, leaving parts of the country without adequate services. Instead of being paid for the removal of fallen stock, knackermen were now being charged. The charge had to be balanced with the opportunity and costs of burial (which were determined by local geography), restrictions imposed by water authorities, the availability of labour and the season. During busy lambing and calving periods some producers dug burial pits, and provided that the carcases were covered every day this complied with regulations. Shared communal burial pits were mostly unacceptable because of the risk of spreading disease.

7.123. Existing knackermen were too busy to take on new customers and the industry was not attracting new trade, so it would ultimately decline further. Private companies were willing to invest in incineration plants but had difficulty obtaining planning permission. Local councils preferred such sites to be situated in neighbouring boroughs. Companies also found the high capital investment difficult to obtain because the charges and size of the market were difficult to assess. Some companies were offering anaerobic digesters, but these were costly and did not comply with regulations.

7.124. In Europe the collection and incineration of carcases was the responsibility of the local authority and was funded by a tax levied on farms. The NCBA thought that this system was unlikely to be adopted here because agricultural property was not subject to local authority tax.

National Farmers' Union

7.125. The National Farmers' Union (NFU) was very concerned that collection charges made by renderers should be kept at reasonable levels. It told us that information provided by LASSA suggested that the charges were higher than would be expected under more competitive conditions.

7.126. The NFU said that the reason given for the imposed charges was the competition between meat-and-bone meal and low-price commodities such as soya bean meal. However, the NFU understood that charges were reintroduced in November 1992, after a period of several months without them, even though at that time there had actually been an increase in soya bean meal prices. The NFU believed that there should be an investigation into competition in the rendering sector, in order to ascertain whether collection charges were set properly and did not reflect any exploitation of a monopsony position.

National Farmers' Union of Scotland

7.127. The National Farmers' Union of Scotland commented that abattoirs and knackers had comparatively few outlets for their waste and that the users of rendered products, such as animal feed manufacturers, had comparatively few sources of supply. While it felt unable to comment authoritatively on whether the present structure of the rendering industry was monopolistic or anti-competitive, it said that it had its suspicions.

United Kingdom Agricultural Supply Trade Association Ltd

7.128. The United Kingdom Agricultural Supply Trade Association Ltd (UKASTA) felt that the handling of waste material, together with the production and sale of meat-and-bone meal, was now very much in the hands of PDM. However, whilst this might affect competition for those supplying waste *into* the processing industry, it could not create an effective monopoly in the supply of the processed product.

7.129. UKASTA felt that the decision as to whether or not a feed manufacturer purchased meat-and-bone meal depended upon the value of that product relative to other raw materials such as cereals and beans. If there was only one company supplying meat-and-bone meal in the UK, it could not command an unrealistic price for the finished product because of competition from other sources of nutrients.

Government departments

Department of the Environment

7.130. The Department of the Environment (DoE) told us that the main nuisance from the rendering industry was smell. Before the EPA, smell was controlled under the Public Health Act 1936. The new controls under Part I of the EPA required renderers to obtain authorization to operate. Authorization was given in line with the concept of BATNEEC (see paragraph 2.44) to prevent, minimize and render harmless emissions. The Secretary of State had issued guidance as to what constituted BATNEEC for the rendering industry. That guidance specified certain standards for existing plant to be met by 1 April 1997. Local authorities must have regard to the guidance under section 7(11) of the EPA, but they were not obliged to implement its every word—rather, it set a framework for them to work within.

7.131. Air pollution from chicken feather processing had hitherto been controlled by Her Majesty's Inspectorate of Pollution (HMIP) (in Scotland HM Industrial Pollution Inspectorate) under the Alkali Act 1906, but would in future be the responsibility of local authorities under Part I of the EPA.

7.132. DoE told us that from April 1992 carriers of controlled waste had to register with their local authorities. UKRA had argued to DoE that renderers were not handling waste and therefore their carriers should not have to register. The local authorities did not accept that view. DoE, MAFF, local authority associations and various trade associations from the industry held a series of meetings but could not resolve this difference. Proposals were then drafted in the draft Waste Management Licensing Regulations issued for consultation in August 1992 to draw the line between various control systems, because any company which was covered by the Animal By-Products Order 1992 already met many of the requirements of the waste legislation.

7.133. If any animal wastes were controlled wastes, renderers might require a waste disposal licence from the local authority, which consulted the National Rivers Authority (NRA) about any possible causes of water pollution. The proposals in the draft Waste Management Licensing Regulations therefore included an exemption from the need to hold a waste management licence for persons keeping or treating animal wastes in accordance with the Animal By-Products Order 1992.

7.134. DoE told us that it had no information to suggest that renderers were not complying with the new legislation on waste or air quality, or that they were facing difficulties in meeting the costs of implementing the new regulations. On the air quality side, the larger players, and possibly some of the smaller ones, were well on line to meeting the standards in their existing plants by 1997.

7.135. On planning matters, DoE told us that planning permission for renderers depended on the local authority, which set out its planning policy in its development plan. There was nothing to preclude development on a greenfield site if the authority believed that it was an appropriate site for a renderer. DoE had endeavoured to separate planning controls from pollution controls, so that the planning authority dealt with matters related to land use and the development plan, and the pollution control authority (either the waste regulation authority or the district council) dealt with the controls on standards under the EPA.

7.136. DoE said that UKRA had commented to it that the UK had been quicker and more diligent to apply the legislation on waste than some other member states. However, the EC Commission was becoming much firmer about ensuring that member states were complying with directives. There was confusion with the waste directive over the definition of waste and how that was interpreted in other countries, and the scope of the directive, particularly in relation to agricultural waste.

7.137. DoE told us that there were two sources of advice. First, its air quality division had a small technical unit in Birmingham which provided help and service to industry and to local authorities. Secondly, there were free help lines provided by DTI which provided four hours' free advice. DoE tended to feed its limited resources into trade associations and local authorities rather than individual firms, although it did deal with individual firms. DoE had received the first draft of a consultancy report which updated guidance on the control of odours from industry.

7.138. The proximity principle, that waste should be disposed of as near as possible to its point of origin, was part of the framework directive. It was up to the local authorities or member states which implemented the regulations to ensure that the proximity principle was adhered to. However, it did not necessarily mean that waste had to go to the nearest place, but that member states had to ensure that there were sufficient installations to enable waste to be disposed of as near as possible to its point of origin.

7.139. DoE told us that it was introducing a new system of strategic waste planning, based on a national statement of waste policy and priorities. This would indicate the need for waste disposal facilities in each region. The local authorities would then be required to take that into account when drawing up their development plans and, therefore, in determining their planning applications. The planning system would not be designed to differentiate between different applicants. The idea was to ensure adequate provision for adequate facilities. It would make it easier for renderers to get new facilities if they applied for them in areas where the need for sites had been identified.

Ministry of Agriculture, Fisheries and Food

7.140. In written and oral evidence, MAFF told us that the pressures recognized in the 1985 report that were causing the rendering industry to rationalize around the most financially viable and dynamic companies had continued.

7.141. The industry had to face ever tighter health and environmental controls which required companies to invest in order to meet the high standards required. Since the late 1980s the industry had had to respond to unexpected health scares such as salmonella. But the biggest difficulty faced by the rendering industry was the emergence of BSE.

7.142. As the probable cause of BSE became clear, the practice of feeding ruminant-based animal protein to ruminants was banned, with effect from July 1988. This effectively cut 10 to 15 per cent off the renderers' market for meat-and-bone meal. The ban also adversely affected the production of blood meal for ruminants. Problems were exacerbated through the loss of export markets because of BSE concerns in former importing countries and reaction to the use of animal protein in pig and poultry rations, where the bulk of material now went.

7.143. These measures had caused major readjustments within the industry. However, of greater impact was the action the Government took to deal with SBO which were most likely to contain the agent which caused BSE. From September 1990, the meat-and-bone meal derived from this material was banned from use in any animal or poultry rations. This followed a ban on its use in human foods in 1989. This created major logistical problems for the industry since the raw material had to be collected and processed separately from other material. This, and the fact that the meat-and-bone meal produced no longer had any end use and had to be buried or incinerated, added to the cost of the rendering operation.

7.144. MAFF felt that without the efforts of PDM there could easily have been serious disruption and SBO left for abattoirs to deal with; but PDM had insisted that they must be collected, albeit at a price, as part of the service it provided. Other renderers had followed suit. PDM had allocated a plant to process SBO from all over England and Wales.

7.145. MAFF told us that PDM also played a major part in one of the priority research projects identified by the Tyrrell Committee on Research into the spongiform encephalopathies. The Government agreed that this research must be undertaken.

7.146. Since the 1985 report, the pressure seen at that time towards a more concentrated rendering industry had continued and intensified. MAFF felt that a company the size of PDM inevitably had advantages, mainly because it had the necessary financial resources for long-term investment plans based on foreseen prices of competing products. It was also better able to withstand unforeseen pressures such as the emergence of BSE. MAFF felt that the need for companies to have the financial backing to meet increasingly sophisticated controls for ensuring statutory standards, and ever stricter product specifications demanded by customers, would mean that the industry would be increasingly dominated by the larger companies.

The Scottish Office Agriculture and Fisheries Department

7.147. The Scottish Office Agriculture and Fisheries Department commented that the rendering industry in Scotland operated under a broadly similar legislative and administrative framework to the industry in England and Wales. There were currently five renderers in Scotland, including two abattoirs processing only their own waste. Forrest was believed to process about 70 per cent of all the red meat waste produced in Scotland, up from just over 50 per cent ten years ago; its approximate 5 per cent share of the UK market was roughly the same as ten years ago. It was understood to be operating perhaps as much as 40 per cent below capacity.

7.148. All the Scottish rendering companies had played their part in the Government's efforts to control BSE and salmonella. The availability of Forrest's large capacity plant able to dedicate one of its three production lines to process exclusively SBO had alleviated a potentially serious difficulty. The environmental controls in Scotland and the guidance issued to enforcement agencies were the same as in England and Wales, and the growing environmental pressures on renderers had taken a similar toll. Tighter environmental standards requiring the input of substantial capital resources, and the depressed markets for tallows and meals, appeared to be the two causes of contraction within the rendering industry.

7.149. The suppliers of animal waste were interested in two factors: the availability of an adequate service and the price offered for their material. Apart from South-West Scotland and parts of the North-East, however, there was little competition to Forrest. In general, the interests of competition were best served if the industry was not dominated by a single company. PDM had tried unsuccessfully to negotiate the take-over of Forrest in 1985, and PDM and Forrest appeared to respect each other's traditional territory. Should PDM acquire either of the two Dundas companies, increased competition might result. It would be a matter of concern, however, if Forrest's viability were undermined and, furthermore, PDM would have an even bigger share of the British market. The maintenance of fair and active competition within the rendering industry in Scotland was very important, but in the absence of that, the livestock industry required to be serviced by at least one efficient and viable renderer of sufficient size.

Others

Humane Slaughter Association

7.150. The Humane Slaughter Association (HSA) is a registered animal welfare charity concerned with the humane destruction of livestock on farms and at abattoirs. It submitted to us a document which it, together with the Universities Federation for Animal Welfare, had drawn up for the House of Commons Agricultural Select Committee.

7.151. HSA said that up to now the knacker industry had provided a valuable service to farmers and horse owners. Its impending demise was already creating a disposal problem and had led to some irresponsible dumping of carcases. Disposal in the past had usually been carried out by knackermen or hunt kennel staff who would, if necessary, kill the animals as well as remove the carcases. When this service was not available carcases would be buried or left to rot.

7.152. Over the past few years, the knacker industry had been under immense financial pressure and many operators had gone out of business. Those remaining now had to charge for their services rather than offer payment to the farmer. This situation therefore led to owners of livestock dumping carcases irresponsibly.

7.153. HSA emphasized the need for a properly-organized on-farm slaughter, carcase collection and disposal system. This would require the collecting personnel to be trained in methods of humane slaughter. It suggested that such a system could be run by a body such as LASSA under the supervision of the State Veterinary Service.

Association of Metropolitan Authorities

7.154. The Association of Metropolitan Authorities (AMA) observed that over many years PDM had 'swallowed up' small renderers as a result of the high cost of handling dead animals and by-products from slaughterhouses. Recent BSE incidents, the restricted use of animal waste and the recession had significantly affected the tallow market, with the result that slaughterhouses now had to pay for the removal of waste and farmers also had to pay for the removal of dead animals. AMA was concerned that farmers would be tempted to dump dead animals, with a consequentially adverse effect on the environment.

7.155. AMA believed that a monopoly situation existed in that there was no competition to obtain this waste. It felt that competition which was both environmentally acceptable and able to provide the capital necessary for adequate plant to handle this waste needed to be encouraged. AMA acknowledged that one of the continual objections to knacker yards was the problem of odour and the siting of yards.

Arfon Borough Council

7.156. Arfon Borough Council (Arfon) told us that in its borough and in adjoining areas one licensed knacker yard acted as a clearing house for the supply of animal waste. The company operating this site was originally part of Granox Ltd but since January 1992 had operated as a wholly independent company under the name of E Clutton & Sons (Marchwiel) Ltd.

7.157. Arfon's concern was that, although this company was keeping to the national trend in charging for the removal of waste and fallen animals, this had led to a problem over the abandonment of dead animals on roadsides and specifically in the area of the licensed yard. The cost of removing these animals had therefore had to be borne by the council.

Gordon District Council

7.158. At a hearing, Gordon District Council told us that it had had numerous complaints over many years regarding smell pollution from Dundas Brothers' rendering plant. In 1990, the Council carried out a detailed inspection of the plant and was advised by its legal services department that it should be reported to the Sheriff Court because too many bye-laws were being breached. Subsequently Dundas Brothers made a great effort to upgrade the premises and so the Council dropped the case. The Council continued to receive complaints about odours, and so in 1991, after inspection, it issued Dundas Brothers with a Public Health Notice. It suspected that the storage of raw material and effluvia extraction and treatment plant were inadequate. It felt that major investment was needed to bring the plant up to date, and that without these improvements it would be unlikely to grant an EPA authorization. However, it felt that a decision to close Dundas Brothers would be a very difficult one.

7.159. The Council told us that farmers were unwilling to pay charges for the removal of fallen stock. There were at least six 'death pits' within its district. The Council was concerned over possible contamination of drinking water and the spread of disease from such pits.

Grampian Regional Council

7.160. Grampian Regional Council told us that, with the threatened closure of Dundas Brothers, the meat industry approached the Council as it was concerned that there would be no facility in the area to dispose of waste. Various options were considered and a decision was reached by the abattoirs, the Scottish Office Agriculture & Fisheries Department, NFU, the regional and district councils and the two local enterprise companies, Murray Badenoch and Strathspey and the Grampian Enterprise, to prepare a business plan for the building of a new rendering plant with a separate incinerator. This was also made a recommendation in a report by the Scottish Agricultural College.

7.161. The Council told us that a New Zealand company named Flo Dry Engineering was interested in developing and part-funding a plant in the Grampian Region. The method to be used for dealing with animal waste seemed more efficient but, as yet, had not been approved by MAFF. Forrest had offered to clear the waste from the abattoirs in the area. The abattoirs, however, were concerned that, with the lack of competition, Forrest could hold them to ransom.

7.162. The Council said that it was rumoured that Hillsdown was getting out of the meat business and that it was worried that, should this occur, Hillsdown might also get out of the rendering business. If this happened, it was likely that PDM would take over Forrest. The Council was concerned that Dundas Brothers might not be able to compete with the bigger players in the market, and thought that its future looked uncertain.

Mole Valley District Council

7.163. Mole Valley District Council sent us a batch of correspondence relating to a dispute in which it had become involved in 1990 between an abattoir (subsequently closed) and PDM, over alleged high charges and inadequate service. It explained that it had done so mainly because it considered that the letters indicated the problems which could arise when a waste producer had no alternative to collection by a monopolistic renderer which could, if it so chose, 'hold that producer to ransom'.

Motherwell District Council

7.164. Motherwell District Council told us that it and the Clyde River Purification Board had made representations to Forrest about the discharge of its effluent into disused mineworkings. In the past, another industry had used similar mineworkings which had burst and contaminated the river. Forrest readily accepted its responsibility. The Council had also received complaints about the smell emitted from Forrest's plant and, as a result, Forrest commissioned a study to determine ways of overcoming the problem.

7.165. The Council found Forrest to be a responsive, co-operative and honest company, nor had it received any complaints from abattoirs regarding Forrest's prices and charges. The Council said that it was simply an enforcer of regulations and legislation and had therefore not considered their implications for competition, eg through potentially forcing renderers to leave the market.

Shrewsbury and Atcham Borough Council

7.166. Shrewsbury and Atcham Borough Council (Shrewsbury and Atcham) was aware that PDM had the largest share of the animal waste processing market, but acknowledged that there was also a number of other established smaller processors. It commented on the concern of the knacker industry over collection charges imposed by the processing industry in the wake of the BSE problem. The 'knock-on' effect of this charge was that the knacker industry had imposed a charge for the collection of animal waste and fallen stock from farms. However, it was understood that the charges had gradually been reduced and that some operators now had their waste removed free of charge.

7.167. Shrewsbury and Atcham felt that if the Government accepted more responsibility, the problems facing farmers and the knacker industry would not be as acute.

Shropshire County Council

7.168. Shropshire County Council sent us costs and other details for September 1991 and September 1992 of the disposal of carcases and animal waste through knackers and hunt kennels within Shropshire. It said that a 'forced' rationalization of the number and operating methods of those who had traditionally served the farming industry had taken place in the last five years as a result of the BSE and other new regulations. The number of knackers had fallen by one-third, in part because of their apparent need to charge for collecting fallen stock following the imposition of steep charges by renderers. Some were surviving by exploiting the BSE controls and utilizing purpose-built incineration plants primarily to cope with BSE carcases. In another five years, however, these plants might cease to be required, and their high level of operating costs meant that they were not viable for fallen stock.

7.169. Waste treatment was a vital environmental function, but charges levied had cost implications on the renderers' end products and, even more so, within agriculture and on operatives within the waste trade. Sustainable, viable alternatives were not currently in place. Therefore keen pricing policies entailing some element of control were required. Increased costs would lead to further knacker closures and a possible reduced intake to hunt kennels, placing further cost burdens on agriculture and raising the risk of disease and to the environment.

8 Evidence of PDM

8.1. Certain comments or representations made by PDM have been reported in earlier chapters, wherever considered most appropriate in our consideration of particular matters falling within the scope of those chapters. In this chapter we summarize PDM's other evidence on further matters bearing on our consideration of the public interest. These relate to competition, the 1986 undertakings, profitability and pricing.

Competition

Share of market

8.2. PDM made it clear that it had never disputed that it acquired for processing in rendering plants at least a quarter of the animal waste so acquired in England and Wales. It pointed out, however, that animal waste was also supplied to pet food manufacturers, producers of gelatine, pharmaceutical and other specialist products, edible fat renderers and waste disposal companies, all of which, therefore, 'competed' with renderers for animal waste. In PDM's submission, the limitation in the reference to the supply of animal waste to renderers created an artificial definition of the market for animal waste. Increasingly animal waste was being diverted from the rendering chain and higher values for it being obtained. This reduced the dependence on the value of substitute commodities for tallow and meat-and-bone meal. Having regard to the continuing uncertainty of traditional markets for rendered products, particularly following the salmonella and BSE crises, it was in the public interest that as much animal waste as possible be used for purposes other than rendering. PDM itself had been the leader in its industry into research and development of alternative products, though its earlier revolutionary efforts had been significantly undermined by the salmonella and BSE crises (see paragraph 4.24).

8.3. PDM acknowledged that it rendered approximately 70 per cent of all animal waste rendered in England and Wales in 1991. It wished to make it clear, however, that the waste it rendered was only approximately 49 per cent of the total of animal waste available, as had been the case, more or less, since 1987.

8.4. PDM put its share of the total poultry waste market at not more than 90 per cent, notwithstanding that it had come to enjoy a natural monopoly as a result of being the only renderer which had set out to process poultry waste and feathers separately. Some 43 per cent of the feathers available in England and Wales went either into landfill, to the bedding industry or to other renderers including poultry producers. Some 45 per cent of other poultry waste was used by the canned pet food industry or by poultry producers still processing and using their own material. PDM had acquired its Nottingham plant from MCP, in September 1986, because it had identified a substantial new market for a pure poultry meat meal (ie free of feathers) which would achieve a substantial price premium over ordinary meat-and-bone meal and so substantially enhanced the price PDM paid to the poultry industry for its waste.

8.5. PDM submitted that there were six other significant renderers in England and Wales: Fats & Proteins, Smith, Gilberts, Hughes, Cheale and Peninsular. Each of these had significantly increased its throughput in the last five years, during which period there had certainly been no increase in the total supply of animal waste.

National service provided by PDM

8.6. Appendix 8.1 reproduces a paper which PDM submitted to us outlining its rise to pre-eminence through acquisition and organic growth against a background of rationalization of the rendering industry. PDM said that the substantial contraction of the rendering industry in England and Wales had imposed almost exclusively on PDM the responsibility for the continued provision of a national waste disposal service for animal and poultry waste. No other renderer had transport facilities or plant capacity (or even perhaps the inclination) to provide such a service. Nevertheless other renderers were able to compete effectively with PDM on a national basis for the larger sources of waste and on a regional basis for smaller quantities.

8.7. PDM said that it provided a fully national service, with the exception of a small area in West Wales. As between each class of its suppliers, the ratio of the number of suppliers to the proportion of the waste they supplied varied greatly. Most significantly, retail butchers, representing 89 per cent of the number of suppliers, provided less than 7.4 per cent of materials, whereas less than 6 per cent of suppliers, ie abattoirs, generated more than 67 per cent of supplies. PDM, however, considered that servicing retail butchers was a necessary obligation in view of the monopoly position it enjoyed, though it was inevitable that the fulfilment of this public service had adverse cost implications for PDM which were not shared by competitors. PDM's vital, effective and unsubsidized national service was made possible by the strategic location of its factories and depots, its fleet of over 400 vehicles and trailers including many specially designed with watertight compartments, and most importantly, the integrated and interdependent nature of its specialized rendering facilities.

8.8. PDM told us that its long-held desire for a high-grade rendering facility in the Midlands had appeared fulfilled through its acquisition of Croda. Significantly reduced availability of suitable material on a national basis, however, obliged it reluctantly to moth-ball the Market Harborough operation in February 1992.

8.9. PDM said that it had clearly demonstrated that its ability to provide a national service for all types of animal waste hinged critically on its ability to transfer large quantities of material to the appropriate specialized PDM processing plant to achieve the following objectives:

(a) maximizing finished product values (high-grade waste);

(b) minimizing environmental impact by processing in large dedicated plants with excellent process and emission controls (low-grade waste);

(c) controlled and proper handling and disposal of proscribed materials to ensure diversion away from the animal feed chain (SBO);

(d) elimination of cross-contamination in different protein meals of different species by operating dedicated process plants (poultry waste); and

(e) the operation of dedicated plants for waste products requiring specific treatment methods (blood and feathers).

8.10. Reasonable levels of profitability in the rendering industry (particularly for PDM) therefore needed to be maintained, to enable PDM to continue to provide its efficient national service. The necessity from time to time for PDM to pay what were unrealistically high prices or to make unrealistically low charges for supplies of waste from its principal sources (as had happened during the 1992 price war) inevitably placed some financial strain on PDM in the fulfilment of its duty to service its thousands of small suppliers.

8.11. It might be said, added PDM, that, in a situation where a universal collection service operated, larger suppliers of waste might be subsidizing the smaller ones. In fact, however, larger suppliers would always be able to command higher prices or lower charges than smaller suppliers. Nevertheless, it was probably the case that were PDM to cease collections from, say, the myriad of butchers' shops, its overall profitability at times would be enhanced.

New entry

8.12. PDM accepted that for anyone wishing to enter the rendering industry there were significant barriers to overcome in the form of planning, environmental and public health controls. It noted, however, that Cheale had entered the industry in 1990 by taking over an existing rendering plant at Canterbury. More recently, too, EUROP had made a planning application for a new rendering plant at Lakenheath (Cambridgeshire). Moreover, PDM had demonstrated that, through its superior skill, industry and foresight, a reasonable return could be made by investing in an industry appearing rebarbative at first sight. This should act as a spur to other entrepreneurs to acquire the necessary expertise and efficiency and to demonstrate the requisite commitment for successful entry into the industry.

8.13. We asked PDM whether it exercised control over the availability of assets of former renderers for sale on the open market, so as to constitute a barrier to entry or growth of existing renderers. PDM categorically denied that it had ever procured the cutting up or the sale abroad of plant or equipment which it did not itself need in order to prevent it from falling into the hands of any would-be or existing competitor. On the contrary, it had on occasion sold surplus equipment to competitors, for example Cheale, Chetwynd, Beeson and MCP.

8.14. We asked PDM whether its exclusive agreement with Hillsdown to render the poultry waste arising from Hillsdown-owned operations was a barrier to entry or the growth of existing renderers. PDM replied that the contract was not in writing and could be terminated on three months' notice. As prices were reviewed on a quarterly basis, the maximum period the contract could legally be expected to exist was three months, though obviously PDM hoped (but without any guarantee) that it would be renewed at each review. Any existing renderer was free to compete for all or part of the business and, indeed, to seek to enter into a contract of longer duration. In these circumstances the agreement could not constitute any barrier to entry or growth.

Competition with Forrest and Peninsular

8.15. We asked PDM whether it had any understandings with the two Hillsdown companies, Forrest and Peninsular, not to encroach on each other's territories. PDM replied that there were no such understandings. It argued that geographical considerations, amongst others, accounted for the fact that it did not presently compete with Forrest in Scotland. There were no significant red meat waste suppliers in Scotland south of the Scottish Lowlands, and Fats & Proteins and Dundas Chemical were more conveniently located than PDM to service suppliers in the Borders. In any event it had never been PDM's practice to compete for supplies from persons with whom it had not traditionally dealt. It would be so difficult to gain adequate supplies of red meat waste in Scotland that PDM could only contemplate re-entering the market on the basis of acquisition. PDM's purchase of Frank Gysels in the late 1970s (see paragraph 4.11) had failed, however, because PDM found it difficult to service the rendering business from England. As to Peninsular, that company had relatively recently won the business of two former PDM suppliers, in Bromsgrove and Bristol.

The 1986 undertakings

8.16. We put it to PDM that it might not have abided fully by the 1986 undertakings, in particular, undertakings 1(iv)*(b)* and *(c)*, relating to its gut-room operations, and undertaking 3, requiring the notification of acquisitions (see Appendix 1.2).

8.17. With regard to undertakings 1(iv)*(b)* and *(c)*, PDM explained that it had informed the DGFT in 1986 that strict compliance with the undertakings would be difficult. It was not possible for audited annual statements together with reconcilable accounts showing the profit and loss of each gut-room contract separately to be prepared until PDM's group audit process had been completed. This itself took considerably longer than three months. This situation had been accepted by the DGFT. PDM currently operated only nine gut-rooms. Weekly administration charges for each gut-room could not be based on anything other than estimates because it was quite impossible and inappropriate to allocate specific amounts of administration costs to these activities. PDM was surprised that it was being said that it had not demonstrated to the DGFT that the weekly administration charge for each gut-room was based on reasonable allocations of overheads. No complaint had been made by the DGFT. PDM conducted its negotiations with abattoirs to purchase their raw material on a day-to-day basis. Invitations (few as there were) which were made to PDM to take over the operation of gut-rooms when they occurred were an integral part of such negotiations. It was simply not possible for anything other than a very broad separate budgeting exercise to be undertaken prior to the quick decision which had to be made as to whether or not a request to take over a gut-room should be accepted.

8.18. PDM had always made it clear that the prior submission of assessments to the DGFT was impracticable in the nature of the way it conducted its business. The complaint made to the DGFT in 1991 that a contract had been taken by PDM on loss-making terms was investigated and found not to have been proven. PDM's attitude to this activity was that if it was asked to take over the operation of a gut-room it did so. It did not seek to do this work. Although, obviously, broad estimates were made at the time as to the throughput and expected yield of the gut-room, it was not and, for the reasons stated above, never had been done in a precise accounting way. PDM said that it did not believe that there had been any cross-subsidization of its gut-room business, or that these matters now gave rise to any public interest concern.

8.19. With regard to undertaking 3, PDM had punctiliously complied with this. In the case of the Nortech acquisition in 1992, PDM was advised that the Nortech business at that time was not a business which was subject to this undertaking. PDM nevertheless notified the DGFT of its acquisition of Nortech, as a matter of courtesy, because PDM had earlier entered into negotiations with the proprietors of Nortech for the purchase of the business at a time when it had included activities subject to the undertaking. So far as the business of Beeson was concerned, PDM had not been involved in taking over any part of the business of that company. The suppliers of raw material to Beeson (mainly independent collectors) had to find other renderers to take their material. PDM had agreed to take some of this material by entering into contracts with those suppliers, who were quite unconnected with the proprietors of Beeson. PDM had also purchased from Beeson, in the ordinary course of business, equipment worth £15,000. Otherwise PDM had not been involved in assisting in the disposal of any plant of the Beeson business, and PDM categorically denied that it had acted in any way which was contrary to the spirit of undertaking 3.

8.20. Concerning the purchase of the small animal waste collection businesses referred to in paragraph 4.48, PDM expressed the view that in the majority of cases pre-notification was not necessary because no acquisition of a business actually took place. In these cases a token payment was made to retiring operators of small bone rounds as a gratuity in recognition of their long-standing but then terminating connection with PDM. None of the recipients of these payments signed any document for sale or entered into any restrictive covenant with PDM about their future activities.

Profitability

8.21. We asked PDM whether its apparent profitability was depressed as a consequence of its end-product sales arrangements with the Jersey-based company, Hi-Cal, which appeared different from, and to incur higher costs than, other renderers' corresponding arrangements. While acknowledging that its arrangements with Hi-Cal 'often quite understandably raise a few eyebrows', and that it had itself heard comments implying a device to hide profits in Jersey, PDM replied that its profitability was not depressed in any way by its sales arrangements, which were not materially different from those made with other brokers by PDM or by other renderers. PDM had explained to the MMC the circumstances which had led it to switch from its previously appointed brokers in 1977. Having regard to the services Hi-Cal performed for PDM (see paragraph 2.77), which in PDM's estimation were equivalent to a requirement for an additional ten personnel, the remuneration of £3 per tonne which PDM paid to Hi-Cal was neither unreasonable nor out of line with the rates paid to other brokers. PDM had no financial interest in Hi-Cal and dealt with it on an arm's length basis. There was no reason why PDM should pay excessive rates of commission to Hi-Cal and it did not in fact do so.

8.22. As regards the adverse impact of its transport costs on its profitability, PDM said that it operated an integrated business of collection and rendering which ran at maximum efficiency and lowest cost as a whole. PDM's pattern of transport reflected its objective, which it achieved, of obtaining the highest net added value from raw materials wherever these may be acquired.

8.23. We also asked PDM whether the profitability of its rendering operations was sufficiently transparent. PDM answered that it complied with its statutory obligations in respect of financial reporting and did not understand in what respect its financial reports might be thought to lack 'transparency' (see paragraph 3.11).

Pricing

8.24. PDM's formulation of its average monthly target prices (and charges) for animal waste has been described in Chapter 6. PDM was at pains to point out that realized prices were affected by such a wide range of factors that no two contracts for the collection of animal waste would be on identical terms. Indeed, no two loads collected were the same.

8.25. PDM told us that the Board of PDM, having first established for internal purposes an overall average target price for each of six broad categories of animal waste, then communicated to its six raw material managers, through the Raw Materials Director, the average level of prices they should endeavour to achieve. The price actually paid for each category of animal waste would then be influenced by other material supply-related factors such as quantity, quality, method of handling, location, collection service required and competition for any of PDM's large suppliers. Generally speaking, each individual supplier and its available raw materials was well known to PDM, and its buying staff in practice thus exercised little latitude.

8.26. Prior to our first hearing with PDM we sent it analyses of the pricing data it had supplied at our request covering each of its suppliers for four categories of waste (fat, bones, offal and SBO) for May and October 1992. In two initial written responses PDM argued that the basis of our analysis of its raw material prices was flawed in several respects, even after allowing for certain errors in its original data.

8.27. First, PDM argued that our use of range and observations methodology was simplistic and potentially misleading for the analysis of what was an extremely complex issue by virtue of the very nature of the market for the supply of animal waste, with its many and variable influencing factors. Notwithstanding its grave reservations on this count, however, PDM prepared a series of histograms for each category of raw material from May and October 1992. These, it believed, graphically and more accurately demonstrated the true degree of price dispersion and relative 'weight' of different price/tonnage relationships. PDM did not deny the existence of ranges of prices but pointed out the clear and meaningful way in which its histograms demonstrated the cluster of its prices around the average.

8.28. PDM wholeheartedly agreed that the main factors affecting price dispersion were quality, quantity, distance and competition. Only in rare cases, however, was a single one of these four variables the only consideration in pricing policy. It was therefore inappropriate, and in PDM's experience impossible, to seek to establish reasons for price dispersion by examining the prices paid relative to one variable in isolation from the others.

8.29. PDM then examined the four main variables. First, as to quality, this meant much more to the renderer than 'freshness' or 'goodness'. Yield by weight, yield by value and other factors, such as the degree of contamination or separation of the abdominal mass carried out by the abattoir could, and did, have a significant effect on the value of raw materials. For example, offal from cattle yielded more than offal from pigs; and an even more dramatic yield by weight variation occurred in the case of SBO, depending on whether the supplier left the large quantity of fat around the intestine or carried out the difficult and costly separation process. Identical raw material would produce different yield by value according to which plant processed it, the standard of handling by the supplier and the rate of degradation.

8.30. Secondly, a wide price dispersion for a given quantity of material could result from a number of influences such as other types and amounts of raw material collected from the same source (if any),

8.44. As regards distance, PDM said that the cost of collecting, say, 200 kilos per day from even a few small abattoirs a given distance away was greater than collecting from one large abattoir at the same distance. This was impossible to analyse and quantify, however, just as was true of the other variables. Prices for supplies from multi-site operators took into account, for example, the increased costs of collecting from a group abattoir down in Cornwall. Similarly, prices for butchers' shops were adversely affected by the relatively high cost of collection, notwithstanding that this was over comparatively little distance. PDM estimated, for example, that it was £10 more expensive to collect 26 tonnes of raw material from a succession of small butchers' shops within 20 miles of one of its plants than to collect the same tonnage in one load from a large abattoir involving a motorway journey of 100 miles.

8.45. In general PDM aimed to establish its average target prices right across the country, because the meat industry was now characterized by a great deal of contact at abattoir and other levels, for example at conferences, or through the MLC and its published monthly price data. But this did not mean there were no regional differences. For example, price seemed less important to suppliers in Cornwall and Devon, or in the North-East of England, than it did to those in the Midlands, where there was strong competition all the time, even for small supplies.

8.46. PDM added that another factor affecting realized prices was, as in any market place, the ability or willingness of the individual supplier to press for a better deal. Apart from a supplier's particular desirability or otherwise to a competitor, his trading fortunes at the time typically had an effect on his keenness to bargain, irrespective of his size. Generally, too, suppliers would have their own internal accounting or other reasons for pressing harder on one type of material than on another. Negotiations were always easier at the season of high kill.

8.47. PDM argued that it was impossible to rank each of the foregoing variables in terms of its relative importance, let alone in terms of £ per tonne. Each factor was relevant but could not be broken down. Taking the whole ranges of these variables into account it could be seen that no two contracts could possibly be compared the one with the other: there was always a special factor some-where. That said, PDM thought that the biggest factor was the raw material itself, which in some way or another was always unique, whether in its mix, the way it was handled, its rendering destination, or what the end product from it was going to be.

8.48. PDM told us that it monitored actual average prices against average target prices on a monthly basis. The variation found could be considerable, particularly at times of a rising or falling market, or of reduced or increased kill affecting the available quantity of high-grade material.

8.49. We asked PDM if at each of its plants there was a list of authorized prices for use in invoicing its suppliers. PDM confirmed that this was so, and that these prices were applied to the tonnages recorded at the weighbridge.

8.50. Following the hearing we wrote to PDM in connection with its reference to the wide ranges of yields about the average (see paragraph 8.41) and asked it to supply details of these ranges for each category of waste. We also confirmed our request for examples of price calculations during the price war (see paragraph 8.38) and the previous 28 months' average target prices lists, and requested copies of authorized prices lists.

8.51. In reply PDM sent us some further notes on factors affecting raw material prices, in particu-lar, quality assessment, quantity, yield by weight and by value, distance and other factors (Appendix 8.2). It stated that there were in fact no break-even (or loss-making) calculations for animal waste: decisions as to whether or not to agree a particular price or charge were taken having regard to all the relevant factors, particularly those set out in Appendix 8.2. The renderer had to pay what the market demanded. Obviously a point might be reached where a particular price asked for, taken on its own, might, *ex post facto*, be seen to be unprofitable to the purchasing renderer. PDM had also explained that at times of price wars, prices generally became unreasonably high, but this did not mean that they were not paid.

8.66. With regard to the distribution of different yielding materials within a particular classification, PDM stated that it was clear from the detailed information provided that it was impossible to quantify, and therefore value separately, the mix of material that would arise within a particular classification. This was especially true in the case of mixed species (ie most) abattoirs, where daily varying quantities of different yielding materials were discharged into the appropriate waste category container. Certain large abattoirs might have sufficient volumes of waste to justify separation into sub-groups (eg heads and feet in one container, soft offals in another). In such situations separate prices/charges could be negotiated, but even in these few cases there would still be a wide variation in the waste supplied, which prohibited the calculation of likely maximum and minimum yields of any consignment let alone of total tonnage supplied in a month.

8.67. In a further written response PDM drew our attention to differences in the energy cost of processing high- and low-yielding raw materials at its various factories. It argued that in assessing value differences in relation to yield variations, these cost disparities must also be taken into account. PDM said that it sensibly operated its business on the basis of average processing costs, and under-pinned this with management by exception.

9 Evidence of Forrest

9.1. Certain comments or representations made by Forrest have been reported in earlier chapters, wherever considered most appropriate in our consideration of particular matters falling within the scope of those chapters. In this chapter we summarize Forrest's other evidence on further matters bearing on our consideration of the public interest. These relate to competition, profitability and pricing.

Competition

The Scottish market

9.2. Forrest believed that there were a number of preliminary points to be made as essential background to any consideration of the Scottish rendering market. These related to the position of the renderer, both generally and particularly in Scotland, and to the management philosophy and commitment to capital expenditure of Forrest's ultimate parent, Hillsdown.

9.3. First, the prices obtained by the renderer for his finished products were determined by the international commodities market.

9.4. Secondly, significant capital expenditure by the renderer on compliance with increasingly stringent environmental controls was required at a time when the industry was suffering from overcapacity and its profitability was already constrained. Compliance with these environmental controls also added to the burden of running costs and to the problem of finding capital for reinvestment.

9.5. The renderer in Scotland was affected by each of these problems. In particular, there was chronic overcapacity in the rendering industry in Scotland and a shortage of raw materials for processing. Forrest's maximum capacity was 55 per cent greater than its current throughput and it believed that its two competitors had considerable spare capacity as well.

9.6. As noted in paragraph 5.18, the capital investment provided by Hillsdown had enabled Forrest to continue where other companies had been forced to close, but Forrest was still failing to produce appropriate profits on the capital employed. This illustrated the difficulties faced by the rendering industry.

9.7. Forrest contended, nevertheless, that there was competition throughout Scotland, be it from the generic alternative, landfill; from Dundas Brothers or Dundas Chemical, which together could potentially cover virtually the same geographical areas as Forrest; or potentially from renderers south of the border establishing depots in Scotland, should they consider it commercially worth their while.

9.8. Forrest accepted, however, that there was a degree of natural monopoly in its favour. It believed that it had around a 70 per cent share of red meat waste rendering in Scotland.

New entry

9.9. Given the difficulties currently facing the rendering industry, without mentioning its inherent unattractiveness, new entry seemed to Forrest an unlikely possibility. Forrest did not believe that its reputation or behaviour gave justification for any concern or acted as a barrier to entry. The main difficulties facing any new entrant would be those arising from the overcapacity of the Scottish rendering industry and the limited supplies of raw materials available. This imbalance was made more acute by the financial and regulatory hurdles resulting predominantly from the increasingly stringent environmental controls and also from the tiny second-hand market for processing equipment.

9.10. So far as Hillsdown's poultry waste agreement with PDM was concerned, Hillsdown did not believe that this constituted a barrier to entry or to the growth of existing renderers. Prior to the agreement, the poultry waste from all but one of Hillsdown's poultry companies was already being supplied to PDM. The agreement was also subject to quarterly review by both parties, in spite of PDM's wish for a longer-term agreement, and Hillsdown did not regard itself as committed to the agreement should a more favourable price and service become available elsewhere, for example through a group of poultry renderers putting forward a composite proposal taking account of their respective locations and capacities. Hillsdown itself had in the past considered doing its own poultry rendering and would do so again if its commercial interest would thus be best served.

Competition with PDM

9.11. Hillsdown told us that the fact that Forrest did not currently obtain raw material in England, and Peninsular did not obtain supplies throughout the whole of England and Wales, was not the result of any understanding or agreement reached with PDM. The areas in which Forrest operated were determined by two principal factors, the location of its depots and plant and the location of its raw material suppliers.

9.12. Forrest did not travel further south than Dumfries or Berwickshire owing to the paucity of materials available for purchase in those areas and further south. Indeed Forrest was considering the viability of collecting from Berwickshire because of the minimal amounts available there (some 3 or 4 tonnes per week, all from butchers' shops), though it was possible that the introduction of a small charge might make the collections sufficiently economic to be continued.

9.13. Most of Forrest's suppliers were to be found in the eastern half of Scotland, where its depots enabled it to collect supplies, albeit in small to medium volumes, from as far north as Dornoch, and to consolidate them into economic loads for transporting to Newarthill usually within 12 hours of collection from the abattoir. Greaves, however, which were entirely unavailable in Scotland, were obtained from England and from both the Republic of Ireland and Northern Ireland.

9.14. Forrest pointed out that, because of its experience of the benefits of its collection depots, coupled with the natural affinity that existed between suppliers and any local renderer, it had tried, but so far in vain, to expand into northern England by acquisition:

— In 1987/88 it investigated the purchase of Tyneside Butchers but concluded that the business lacked adequate management and was too far from Motherwell to be managed from there.

— Also in 1987/88 it considered purchasing Blackburn Products Co Ltd but concluded that it was too small and faced serious environmental problems which were compounded by its location in the town centre.

— In early 1988 it wished to purchase Wildriggs, in Penrith. After agreeing the purchase price with its owners, the offer for sale was withdrawn and the business subsequently sold to a pet food manufacturer. [*Details omitted.*
See note on page iv.   ]

— In July 1991 Forrest agreed the price for the acquisition of Wells By-Products, about 25 miles distant from Doncaster. However, the business was sold instead to PDM.

9.15. Nor did Hillsdown have any agreements, formal or informal, with PDM other than the poultry waste agreement already referred to.

9.16. For all these reasons it was Forrest's contention that the fact that it did not currently operate in England resulted from its proper evaluation of a number of commercial and economic factors and not from any agreement or understanding with PDM. If, in Forrest's opinion, it became commercially viable for it to do so, Forrest would expand its operations into England and so increase the availability of raw materials, with the potential benefits to its throughput.

9.17. As regards Peninsular, its major suppliers were located in the South-West and were served by good road networks. Peninsular's suppliers provided it with sufficient raw material to operate at maximum capacity when the plant was running (which it did not do at weekends, for environmental and maintenance reasons), and it had no wish for any greater volumes of raw materials. Peninsular, however, was mindful of the fact that it could at any moment lose any of its supplies to a third party, or through a supplier's withdrawal from the market. Therefore it was constantly in contact with other potential suppliers so that it could replace any lost supplies if need be. Peninsular's relationships with potential suppliers had stood it in good stead following the uprating of its capacity in 1992. Of the abattoirs presently serviced by Peninsular, five remained out of eleven originally captured from PDM.

Profitability

9.18. Forrest denied that its financial results reflected higher charges and lower payments than would have been the case in a more competitive market. On the contrary, its ROCE had been distorted as a result of some exceptional movements, including the approach that had been adopted to the valuation of the property and to capital corporation tax. In reality, after appropriate adjustment, the level of profitability of Forrest did not increase as dramatically as its statutory accounts might suggest.

9.19. Forrest calculated its ROCE for the five years to 1992 as 33.02, 21.91, 28.47, 27.24 and 12.26 per cent respectively. These results, it said, showed a relatively consistent trend from 1988 to 1991, followed by the obvious downturn in 1992 when, *inter alia*, capital employed increased by almost 50 per cent.

9.20. Looking at these returns on what it described as 'management capital employed', rather than capital employed according to the statutory accounts, which in Forrest's case it believed was not particularly meaningful, Hillsdown said that it was none too happy with the trend and would be looking for improvement in 1993. Although it regarded rendering as a medium- rather than a high-risk business, it was one which entailed an enormous and continuing cash requirement, not least to expend on compliance with environmental controls at nil return on capital. Hillsdown therefore considered between 25 and 27 per cent an appropriate rate of return.

9.21. The improvement in its profits in 1990 as compared with 1989, despite the BSE crisis, Forrest commented, was due to the increased throughput arising from its acquisition of Elgin Animal By-Products in April 1990. Forrest indicated, however, that in 1991, when its end-product sales fell by £9.40 per tonne of raw material and its costs increased by £2.35 per tonne, the fact that its profits fell by only £1.11 per tonne reflected the Forrest policy of relating raw material prices to the value of the end product.

9.22. The most important single element in price-setting was the selling price of the renderer's end product. If that price fell, it was inevitable that less must be paid or more must be charged for the raw material needed to manufacture it. This was reasonable and sensible because the renderer had no rationale for carrying on his business unless he could obtain from the abattoir industry what he felt necessary in order to make what he regarded as a reasonable profit. Whilst the creation and sale of animal by-products was not the principal business of the abattoir owner, it was the inevitable consequence of conducting that business. As such, the prices which may be obtained or charged for the by-products were constantly taken into account by the abattoir owner when assessing his profitability and the prices he paid for the animals he purchased. In the UK, in contradistinction to certain other European countries where governmental subsidies may apply, the value of animal waste was necessarily dictated by its value to the renderer bearing in mind what he could get for his finished products, which in turn was governed by international commodities markets. In reality, therefore, the abattoir owner was left with a by-product which may or may not have a value. The issue here was not one of competition but of the structure of the market and people's place in the supply chain.

9.23. Forrest commented further that its total tonnage processed had remained fairly static in the last two years whilst its profitability had declined. This was not what one would expect if the renderer was able to demand what he liked from the abattoir owner. Moreover, end-product sales prices had increased by about £14 per tonne in 1992.

Pricing

9.24. Forrest's formulation of its prices and charges for animal waste has been described in Chapter 6. Essentially, Forrest said, these were determined by reference to its standard yield percentages against market or sales values of the end product, less costs based on an assumed annual throughput of [*] tonnes and a gross profit per tonne ideally of £5 to £10. Prices were revised as often as changes in end-product values required. Around 10 per cent of agreements with suppliers were based on contracts (for a predetermined period) confirmed in writing.

9.25. Before our first hearing with Forrest, we sent it analyses of the pricing data it had supplied at our request covering each of its abattoir suppliers for four categories of waste (fat, bones, SBO and other offal) for May and October 1992. After correcting errors in the data which it had supplied, Forrest explained that in assessing its prices for its individual suppliers it had constant regard to the value of each category of raw material to Forrest in the context of the comparatively high threshold of its continuous process operation (as compared with a batch cooking operation) and the need to obtain sufficient volume of raw materials to enable it to operate profitably. Whilst all volumes were important to Forrest, it might pay less for smaller quantities because of economies of scale and costs of collection.

9.26. Forrest expanded on this point by describing how, realizing that its throughput had fallen below the critical weekly break-even level between March and July 1992 and that it was trading at a loss, it had been obliged to attempt to increase its throughput, if necessary by offering higher prices. These higher prices would then be mitigated by the fact that its fixed costs could be spread over a greater throughput. Hence Forrest approached large-volume suppliers because that materially increased throughput at once, whilst at the same time these volumes were collectable in convenient and therefore economic loads.

9.27. Additional factors which Forrest said accounted for price differentials were size of uplift (collection) and, in particular, whether the supplies of each type of raw material could be collected conveniently and economically; quality differences in the raw materials; the prices offered by other renderers; contracts made at different times or for different periods against the background of a rising or falling market; and the negotiating skills of the individual supplier, or group of suppliers.

9.28. At our first hearing with Forrest we discussed an analysis which Forrest had prepared of the various considerations relevant to the prices offered for raw materials in October 1992 to each of its abattoir suppliers. This analysis showed the volumes of beef fat, bones, SBO and other offal supplied, accompanied by comments relating, for example, to the quality or particular characteristics of the raw material, size of uplift, collection distance or costs and the effect of group price negotiations.

9.29. Forrest stated that the prices that it was prepared to pay were affected by quality differences, which translated into higher or lower yields, such as whether offals included significant amounts of water; whether fat had been hung and dried in the abattoir or simply tossed hot into the waste skip, or was dirty (eg covered in manure); whether bones included fat, or pig heads, or were clean and fresh; and whether SBO had had all the fat removed. These differences in quality affected both processing costs and achievable end-product values and consequently, in turn, Forrest's raw material prices. Forrest thought that the maximum differential arising from quality differences in fat, for a given quantity, would be about £10 to £15 per tonne.

9.30. Forrest presumed that abattoirs would normally be operating in the same basic manner week after week, with no more than minor variances in the value of their raw materials to Forrest as a result. However, Forrest had a Raw Materials Manager who spent about two or three days a week touring abattoirs regularly, particularly the larger ones. In addition, exception reports would normally be received in the first place from Forrest's drivers.

---

*Figure omitted. See note on page iv.

9.31. The economics of collection varied naturally with both the overall volumes supplied and the size of the individual uplift. On the one hand, an abattoir might supply on a regular and frequent basis raw materials which were collectable in one load, be it of one type of raw material or more. On the other hand, butchers' shops necessitated a 'milk round' picking up variable and irregular quantities of raw materials. Disregarding the latter, the maximum differential arising from collecting different quantities of fat was probably about £40 to £50 per tonne.

9.32. Group prices were applied directly to FMC's three Scottish abattoirs. In addition, some small and remote abattoirs were treated as a group and received prices set to take account of the average weight and collection distance.

9.33. Forrest believed that competition was a further consideration. The negotiating skills of the abattoir owner, however, were a very influential factor given the inherent stability, or lack of desire to switch, between abattoir and renderer. Nevertheless, whilst an abattoir owner had to be very concerned at the service it was receiving before being minded to switch, this did not remove the threat or possibility that he might switch if he considered that it was in his best interests to do so. The strength of the abattoir owner lay in merely being aware of the prices which other abattoir owners were receiving throughout the UK, as indeed he tended to be through frequently talking or meeting with other owners: he did not actually have to switch to take advantage of this situation.

9.34. Further, abattoir owners hardened their negotiating stance in the face of pressure on their margins and became more determined. In the case of one large abattoir with top quality raw material and substantial daily uplifts, Forrest had allowed a temporary 'no-charge' period until January 1993 to help it to re-establish after going into receivership.

9.35. In order of priority, said Forrest, market forces had most bearing on its prices, because if other renderers were offering more favourable rates Forrest would be unable to maintain adequate throughput. This did not mean, however, that there was no limit to what Forrest would be prepared to pay to obtain the volume it needed. For example, in October 1992 Forrest had lost its fat contract with British Beef at Hawick because it would have had to pay £125 or £130 per tonne and this would have resulted in a loss of some £12 per tonne. (Forrest had also lost the offals contract with this abattoir in March 1992.) Whilst Forrest, on occasion, was prepared to bid for raw material at break-even prices where there was an extreme paucity, or abnormally low levels, of raw material supplies, it would not go beyond that, and would go thus far only after taking into account market trends. Exactly how far it would be prepared to go in a given instance would be influenced by the importance of the contract for maintaining Forrest's break-even throughput.

9.36. Forrest said that it had never carried on business with the objective either of removing business from other renderers—other than through the normal competitive process where it needed the throughput and set its prices so as to obtain raw material without incurring losses—or of forcing a competitor out of business, or of deterring potential competitors. As regards the complaints about Biggar, Buchan Meat and ISM, for the reasons explained in paragraph 9.26, Forrest sought raw material from these three suppliers because they offered sufficient volume to ensure Forrest's return to profitability. Although the problem had occurred in the second quarter of 1992, supplies could not be obtained before the third quarter, and thereafter Forrest's throughput increased.

9.37. Forrest stated that it did not set its prices at levels such that the expected additional revenue from the increase in sales was insufficient to cover average costs. It was only too conscious of the level of fixed costs it bore and the importance of a sufficient throughput to enable it to trade profitably. Nevertheless, in difficult circumstances and where there was paucity of raw materials available for purchase, it was prepared to accept a situation where the expected additional revenue covered incremental costs plus only a partial contribution to overheads, because it could otherwise lose a substantial amount of business. Even so, all the prices agreed with Biggar, Buchan Meat and ISM were profitable by up to £10 or £11 for each type of material.

9.38. Commenting on a further analysis that we had carried out which sought to disentangle the effect on prices of competition as against other factors, in particular quantity and quality, Forrest argued that the analysis could not possibly support any conclusion that Forrest practised discriminatory pricing.

9.39. First, Forrest believed that the MMC's approach was fundamentally flawed, not only because it assumed that quality and quantity were the *only* relevant criteria, but also because the effect of adopting broad categories of quality viewed in isolation was to oversimplify the analysis which Forrest undertook when considering the prices it was to offer. The value of raw materials to Forrest was determined by additional variables already described, such as the economics of collecting and processing and the wider range of variability of quality of the raw material. Thus neither quality nor quantity could be viewed in isolation but must be viewed together with the particular features of each individual contract.

9.40. On the basis of these analyses, Forrest produced revised price dispersion ranges for the prices it paid for beef fat, bones, SBO and other offals in October 1992. In each case these showed the ranges not explained by factors other than competition in single figures. In Forrest's view this showed that its approach to pricing was rational and logical and that, contrary to the conclusion reached in the MMC's analysis, it was neither predatory, discriminatory nor otherwise improper.

10 Conclusions

Introduction

10.1. Under the references dated 30 September 1992, as varied on 1 December 1992, we are required to report whether a monopoly situation exists in relation to the supply of animal waste in England and Wales, and in Scotland, and if so:

(a) by virtue of which provisions of section 6 to 8 of the Fair Trading Act 1973 (the Act) that monopoly situation is taken to exist;

(b) in favour of what person or persons that monopoly situation exists;

(c) whether any steps (by way of uncompetitive practices or otherwise) are being taken by that person or those persons for the purpose of exploiting or maintaining the monopoly situation and if so by what uncompetitive practices or in what other way;

(d) whether any action or omission on the part of that person or those persons is attributable to the existence of that monopoly situation and if so what action or omission and in what way it is so attributable; and

(e) whether any facts found by the MMC in pursuance of their investigations under the preceding provisions of this paragraph operate or may be expected to operate against the public interest.

Full details of the references are set out in Appendix 1.1.

10.2. For the purposes of the references, 'the supply of animal waste' means the supply of animal material which is acquired for processing in rendering plants. The variations in the references brought a substantial volume of poultry waste within this definition. Fish waste is excluded unless it is part of butchery waste.

10.3. We first consider the existence of monopoly situations and the persons in whose favour the situations exist (questions *(a)* and *(b)*). In paragraphs 10.12 to 10.34 we describe the background to the inquiry, including the MMC's two earlier reports concerning the animal waste industry, and more recent developments. We turn to the rendering markets and barriers to entry in paragraphs 10.35 to 10.48. The subsequent questions *(c)* to *(e)* above are dealt with from paragraph 10.49 onwards.

The monopoly situations

England and Wales

10.4. Under section 6(1)*(b)* of the Act a scale monopoly situation would exist if at least one-quarter of the animal waste supplied in England and Wales were supplied to members of one and the same group of interconnected bodies corporate. As we have shown in paragraph 2.18, Prosper De Mulder Ltd and its subsidiary companies John Knight (Animal By Products) Ltd, Granox Ltd, De Mulder &

Sons Ltd, J L Thomas & Co Ltd and De Mulder (Market Harborough) Ltd[1] together acquired for processing in rendering plants over a quarter of the animal waste so acquired in England and Wales in 1992. There has been no material change since then. We conclude therefore that a monopoly situation exists by virtue of section 6(1)(b) of the Act.

10.5. We further conclude that this monopoly situation exists in favour of Prosper De Mulder Ltd and the following subsidiary and related companies:

Subsidiary companies

John Knight (Animal By Products) Ltd
Granox Ltd
De Mulder & Sons Ltd
J L Thomas & Co Ltd
G E and H Mitchell Ltd
Beacon Research Ltd

Related companies

Frazer (Butchers) Ltd
Chettles Ltd
Prosper De Mulder Transport
Prosper De Mulder Services
Oracle Motors Ltd
Francis Investments Ltd

All the above subsidiary and related companies benefit from their relationship with Prosper De Mulder Ltd. They are all owned by the De Mulder family and managed as a single entity. In this chapter we refer to Prosper De Mulder Ltd and its subsidiary and related companies as PDM.

Scotland

10.6. Under section 6(1)(a) of the Act a scale monopoly situation would exist if at least one-quarter of the animal waste supplied in Scotland were supplied to any one person. As we have shown in paragraph 2.24, William Forrest & Son (Paisley) Ltd (Forrest) acquired for processing in rendering plants over one-quarter of the animal waste so acquired in Scotland in 1992. There has been no material change since then. We conclude therefore that a monopoly situation exists by virtue of section 6(1)(a) of the Act.

10.7. We further conclude that this monopoly situation exists in favour of William Forrest & Son (Paisley) Ltd and its ultimate holding company, Hillsdown Holdings plc (Hillsdown).

Definition of the market

10.8. PDM submitted that the limitation of the terms of the reference to the consideration of the supply of animal waste to renderers created an artificial definition of the market for animal waste. Our studies show that the supply to renderers is about 73 per cent of the total supply. The rest is accounted for by sales to pet food manufacturers (15 per cent), disposal as waste (8 per cent)—the main items disposed of being blood and feathers—and sales of special items to manufacturers of particular types of food, pharmaceuticals and other products (4 per cent). PDM's share of total animal waste is around 50 per cent compared with a share of some 69 per cent of supplies to renderers.

---

[1]The Market Harborough rendering plant was closed in February 1992.

10.9. From a competition point of view it is in our view reasonable to focus on the supply of waste to renderers, the subject of the reference. Rendering accounts for the majority of waste, and there are a number of other pertinent considerations. By law, abattoirs must dispose of their waste within 48 hours, and they need in practice to do so within 24 hours. They are thus not able to operate in a normal commercial way and sell what they can and dispose as they wish of the rest. Being able to sell certain high-grade materials to pet food and other manufacturers does not therefore have much effect on the arrangements they make for the sale of the main part of the waste material to renderers. Nor does the possibility of disposing of blood (by spreading on the land) and feathers (to a land-fill site) have much impact on those arrangements. The one effect of significance is that the alternative disposal methods do set some upper limit on the charges that renderers can make to abattoirs.

10.10. We conclude that we should not regard the total supply of animal waste as the relevant market for examining the economic relationship between renderers and their suppliers. The market strengths of PDM and of Forrest are best represented by their shares of supplies to renderers alone.

10.11. PDM also argued that the manufacture of edible fats for human consumption was not part of the animal waste rendering industry (see paragraph 3.13). We accept this, and so far as possible we have excluded such material from our calculations of market shares. In paragraphs 10.35 to 10.41 we deal separately with the red meat waste rendering and poultry waste rendering markets.

Background to the inquiry

General

10.12. Red meat waste supplied to the rendering industry in 1992 amounted to almost 1 million tonnes in England and Wales and 150,000 tonnes in Scotland. In the same year poultry plants in Great Britain provided commercial renderers in England with over 300,000 tonnes of waste. There is no commercial rendering of poultry waste in Scotland.

10.13. The main categories of animal waste for commercial purposes are offal, best fat, other fat, bones, blood and poultry carcases and feathers. In accordance with Government regulations to control bovine spongiform encephalopathy (BSE) special arrangements are made to deal with offals of certain categories (known as Specified Bovine Offals—SBO).

10.14. The principal sources of red meat waste are abattoirs; fat and bones are also provided by butchers and boning-out plants; and knackers and others provide material from diseased or fallen animals. Some abattoirs, mainly the larger ones, operate a 'gut-room' where the different types of product such as tripes and pancreases are carefully segregated, and they sometimes contract out the operation to specialist companies, of which PDM is one. But frequently only a basic form of separation takes place at the abattoir.

10.15. The number of abattoirs in Great Britain has declined from 2,062 in 1968/69 to 709 in 1991/92, when 11 per cent of the abattoirs accounted for almost 63 per cent of slaughtering through-put (see paragraphs 2.9 and 2.11).

10.16. Virtually all red meat waste is removed from abattoirs within 24 hours of slaughter and the same applies to waste from poultry processing plants. Supplies vary seasonally and by day of the week and all must be cleared, bringing capacity implications for the renderer. It is a tribute to the industry in the discharge of a vital function that we received minimal complaint about the quality of services provided.

10.17. The principal products from rendering animal waste (a mechanical and heat treatment process) are meat-and-bone meal, and tallows of various grades. Greaves are a part-processed material, after extraction of some of the tallow, but before drying and milling to produce meat-and-bone meal. Greaves can be stored and are therefore a useful means of smoothing production when animal waste is in short supply; they are also used for pet food. An estimated 390,000 tonnes of meat-and-bone meal (valued at £53 million) was produced in the UK in 1992 for use mainly in animal feed.

Tallow production amounted to an estimated 195,000 tonnes (value £36 million) in that year. Tallows are variously used for soap manufacture, for animal feed, or in the production of chemicals. There are close substitutes for both meat-and-bone meal and tallow in most of these uses.

10.18. The charges made or prices paid for an abattoir's waste will reflect on the one hand the types of material, and their quality, quantity, distance from the processing plant and the extent of competition between renderers, and on the other hand the prices for end products. Sometimes there is just one overall price (or charge) which reflects the mix of the waste. Some types of material are of much less value to renderers than others, and this is reflected in the transactions. For low-yielding products, such as blood and offal, the abattoir generally pays a collection charge to the renderer; for high-yielding products, such as fats and poultry carcases, the renderer pays the abattoir. Over the years, bones and poultry offal have sometimes been in the one category and sometimes in the other.

10.19. Renderers operate under strict regulatory controls both as regards the safety of their products and the environmental effects of their plants. The need for environmental protection relates mainly to the effluent and odours created by the process. It is now possible to treat effluent so successfully that discharge into a river can be accepted. As for odour control, the design of both process plant and the building housing it can substantially reduce obnoxious output. Standards laid down in legislation, in particular the Environmental Protection Act 1990 covering effluent and emissions, are monitored by local authorities who have a duty to ensure that the standards are attained (see paragraph 10.34). The plant and facilities of a rendering factory are also affected by the recent EC Directive (90/667/EEC) which seeks to harmonize the arrangements for the processing and disposal of animal waste and came into force at the start of 1993. Additional regulations have been made by the Ministry of Agriculture, Fisheries and Food (MAFF) in response to the threats to health from salmonella and BSE (see paragraph 10.26).

Previous inquiries

10.20. This is the MMC's third report concerning the rendering industry. The first report,[1] submitted in January 1985, was on the supply of red meat animal waste (ie it excluded poultry waste) in Great Britain as a whole (the 1985 report). We are now, as already indicated, required to consider separately the supply of animal waste in England and Wales, and in Scotland, and to include poultry waste. The second report,[2] submitted in June 1991, was on the merger of Prosper De Mulder Ltd and Croda International plc (the Croda report).

10.21. Despite the groundwork of these earlier reports, we did not find it easy to assemble the facts and figures necessary for our wider inquiry. The rendering industry is not large, and contains a number of quite small family firms which have difficulty in providing data, particularly going back over a period of time. Business tends to be conducted informally with a minimum of paperwork; for example, written contracts for the supply of waste material for processing are rare. We outline below the findings of the earlier reports and the market environment they described. We then deal with subsequent developments and set out our current findings.

The 1985 report

10.22. The 1985 report (see Appendix 4.1) into red meat waste in Great Britain considered that the public interest had three main requirements of the rendering industry:

(a) most importantly, that it should provide an effective and reliable waste disposal service to the meat industry;

---

[1]*Animal Waste: a Report on the supply of animal waste in Great Britain*, Cmnd 9470, April 1985.

[2]*Prosper De Mulder Ltd and Croda International plc: a report on the merger situation*, Cm 1611, August 1991.

(b) that the collection, transportation and processing of animal waste should be carried on without unduly polluting the environment; and

(c) that the industry should be economically efficient.

While the report found that PDM satisfied the first two of these requirements, it was unable to reach firm conclusions on PDM's efficiency because the variability of conditions in the industry made comparisons difficult and PDM's management information systems were not well developed. It found no basis, however, for criticizing PDM's processing efficiency.

10.23. The report noted that PDM pursued a strategy of growth through acquisition, but found no evidence that it had deliberately eliminated competitors, nor did it consider that PDM's growth had been harmful to abattoirs. The report did, however, find that PDM used its market power to respond aggressively to competitors seeking to capture its raw material sources. It found that PDM's pricing policy was designed to exploit or maintain its monopoly and might be expected to operate against the public interest by restricting competition in rendering.

10.24. As a result of the report, PDM gave three main undertakings (the 1986 undertakings—see Appendix 1.2):

(1) that it would not enter into gut-room contracts[1] at a loss or engage in cross-subsidy between its gut-room business and its other activities;

(2) that it would not make the collection of any grade of animal waste conditional on that customer also supplying higher-grade waste to PDM; and

(3) that it would notify the Director General of Fair Trading (DGFT) at least one month before it made any future acquisitions of animal waste enterprises.

The Croda report (submitted in June 1991)

10.25. The Croda report (see Appendix 4.2) found that the rendering industry had been experiencing difficult and turbulent trading conditions. First, the prices of tallow and meat-and-bone meal, which had been at peak levels in 1984, had fallen back sharply by 1986, and after stabilizing for a time had dropped even further in 1990. These price movements were initially due to reductions in the prices of competing commodities such as palm oil and soya meal which were in world-wide surplus.

10.26. Secondly, the industry had been hit by two major health scares. Concern over the extent of salmonella in animal feed had led to the imposition of tighter controls under the protein processing legislation in 1989. More important had been the impact of BSE, first identified in late 1986. The practice of feeding ruminant-based animal protein to ruminants had been banned from July 1988, effectively cutting off 10 to 15 per cent of the market for meat-and-bone meal. Further regulatory action had been taken in September 1990 when SBO material had been banned from being incorporated in meat-and-bone meal for use in any animal or poultry rations. As a result of the new regulation, SBO material had to be collected and processed separately from other material; and while rendering was still necessary to sterilize the specified material, the meat-and-bone meal produced no longer had any end use (the tallow still had a market in uses other than animal feed).

10.27. As a result of these developments, renderers had had to cut the prices they paid for high-grade waste and introduce progressively higher charges for collecting low-grade waste, and implement a high charge for collecting SBO material. At the same time growing public awareness of environmental issues had put pressure on the rendering industry to achieve higher standards of odour and effluent controls. For those renderers who wished to remain in business this had led to a need for capital investment on a scale which was substantial in relation to the turnover and profits which they could reasonably expect to achieve.

---

[1]See paragraph 10.14.

10.28. The report also found that concentration in the rendering industry had continued. Whereas the 1985 report had calculated that the number of rendering companies in Great Britain in 1983 was 57 (down from about 160 in the 1950s), the number trading early in 1991 was down to around 30, of which three operated only in Scotland and four processed edible fats only. Since the 1985 report PDM had acquired a further seven animal waste businesses. Only two cases of new firms entering the market since 1985 had come to the MMC's attention: B & E (Rassau) Ltd which had opened a rendering plant in South Wales in 1988 (since closed), and Cheale Meats Ltd, an abattoir company which had acquired a small plant near Canterbury in 1990 from a firm which was leaving the industry.

10.29. Over the same period PDM had further developed its strategy of concentrating production on a few large plants which specialized in processing high-grade waste, while Doncaster, Nuneaton (Hartshill) and Exeter concentrated on low-grade. Since the 1990 BSE regulations, PDM had dedicated the Nuneaton plant to processing solely SBO, knacker and other condemned material. This specialization had caused PDM's transport costs to rise as material had to be hauled longer distances to the appropriate plant; SBO material, in particular, was brought to Nuneaton from all parts of England and Wales.

10.30. The Croda report found that the merger had an adverse effect on competition in the collection of high-grade waste in the South-West and South-East of England, and had modestly enhanced PDM's position in the overall waste collection market in England and Wales. But these effects were marginal in relation to the structural defects in competition which existed before the merger. Moreover, Croda was a declining competitive force (see Appendix 4.2, paragraph 36). The report considered that the merger was likely to improve PDM's efficiency and bring wider public health and environmental benefits. These effects, though also modest, would assist PDM in carrying out functions which represented an important public service as well as a commercial activity. Having taken account of the limited adverse effects on competition on the one hand, and the important public issues of health and the environment as well as efficiency gains on the other hand, the MMC concluded that the merger did not and might be expected not to operate against the public interest.

10.31. The report went on to make certain observations. First, the report noted that the issues which arose in this industry concerned not only competition but also the relationship between its commercial and public service aspects. The monopoly powers under the Act and the provisions of the Competition Act 1980 dealing with anti-competitive practices might therefore not be appropriate for dealing with the whole range of these issues: a different kind of inquiry might be necessary to address the various questions relating to public health and the environment. Secondly, the report stated that it would be advantageous if, in the case of any future proposed acquisition by PDM of businesses engaged in the collection or rendering of animal waste, a longer period of notice of the proposed transaction, possibly three months, was given to the DGFT than the one month provided for in the current undertakings. Thirdly, the report also noted that PDM's published accounts did not cover the whole of the group's animal waste business. It suggested that a group of companies playing such a crucial role as PDM in an important market should arrange its financial affairs in such a way that its published accounts were sufficiently transparent and complete to give a full picture of its trading fortunes.

Developments since the Croda report

10.32. When publishing the Croda report, the Department of Trade and Industry announced that it would be working with MAFF and the Department of the Environment (DoE) to ensure that the regulation of the rendering industry following the implementation of the EC Directive on animal waste would, as far as possible, be organized so as to allow the development of effective competition in the industry. Essential public health and environmental interests would be safeguarded. The DGFT would also continue to keep the industry under review. The other observations mentioned in paragraph 10.31, which in the absence of an adverse finding were not enforceable, were not pursued.

10.33. PDM has since purchased a number of small animal waste collection businesses without pre-notifying the acquisitions to the DGFT (see paragraph 10.70). Meanwhile PDM has ceased production at the high-grade waste rendering plant it acquired from Croda and moth-balled the plant. In the half-year immediately preceding the acquisition, the plant processed an average of 1,000 tonnes of fat and bones a week. PDM told us that the decision to close the plant reflected the decline in high-grade material available for rendering.

10.34. By virtue of Part I of the Environmental Protection Act 1990 and Schedule 1 to the Environmental Protection (Prescribed Processes and Substances) Regulations 1991, which consolidated earlier provisions, no new rendering process or substantial change is permitted without local authority authorization. In issuing any authorization, local authorities must have regard for guidance produced by the Secretary of State for the Environment on appropriate air pollution standards for rendering plants, in compliance with the BATNEEC concept (Best Available Techniques Not Entailing Excessive Cost). Existing plants are to be allowed until 1 April 1997 to comply with the conditions governing their authorization. DoE told us that in most cases it was likely that authorizations would be issued specifying that an upgrading programme must be submitted demonstrating how compliance was proposed to be achieved by the due date (see paragraphs 7.130 *et seq*).

The rendering market: red meat waste

England and Wales

10.35. For many years the largest purchaser and renderer of animal waste in England and Wales has been PDM. It had an estimated 50 per cent of supplies for rendering in 1982 and about 64 per cent in 1992, a proportion similar to that estimated in the Croda report for 1990. In 1992 PDM processed 621,000 tonnes of red meat waste, which may be compared with an estimated half a million tonnes in 1982.

10.36. PDM has eight animal waste rendering plants and provides a collection service covering the whole of England and Wales apart from West Wales. The high-value business of rendering fat and bones is undertaken at Widnes and Silvertown; clean offal with fat and bones is processed at Doncaster and Exeter; and 'dirty offal' (ie SBO and knacker material) together with fat and bones is rendered at Hartshill. The Widnes plant handles all blood and some poultry waste, but the bulk of the poultry waste is dealt with at Ditchford and Nottingham. As already mentioned, the Market Harborough plant is currently moth-balled. PDM told us that it operated as an integrated business and that the strategic location of its plants and the specialized production processes gave it an advantage because it was able to produce final products with higher values than those of its competitors.

10.37. Each of the other renderers in England and Wales has one plant. The main companies and their shares are Fats & Proteins (UK) Ltd (7 per cent), Smith Brothers (Hyde) Ltd (6 per cent), Gilberts Animal By-Products Ltd (Gilberts) (5 per cent), A Hughes & Son (Skellingthorpe) Ltd (5 per cent) and Peninsular Proteins Ltd (Peninsular—a subsidiary of Hillsdown) (4 per cent). There are in addition a number of smaller operators who between them have a market share of approximately 9 per cent. Forrest does not collect red meat waste in England or Wales, nor does PDM collect such waste in Scotland. In fact very little red meat waste is transported across the border between England and Scotland. Most rendering plants are some distance from the border, and there are few major abattoirs in the border areas. We conclude that for most practical purposes England and Wales on the one hand and Scotland on the other may be regarded as two separate markets.

Scotland

10.38. There are only three commercial red meat waste renderers operating in Scotland. The largest is Forrest, which in 1992 processed over 100,000 tonnes of red meat waste at its Motherwell plant, about 71 per cent of all such waste rendered in Scotland. The two others are Dundas Brothers Ltd (Dundas Brothers) with a plant in the North-East of Scotland and Dundas Chemical Company (Mosspark) Ltd (Dundas Chemical) with a plant in the Borders. In 1992 Dundas Brothers rendered approximately 25,000 tonnes, a share of some 18 per cent, and Dundas Chemical 16,000 tonnes, a share of around 11 per cent.

10.39. Forrest has been becoming increasingly dominant in Scotland: ten years ago it had only around 50 per cent of the market compared with its current 71 per cent. Forrest is, however, a small producer compared with PDM and processes the equivalent of only around 10 per cent of all the waste processed by PDM.

The rendering market: poultry waste

10.40. Four of the main poultry producers process their own waste, and they may sell the product as feed for pigs and sheep. Not all of them use it to feed their poultry because of the risk of cross-contamination perceived by poultry retailers. They are not allowed under animal health regulations to dispose of the waste for other purposes and have no interest in competing with the renderers to process the waste of other poultry producers.

10.41. Since 1989 there has been an obligation to process poultry waste separately from red meat waste. There are only four significant commercial poultry waste renderers. PDM is by far the largest, with an estimated share of over 80 per cent of the commercial market of 300,000 tonnes. PDM has an agreement with Hillsdown, the largest poultry producer in the UK, enabling it to acquire all of Hillsdown's poultry waste (see paragraph 10.73). The other significant operators are Wildriggs Proteins Ltd (Wildriggs) in Cumbria, Mid-Norfolk Proteins and Hughes. All poultry waste produced in Scotland that requires commercial rendering is processed in England. PDM and Wildriggs collect poultry waste in Scotland.

Barriers to entry

England and Wales

10.42. There has been no significant entry into the rendering industry in England and Wales for many years. An important barrier appears to have been created by the health and environmental concerns that have led to the more demanding standards for the industry we have noted in paragraph 10.19 together with a reluctance on the part of the authorities to approve sites. Even if all the difficulties presented by environmental regulation can be overcome it is likely to take an entrant two or three years to gain all the requisite permissions.

10.43. Although we found little agreement between renderers as to the cost of entry, it is clear that environmental regulation has added substantially to that cost. Excluding very small renderers, cost estimates provided by renderers in England and Wales ranged from £2.5 to £10.0 million. Peninsular, which has had recent experience of re-equipping a plant with the latest technology, thought that the minimum cost would be £2.5 to £3.0 million.

10.44. Acquiring waste material would be a serious problem for an independent new entrant. The supply of red meat waste is at best static and probably declining (see paragraph 2.6); a new entrant can therefore only acquire material at the expense of an existing renderer. Here, PDM's reputation for taking vigorous action to safeguard its supplies is likely to discourage independent entry. The position is even less encouraging in respect of poultry waste; PDM has over 80 per cent of the commercial market and has reinforced its position by its agreement with Hillsdown to process all Hilldown's poultry waste. The agreement is perceived in the industry to be a long-term arrangement (see paragraph 10.73).

10.45. PDM, as we have already indicated, has been active in the acquisition of rendering businesses. For the most part, the rendering plants PDM acquired were closed, and the machinery scrapped or used by PDM itself or sold, sometimes to overseas customers. We were told that other renderers often had no opportunity to bid for the business. In the case of Croda, we note that PDM acquired the rendering business and subsequently moth-balled the plant (see paragraph 10.33).

10.46. Our surveys produced some evidence that abattoirs have considered diversifying into rendering over the years; and some abattoirs indicated that, for them, this remained at least a possibility. We were also told of two examples of such diversification (see paragraph 7.68). We have

236197 H2

heard that a New Zealand company has expressed interest in establishing a large integrated abattoir and rendering plant in Anglesey or southern Scotland on the sites of former abattoirs, but the market opportunity for such a plant is unclear. The disposal of animal waste by incineration, which might encourage entry, does not appear to represent a viable alternative to large-scale rendering. We understand that European Organic Processing Ltd is seeking planning permission for a site to open a combined maggot breeding, rendering and organic waste disposal plant and, with the support of MAFF, has applied for a grant from the EC (see paragraph 2.92).

Scotland

10.47. There has been no entry into the industry in Scotland for several years. The preceding comments on the difficulties of entering the industry in England and Wales apply similarly to Scotland, given Forrest's dominance.

10.48. We were, however, told of a possible joint venture for a proposed new rendering plant and associated incinerator in the Grampian region of North-East Scotland. This was seen as a contingency plan against possible future closure of Dundas Brothers notwithstanding the latter's determination to remain in business as a renderer (see paragraphs 7.83 to 7.84). The current situation was that Grampian Regional Council, which was a party to the joint venture, was committed to the point of selecting the most appropriate site for such a plant. Ultimately there was a political decision to be made on the matter. In addition, MAFF told us that it was currently assessing the new technological aspects of the scheme against the requirements of the Animal By-Products Order 1992, prior to any decision about putting it forward to the EC for consideration for grant.

The public interest issues

10.49. Public interest issues arise, both in England and Wales and in Scotland, with regard to pricing, market arrangements and behaviour, profitability and efficiency. There are further issues in England and Wales concerning the fulfilment by PDM of the 1986 undertakings, and concerning the transparency of PDM's financial performance. We found that the public service of animal waste disposal by the renderers and the arrangements in train in the industry for the protection of the environment were both working well.

England and Wales

10.50. We compared the complaints and allegations about PDM received during our earlier monopoly inquiry into animal waste (see paragraph 10.20) with those received during this inquiry and found a marked increase from 9 or so to 43 (see Chapters 6 and 8 and Appendix 6.1 in the 1985 report and Chapter 7 and Appendix 7.1 in this report).

Pricing

10.51. The main public interest issues concern PDM's pricing (including charging) policy and practices, and in this respect little has changed since the 1985 report. As before, we are concerned about the prices paid by PDM to its suppliers for high-grade waste and its charges for low-grade waste, and not about prices charged for its end products. The latter are, we believe, restrained by the international price of tallow, and by prices of palm oil and soya meal, which are close substitutes for tallow and meat-and-bone meal and are also traded internationally. There have been allegations from competitors that PDM engages in predatory pricing for supplies of waste, and from suppliers that PDM takes advantage of its dominant position by imposing excessive charges for collection of material such as offal or paying unduly low prices for the better material such as bones and best fat.

10.52. We considered PDM's pricing practices under two main headings: predatory pricing and discriminatory pricing. By predatory pricing we mean setting payments and charges for animal waste at levels that imply a financial loss (when other costs and expected sales revenues are taken into account) and doing so with the intention of prejudicing the survival of a competing renderer. By discriminatory pricing we mean that there is a substantial difference between prices paid to different suppliers for material of comparable quality and entailing similar collection costs. A firm that is dominant in the market can exploit its strength through discriminatory pricing.

10.53. We studied five cases of possible *predatory pricing* by PDM. One arose from a complaint by Imperial Meat Company Ltd (IMC) and related to PDM's undertakings in respect of gut-room operations. It is dealt with in paragraphs 10.64 to 10.68. The other four cases are described in Appendix 6.2. In one of these, described in paragraphs 2 to 12 of the appendix, the prices offered by PDM were likely to lead to significant losses. We did not, however, find any clear evidence that PDM was seeking by this means to drive the competing renderer (in this case Gilberts) from the market: PDM's behaviour was consistent with, and explicable by reference to, its avowed intention of maintaining its level of supplies. We have not, therefore, been able to identify any cases that are predatory in the sense of which we are using the term.

10.54. Regarding *discriminatory pricing*, we carried out a detailed analysis in order to examine the extent to which suppliers to PDM whose supplies entailed similar collection costs experienced different payments/charges for material of comparable quality. The main aim of the analysis was to compare the range of actual payments/charges with the range that could in theory result from variations in quality or differences in collection or processing cost. This proved to be a long and complicated exercise, mainly because of the breadth of the quality range within each category of material. We had extensive discussions with PDM about facts and figures used in the analysis and about the methodology. PDM was highly critical of our approach and suggested a number of changes. We have been able to reflect a number of PDM's suggestions in the analysis; others we have not accepted. After taking careful account of PDM's representations, we are satisfied that the analysis is robust. To a significant extent variations in payments/charges cannot be explained by reference to variations in yields of end products or by other physical factors, even when combined with a reasonable degree of variation to account for ordinary competition. The details of the analysis are set out in Appendix 6.1.

10.55. In order to check whether the range of prices paid by PDM was greater or smaller during the period of more intense competition in the middle months of 1992 than at other times, we examined the range of PDM's prices in April 1993 and compared them with those of May and October 1992. We found that there was no significant difference between April 1993 and October 1992 and little difference between April 1993 and May 1992. Our various studies show, in sum, that:

(a) PDM's payments/charges varied widely in a way that was not always related to physical factors (see paragraph 6.9 and Appendix 6.1);

(b) PDM sometimes made significantly lower charges or paid significantly higher prices when another renderer bid for an abattoir's supplies (see paragraph 6.7 and Appendix 6.2);

(c) at times of acute competition PDM sometimes lowered its charges or raised its payments to a level that meant that it made losses on the contracts (see paragraph 6.14 and Appendix 6.2, paragraph 12); and

(d) PDM negotiated a single set of charges/payments with some large suppliers operating from a number of locations, and therefore did not make charges or payments that reflected the economic value to it of the supplies it collected from each of those locations as it would for single-location suppliers (see paragraph 6.3).

10.56. We also considered whether PDM's practice of offering package deals to abattoirs for different types of material was anti-competitive (see Appendix 6.1, paragraphs 18 and 19). PDM assured us that it only offered such deals at the request of its suppliers, and the evidence we have found is insufficient to support a conclusion that the deals were damaging competition.

10.57. We conclude that PDM has engaged in discriminatory pricing. The wide range of charges/ payments we have found is to a significant extent unaccounted for by physical factors, even when combined with a reasonable degree of variation to account for ordinary competition. PDM has been able to set different charges/payments unrelated to cost differences. It has admitted that in some cases it set charges/payments which resulted in a loss in the price war during the middle months of 1992; this behaviour fell short of predatory pricing in the cases we studied (see paragraph 10.53), though we believe that PDM will generally have been aware when prices offered would mean that the contract would be loss-making (see paragraph 6.14).

10.58. PDM and Gilberts both say that the origin of the price war was Gilberts' acquisition of material from certain of PDM's suppliers. We understand that the war affected other renderers, particularly in England and Wales, but also to a limited extent in Scotland because suppliers, notably the larger firms with operations in both Scotland and England, compared charges/payments and sought parity of treatment. PDM assured us that it was not in the normal course its policy to compete for another renderer's supplies. It tended, however, to retaliate if its own supplies were under threat. We were told that this latest price war ended after a telephone conversation between PDM and Gilberts, which was initiated by PDM.

10.59. It might be thought that the intermittent price wars which occur in the industry are indicative of a healthy climate of competition. It seems to us, however, that there is generally little competition amongst renderers. As we have noted in the preceding paragraph, PDM admits that it does not normally compete for other renderers' supplies, and we believe that for the most part its policy of selective retaliation keeps other renderers in their place, allowing PDM to become increasingly dominant (see paragraphs 8.34 and 8.36).

10.60. As to the telephone conversation between PDM and Gilberts referred to in paragraph 10.58, it appears to us that this may have given rise to an agreement which is subject to registration under the Restrictive Trade Practices Act 1976. Section 54(5) of the Fair Trading Act 1973 directs the MMC to exclude from their investigation consideration of whether an agreement which is subject to registration under the Restrictive Trade Practices Act 1976 operates against the public interest. We are therefore debarred from reaching any public interest conclusions on this matter. No doubt the DGFT will take any action he considers necessary.

10.61. PDM's pricing practices need to be seen in the context of the company's position in the industry. It is the only renderer that obtains supplies from the whole of England and almost the whole of Wales; it is a much larger company, and has much greater financial strength, than other renderers; and the size of its acquisitions of animal waste is such as both to make it much less vulnerable than other renderers to the loss of individual large suppliers and to provide it with opportunities for discrimination between customers of different types and locations. The practices set out in paragraph 10.55 show that PDM has market power which it exercises over-zealously to protect its supplies. By engaging in price discrimination, it squeezes smaller competitors, particularly any competitor which attempts to gain supplies at PDM's expense.

10.62. We conclude that PDM's practice of discriminatory pricing (see paragraph 10.57) is a step taken for the purpose of exploiting and maintaining the monopoly situation and that this constitutes a fact which operates and may be expected to operate against the public interest. The particular effect adverse to the public interest is the restriction of competition in rendering.

The 1986 undertakings

10.63. We have been concerned about certain aspects of PDM's undertakings, which are set out in full in Appendix 1.2.

Gut-room undertakings

10.64. Undertaking 1(iv)*(b)* requires PDM to provide to the DGFT in respect of each gut-room contract into which it proposes to enter a statement providing estimates of throughput, yield of product and expenses. It is clear that this undertaking requires a budget to be submitted to the DGFT *before* PDM enters into a new contract. PDM has not done this. Therefore when IMC, a specialist gut-room operator, complained to the DGFT in 1991 that a contract at West Devon Meats, Hatherleigh, had been taken on by PDM at uneconomic prices in breach of the 1986 undertaking, the DGFT had no budget to hand against which to check the complaint. In this instance PDM supplied a budget 20 weeks after the contract had begun (see paragraph 7.47 and Appendix 6.3).

10.65. Undertaking 1(iv)*(c)* requires PDM to submit to the DGFT 'an audited annual statement, within three months of the end of the relevant accounting reference period, of the profit and loss of its gut-room business, together with reconcilable management accounts showing the profit and loss of each gut-room contract separately'. PDM's actual returns to the DGFT have comprised a list of the profits for each gut-room and an audited profit and loss account statement for the gut-room business as a whole, but without 'reconcilable management accounts' for each gut-room. Revenues and expenses from transactions with PDM's other businesses have not been shown separately from revenues and expenses from transactions with third parties. It follows that, as a large proportion of the sales, most of the haulage expense and all of the administration charges are of this nature, there is no basis for determining whether such revenues and expenses are on an arm's length basis. Moreover, PDM has not demonstrated to the DGFT that the weekly administration charge of £50 for each gut-room is based on a reasonable allocation of overheads, as required by undertaking 1(iii)*(a)*. We also note that the returns have generally been submitted late, usually in October, six months after the 31 March year-end, and that the statement for 1991/92 was not submitted until January 1993 (see Appendix 6.3).

10.66. We have found that PDM has failed to adopt and operate accounting systems and accounting procedures in the manner required by undertaking 1(iii). In particular:

(a) PDM's administration charge of £50 per week for each of its gut-rooms is only sufficient to cover the direct administration costs. It is not sufficient to cover indirect costs, as required by undertaking 1(iii)*(a)*.

(b) We do not believe that PDM's inter-company transfer prices for the Hatherleigh gut-room were equal to those that would be credited in respect of an equivalent transaction at arm's length, as required by undertaking 1(iii). When we costed the Hatherleigh gut-room using the prices paid to IMC and charges made to its associated abattoirs by PDM for similar material, we found that the gut-room had operated at a loss.

10.67. There is no evidence that PDM deliberately took on the Hatherleigh gut-room on loss-making terms with the intention of damaging IMC, which would be necessary to sustain a charge of predatory pricing. However, PDM has been cross-subsidizing its gut-room operations in breach of undertaking 1, thus continuing the effect, identified at paragraph 9.42 of the 1985 report, that PDM has been enabled to pay prices or make charges which a gut-room operator who is not also a renderer might not be able to match.

10.68. We conclude, therefore, that PDM is in breach of undertaking 1 through failure to adopt and operate accounting systems and accounting procedures in the manner required, through failure to charge adequate administration costs to its gut-room operations and through failure to make arm's length payments/charges for the collection of raw materials from abattoirs where it operates gut-rooms. These are steps taken for the purpose of maintaining the monopoly situation and constitute facts which operate and may be expected to operate against the public interest. The particular effects adverse to the public interest are that the DGFT has been deprived of information concerning the financial results of PDM's gut-room activities which would have enabled him to intervene with timely measures to protect competition in the operation of gut-rooms and in rendering, and that competition in the operation of gut-rooms and in rendering has been restricted.

Undertaking to notify intended acquisitions

10.69. Undertaking 3 requires PDM to notify the DGFT at least one month before the date on which PDM or its subsidiaries (as the case may be):

(a) acquire directly or indirectly or do anything with the intent that an associated person will acquire directly or indirectly any animal waste enterprise; or

(b) do anything alone or with others which would result in any animal waste enterprise ceasing to be distinct (within the meaning of section 65, interpreted, where appropriate, in accordance with section 77, of the Fair Trading Act 1973) from any enterprise carried on by or under the control of PDM or any of its subsidiaries.

10.70. PDM has failed to notify 12 small acquisitions of the goodwill of certain businesses (all but one being a collector), with a total value of £168,250 and involving some 180 tonnes of animal waste a week (see Appendix 4.3). This amounts to nearly 1 per cent of the supply of red meat waste in England and Wales, not an insignificant tonnage to the smaller renderers. Such acquisitions illustrate the problem of creeping purchases: individually they may be insignificant but collectively they enhance PDM's market dominance. PDM has argued that 'in the majority of cases pre-notification was not necessary because no acquisition of a business actually took place' (see paragraph 8.20). In our view, by purchasing the goodwill of the businesses, PDM acquired animal waste enterprises as defined in the undertaking.

10.71. We conclude, therefore, that PDM is in breach of undertaking 3 through failure to notify acquisitions of animal waste enterprises, and that this is a step taken for the purpose of maintaining the monopoly situation which constitutes a fact that operates and may be expected to operate against the public interest. The particular effects adverse to the public interest are that the DGFT has been deprived of information which would have enabled him to intervene with timely measures to protect competition in rendering, and that competition in rendering has been restricted.

10.72. In our view, these failures to fulfil undertakings given to the DGFT following the 1985 report (see paragraphs 10.68 and 10.71) are a serious matter.

Market arrangements and behaviour

PDM's agreement with Hillsdown

10.73. In October 1992 PDM entered into an agreement with Hillsdown, whereby PDM agreed to collect all of Hillsdown's UK poultry by-products. Prior to the agreement all but one of Hillsdown's processing plants were serviced by PDM. Hillsdown and PDM agreed a uniform price for each product (with some exceptions), which we understand was similar to that already being paid to the majority of the poultry companies. To reflect the volume of materials to be supplied by Hillsdown and the value of those materials to PDM, PDM agreed that it would make an additional payment of £3 per tonne, quarterly in arrears. We were informed by the parties that these arrangements did not form the subject of a written contract and that it was intended that the agreement would be reviewed on a quarterly basis. We found no support for the common belief in the industry that the agreement was set to last for five years, but noted that both parties expected it to be ongoing.

10.74. Hillsdown was able to produce notes of meetings and other documentation concerning the agreement. We asked PDM for its records of the same agreement, but were told that it had no such documentation. Given the importance of the contract in securing a large volume of poultry waste for PDM, we found this unsatisfactory, and it adds to our concern about the lack of transparency in PDM's activities (see paragraphs 10.82 to 10.87).

PDM's informal links with other companies

10.75. Three competitors alleged that PDM enhanced its dominance of the supply of animal waste in England and Wales by informal links with other enterprises in the industry such as the Klein family and G H Klein & Son Ltd (the Kleins), Specialpack Ltd and E Clutton & Sons (Marchwiel) Ltd. We looked carefully into PDM's dealings with these enterprises but were unable to find any evidence of informal links that were detrimental to competition (see paragraphs 4.49 et seq).

10.76. We found that PDM's arrangements with the Kleins were particularly complex. Various allegations were made to us that the Kleins acted as agents for PDM. The allegations are no doubt partly based on the Kleins operating from a temporary building on PDM's Silvertown site, having their vehicles maintained by PDM, and generally making use of PDM's Silvertown facilities (for which they are invoiced by PDM). The most serious of the allegations was that the Kleins were acting on behalf of PDM when in 1991 they acquired and sold the rendering assets of Faversham Animal By-Products Ltd. PDM told us that it did not in any way encourage the Kleins to acquire these assets. It was only later when G H Klein & Son Ltd had liquidity problems that PDM decided to grant that company an interest-free loan of £200,000. PDM said that it was motivated by a desire to support an animal waste collector with whom it had been connected for more than 20 years, and that it was concerned to protect its investment in the building site owned by Stannard & Co (1969) Ltd, a non-trading company jointly owned by PDM and the Kleins.

PDM's relationship with Hi-Cal Proteins Ltd

10.77. Over 40 per cent of PDM's sales are made through Hi-Cal Proteins Ltd (Hi-Cal), a Jersey-based broker. Under the arrangements PDM sells meat-and-bone meal to Hi-Cal and that company invoices PDM's customers and provides a sales force through its UK agent, Thomas Mawer Ltd. PDM told us that the arrangements 'often quite understandably raise a few eyebrows'. It had itself heard comments implying a device to hide profits in Jersey. In fact they were long-standing arm's length arrangements for which Hi-Cal made a reasonable charge of some 2.2 per cent of sales. We asked PDM whether it had any interest in Hi-Cal directly or indirectly, and it said that it had no such interest. Nevertheless these offshore arrangements for products which are primarily sold in the UK add to the lack of transparency which is not infrequently associated with PDM's activities.

PDM's surveillance of a competitor's premises

10.78. Our attention was drawn to PDM's surveillance of a competitor's premises (see paragraph 7.56). We did not find PDM's explanation entirely convincing (see Appendix 7.1, paragraph 11(c)), but as no current instances of such conduct were brought to our attention, we did not consider that it was necessary to pursue this matter further.

Alleged collusion between PDM and Hillsdown's subsidiaries

10.79. It was put to us that PDM and Hillsdown's subsidiaries, Forrest and Peninsular, had reached understandings not to encroach on each other's territories. The parties strongly denied that there were any such arrangements.

10.80. So far as PDM and Peninsular are concerned, we found that following re-equipment of its West Country plant in 1991/92 Peninsular had acquired sufficient suppliers to absorb the plant's peak capacity, and that it had gained some supplies at the expense of PDM. While we saw no indication that PDM had competed strongly with Peninsular, there was no evidence of any understanding between the companies.

10.81. So far as PDM and Forrest are concerned, we found that Forrest did not in the normal course of business attempt to collect material in England and Wales. Forrest argued that it was apparent from the location of renderers in southern Scotland and northern England and the volumes of raw materials available to those renderers that there was a natural geographic division at or about the border between England and Scotland. It would find it difficult to collect material in England unless it could establish a base south of the border, in practical terms by taking over an existing licensed plant. It had tried to acquire such a base, so far without success (see paragraph 9.14). We found no evidence of collusion with PDM. We deal with PDM's activities in Scotland in paragraph 10.106.

Transparency and profitability

10.82. We considered whether the results of PDM's rendering operations (carried on by Prosper De Mulder Ltd and its subsidiary and related companies) were sufficiently transparent.

10.83. PDM told us that as a private limited company it wished to keep its financial performance private. We found that it had achieved this by splitting itself into six separate companies, of which four were important:

Prosper De Mulder Ltd and subsidiaries;
Prosper De Mulder Transport (an unlimited company);
Prosper De Mulder Services (an unlimited company); and
Frazer (Butchers) Ltd and subsidiaries.

10.84. The unlimited companies which do not file accounts with the Registrar of Companies incur expenses on behalf of the other companies which they rebill with a mark-up. The existence of this mark-up depresses the reported profits of the other two companies which do file accounts. The retention of profits in the unlimited companies and the existence of loans between the various companies (which are not described in the accounts of the individual companies as being due to or from associates) give an incomplete impression of PDM's overall profitability and of its financial position to any person who has to rely on publicly available sources (see paragraph 3.11). By disclosing only part of its profits in Prosper De Mulder Ltd, PDM is less likely to face pressure from suppliers for improved prices for raw materials or to alert potential entrants into the rendering industry of the profitability of rendering. The authorities are also left in ignorance of PDM's true financial performance.

10.85. PDM calculated for us its return on capital employed (ROCE) by all its companies engaged in the rendering business for the five years ended 31 March 1992. These figures may be compared with the ROCE of *(a)* 56 food manufacturers and *(b)* 10 meat processors, as shown in Table 10.1.

TABLE 10.1 **PDM's ROCE compared with food manufacturers' and meat processors'**

				per cent
	PDM		Food manufacturers	Meat processors
1987/88	16.0	1988	19.1	13.9
1988/89	21.2	1989	21.3	16.9
1989/90	11.9	1990	23.3	18.5
1990/91	17.8	1991	22.6	17.6
1991/92	30.3	1992	23.3	9.8
1987/88 to 1991/92	19.4	1988 to 1992	21.9	15.3

Sources: PDM; MMC from MicroEXSTAT.

10.86. PDM's ROCE of 30.3 per cent in 1991/92 is high, but the average over the five years is much lower, at 19.4 per cent. Moreover, we have examined PDM's unaudited management accounts for 1992/93; they clearly indicate that the price war in that year has been costly (see paragraph 3.26) and that there will be a sharp fall in the ROCE compared with 1991/92. We have already referred to the suggestion that PDM's arrangements with Hi-Cal may allow PDM to understate its profits in the UK (see paragraph 10.77). There is, however, no evidence that such understatement has taken place, and we therefore conclude that there are no grounds for an adverse public interest finding on PDM's level of profits.

10.87. Nevertheless, we conclude that, for the reasons stated in paragraph 10.84, PDM's arrangement of its accounts in such a way as to avoid disclosure of the true profitability of its rendering business is a step taken for the purpose of exploiting and maintaining the monopoly situation and that this constitutes a fact which operates and may be expected to operate against the public interest. The particular effects adverse to the public interest are that it deprives PDM's customers and potential competitors of information which could help to redress the market imbalance resulting from PDM's dominance, and deprives the relevant authorities of a clear picture of PDM's continuing ability to make a major contribution to the provision of a vital public service.

Efficiency

10.88. We compared PDM's financial results with the weighted averages of three smaller renderers in England and Wales, and with those of Forrest, over the three years 1989 to 1991, on the basis of £ per tonne processed (see paragraphs 3.46 to 3.62).

10.89. We calculated three components of cost: transport, processing and other operating costs. PDM's costs under all these headings were significantly higher than those of the smaller renderers, and its total operating costs were higher than those of Forrest and the weighted average of the smaller renderers. As PDM told us that it incurred higher costs because of its separation of raw materials and the expense of transporting them to specialist plants, but that these costs were more than offset by higher yields of grade 2 tallow and of other high-grade products, we deducted end-product sales from operating costs to give a 'processing margin'. We found that PDM had a lower processing margin than Forrest and the smaller renderers.

10.90. We also found that PDM had paid less on average for its materials than the smaller renderers, but some allowance needs to be made for the different mix of materials purchased by PDM. PDM's profit before interest and tax (PBIT) was on a rising trend while that of the smaller renderers was falling.

10.91. We looked at the components of capital employed. The net book value of PDM's plant and machinery, per tonne processed, was much lower than that of the smaller renderers.

10.92. A review of processing costs suggested that PDM had higher energy and repair costs per tonne processed, but a lower depreciation charge than the smaller renderers. Other fixed assets were lower for PDM than for the smaller renderers. This reflected lower net book values for land, buildings and vehicles. Overall the net book value per tonne processed of fixed assets of the smaller renderers was almost three times that of PDM.

10.93. The overall comparison showed that PDM's ROCE had averaged 20 per cent and was on a rising trend, while that of the smaller renderers was 13 per cent and declining despite their lower operating costs. The average ROCE of the smaller renderers disguised a very wide range of performance.

10.94. PDM was critical of our analysis of comparative performance of renderers. In its view 'the business of PDM cannot be compared with those of other renderers on pure financial grounds because they are different in so many fundamental respects from those of the other single plant renderers in England and Wales'. We have given careful consideration to PDM's arguments and we acknowledge that there is some force in them. Nevertheless we believe that limited conclusions can be drawn from the analysis. We had expected that PDM's practice of channelling materials to particular specialized plants in order to maximize the value of end products would result in higher transport costs, but were surprised that its processing margin was lower than the other renderers.

10.95. We conclude that there is little indication in our analysis that PDM is more efficient than the smaller renderers, and there must be at least some doubt whether it achieves the network benefit claimed from its multi-site operation.

10.96. The 1985 report noted, at paragraph 9.18, a lack of formality in PDM's information systems and felt that a rather more formal style of management was becoming appropriate. We have already commented on the lack of records concerning the Hillsdown agreement (see paragraph 10.74). It also became clear to us in the course of our inquiry that PDM did not have the information readily to hand to justify its pricing decisions, but had to carry out special studies in order to attempt to justify its pricing decisions some time after the events. We do not go so far as to make an adverse public interest finding with regard to PDM's record-keeping, but we note that PDM's management information systems fall well short of best management practice.

Scotland

10.97. There were eight complaints concerning Forrest. These included particularly detailed allegations of predatory pricing from its two competitors in Scotland, Dundas Brothers and Dundas Chemical (see Appendix 6.5). We comment further on these allegations in paragraph 10.99.

Pricing

10.98. The main public interest issues concern Forrest's pricing policy and practices. We are concerned about the charges made and prices paid by Forrest to its suppliers, and not about prices charged for its end products. As mentioned in the preceding paragraph, there have been complaints from competitors that Forrest engages in predatory pricing, and the evidence shows that Forrest makes a wide range of charges and payments for the collection of low-grade waste and pays a wide range of prices for high-grade material. We adopted the same approach to studying Forrest's pricing practices as we took for PDM (see paragraphs 10.52 *et seq*).

10.99. We studied four cases of alleged *predatory pricing* by Forrest (see Appendix 6.5). The studies show that Forrest has competed hard for supplies necessary to maintain what it considers to be an adequate level of profitability, and that in two cases it made losses on the relevant contracts, but there was no evidence that Forrest intended to prejudice the survival of its competitors.

10.100. Regarding *discriminatory pricing*, we carried out a detailed analysis in order to examine the extent to which there was variation between the charges/payments experienced by different suppliers to Forrest whose supplies were of comparable material, entailing similar collection costs. As with PDM this was a difficult exercise because of the quality variation within each category of material. Details of the study are set out in Appendix 6.4.

10.101. Our various studies show:

(a) Forrest's charges/payments varied substantially in a way that was frequently not attributable to physical factors (see paragraph 6.18 and Appendix 6.4);

(b) Forrest sometimes made significantly lower charges or paid significantly higher prices, not related to costs, when another renderer bid for an abattoir's supplies (see paragraph 6.19 and Appendix 6.5); and

(c) at times of acute competition Forrest sometimes lowered its charges or raised its payments to a level that meant that it made losses on the contracts (see paragraph 6.20).

10.102. Forrest pointed to physical factors that explained many of the charges/payments variations, but accepted that it sometimes made offers that varied according to the existence or extent of competition from other renderers. Such offers sometimes resulted in losses on particular contracts. Having carefully considered all the evidence we are satisfied that many individual payments/charges cannot be explained by differences in physical factors even when combined with a reasonable degree of variation to account for ordinary competition.

10.103. As with PDM, Forrest's pricing practices need to be seen in the context of its position in the industry. It is the only renderer that obtains supplies from the whole of mainland Scotland, and the only significant competitive pressure it faces is from Dundas Brothers and Dundas Chemical. Forrest is a much larger company than these competitors, has much greater financial strength and the size of its acquisitions of red meat waste is much larger than theirs. These factors make it much less vulnerable to the loss of individual large suppliers and provide it with opportunities for discrimination. Forrest's practices show that it has market power which it exercises over-zealously to protect its supplies. It exploits this by engaging in price discrimination, which has the effect of squeezing its two smaller competitors.

10.104. The low marginal cost of processing animal waste associated with the kind of continuous plant operated by Forrest and the other large renderers provides a powerful incentive to seek extra tonnage by price discrimination. When a dominant supplier, such as Forrest, engages in this practice, it is likely to damage smaller competitors to the extent that they are forced out of business. This would be particularly detrimental to competition in Scotland, where there are only two such competitors.

10.105. We conclude that Forrest's practice of discriminatory pricing (paragraph 10.103) is a step taken for the purpose of exploiting and maintaining the monopoly situation and that this constitutes a fact which operates and may be expected to operate against the public interest. The particular effect adverse to the public interest is the restriction of competition in rendering.

Market arrangements and behaviour

10.106. We referred in paragraph 10.79 to the belief in the industry that PDM and Forrest had reached an understanding not to encroach on each other's territory. We noted in the course of our inquiry that PDM collected poultry waste in Scotland for processing in Widnes, and enquired why PDM had not adopted a similar strategy for red meat waste. PDM told us that its entry in the late 1970s into the red meat waste market in Scotland had not been a success. It had found it difficult to service the rendering business from England, and had sold out after three or four years. It would be so difficult to gain adequate supplies of red meat waste in Scotland that it could only contemplate re-entering the market on the basis of acquisition (see paragraph 8.15). As we say in paragraph 10.81, we found no evidence of collusion between PDM and Forrest.

Profitability

10.107. We calculated Forrest's ROCE for the five years ended 31 December 1992 on the basis of the company's audited accounts. The ROCE averages 41.1 per cent over the period. Forrest told us that an independent valuation of its property in 1987, on the basis of open market value for existing use, had reduced the value by nearly £1 million, and that the revaluation had been incorporated into the statutory accounts. It argued that the ROCE should be adjusted to take account of the revaluation, reducing the return to an average of 28.2 per cent over the five years. The results of the alternative calculations are set out in Table 10.2.

TABLE 10.2 **Forrest's ROCE**

	Unadjusted	Adjusted
1988	47.1	37.3
1989	36.6	23.1
1990	43.8	29.3
1991	50.7	33.8
1992	27.1	17.3
1988 to 1992	41.1	28.2

Source: Forrest.

10.108. In our view it is generally advisable when considering the profitability of companies to adopt the conventions and information in the audited accounts. Here, however, we see no need to come down on one side of the argument or the other. On either basis of calculation the average level of profitability exceeds by a wide margin the 19.4 per cent achieved by PDM, or the average returns achieved by food manufacturers (21.9) or meat processors (15.3) (see Table 10.1). Forrest told us that its profitability declined in 1992 partly because of repercussions from the price war in England and

Wales (see paragraph 10.58). We are, however, still inclined to our view that the markets for red meat waste in England and Wales, and Scotland, are separate (see paragraph 10.37). Looking to the future, Forrest's forecasts indicate, perhaps conservatively, that ROCE of [*], [*] and [*] per cent will be achieved in the years 1993, 1994 and 1995 respectively and that purchases of fixed assets would be [*], [*] and [*] per cent of operating cash flow respectively in those years, indicating that the expenditure would be well covered.

10.109. We conclude that Forrest's profitability reflects higher charges and lower payments for animal waste than would have been the case under more competitive conditions, and that such a level of profitability is likely to continue. These higher charges and lower payments are steps taken for the purpose of exploiting and maintaining the monopoly situation and constitute facts which operate and may be expected to operate against the public interest. The particular effects adverse to the public interest are that charges have been higher and payments lower than they would have been under more competitive conditions, and that this situation may be expected to continue.

Efficiency

10.110. For reasons of confidentiality concerning Forrest's two competitors in Scotland we compared Forrest's financial results over the three years 1989 to 1991 with the weighted averages of the same three renderers we used in the PDM comparison (see paragraph 10.88), again on the basis of £ per tonne processed.

10.111. We calculated three components of cost: transport, processing and other operating costs. Forrest's transport and processing costs per tonne were significantly higher than those of the smaller renderers. The long distances travelled and the costs of Forrest's two depots may explain the higher transport costs. However, Forrest's processing costs were higher than those of any individual renderer included in our calculations. We note that Forrest's capacity utilization at about 45 per cent was below that of any of the smaller renderers and far below the 85 per cent achieved by PDM. Forrest had the additional expense of its solvent extraction plant (now closed) which gave higher yields of tallow than the plants of the smaller renderers and PDM.

10.112. We deducted end-product sales from operating costs to give a 'processing margin', to see if the higher operating costs were offset by a higher value of end products. It appeared that this was the case for Forrest, because its processing margin is similar to the average for the smaller renderers. Forrest paid less for its materials than the other renderers (much less if the purchases of greaves are taken into account), so that it has enjoyed higher profits. PBIT has remained level while that of the smaller renderers has fallen.

10.113. We looked at the components of capital employed. The net book value per tonne of Forrest's plant and machinery (before deduction of investment grants) was much lower than that of the smaller renderers.

10.114. Other fixed assets per tonne processed were lower for Forrest than for the smaller renderers, even if adjustments were made to restate leasehold properties at historical cost and to add back £3 or £4 per tonne for investment grants. Overall the net book value of fixed assets per tonne of the smaller renderers was about two and a half times that of Forrest.

10.115. The overall comparison showed that Forrest's ROCE averaged 43 per cent and was on a rising trend, while that of the smaller renderers was 13 per cent and declining, in spite of their lower operating costs. Forrest had high operating costs, particularly for processing. It had paid less for its materials than the smaller renderers and, with its low asset base, had enjoyed much higher returns.

---

*Figures omitted. See note on page iv.

10.116. Forrest told us that it did not consider it appropriate or sustainable to compare Forrest with smaller renderers and simply to apply a weighting in terms of tonnes processed (see paragraph 3.51). We have carefully considered Forrest's detailed comments on our analysis, and have taken them into account in reaching our conclusions.

10.117. Forrest has higher operating costs than the average of the three smaller renderers. Given the long distances over which it has to transport much of its waste, we can understand that it has high transport costs. But its average processing costs were significantly higher than those of the average of the smaller renderers. Unlike PDM, Forrest did achieve higher selling prices for its end products in 1989 and 1990 benefiting from its use of solvent extraction (see paragraph 10.111) to obtain higher tallow yields. In 1991, when its end products achieved less of a premium, it paid less for its materials than the small renderers, so that in all three years, assisted by the relatively low level of its capital employed, it earned the highest ROCE of all the renderers.

Summary of conclusions

England and Wales

10.118. We have concluded that the following steps taken by PDM for the purpose of exploiting and/or maintaining the monopoly situation constitute facts which operate and may be expected to operate against the public interest:

(a) PDM's practice of discriminatory pricing, which has the particular adverse effect of restricting competition in rendering (see paragraph 10.62);

(b) PDM's breach of undertaking 1 through failure to adopt and operate accounting systems and accounting procedures in the manner required, through failure to charge adequate administration costs to its gut-room operations and through failure to make arm's length payments/charges for the collection of raw materials from abattoirs where it operates gut-rooms, which have the particular adverse effects that the DGFT has been deprived of information concerning the financial results of PDM's gut-room activities which would have enabled him to intervene with timely measures to protect competition in the operation of gut-rooms and in rendering, and that competition in the operation of gut-rooms and in rendering has been restricted (see paragraph 10.68);

(c) PDM's breach of undertaking 3 through failure to notify acquisitions of animal waste enterprises, which has the particular adverse effects that the DGFT has been deprived of information which would have enabled him to intervene with timely measures to protect competition in rendering, and that competition in rendering has been restricted (see paragraph 10.71); and

(d) PDM's arrangement of its accounts in such a way as to avoid disclosure of the true profitability of its rendering business, which has the particular adverse effects that it deprives its customers and potential competitors of information which could help to redress the market imbalance resulting from PDM's dominance, and deprives the relevant authorities of a clear indication of PDM's continuing ability to make a major contribution to the provision of a vital public service (see paragraph 10.87).

10.119. We have found no actions or omissions attributable to the monopoly situation (see paragraph 10.1(d)).

Scotland

10.120. We have concluded that Forrest's practice of discriminatory pricing is a step taken by Forrest for the purpose of exploiting and maintaining the monopoly situation and that this constitutes a fact which operates and may be expected to operate against the public interest. The particular adverse effect is the restriction of competition in rendering (see paragraph 10.105). We have further concluded that Forrest's profitability reflects higher charges and lower payments for animal waste than would have been the case under more competitive conditions, and that such a level of profitability is likely to continue. These higher charges and lower payments are steps taken for the purpose of exploiting and maintaining the monopoly situation and constitute facts which operate and may be expected to operate against the public interest. The particular adverse effects are that charges have been higher and payments lower than they would have been under more competitive conditions, and that this situation may be expected to continue (see paragraph 10.109).

10.121. We have found no actions or omissions attributable to the monopoly situation (see paragraph 10.1(d)).

Recommendations

Introduction

10.122. Having identified particular effects adverse to the public interest concerning the conduct of PDM in England and Wales (paragraph 10.118) and Forrest in Scotland (paragraph 10.120), we have to consider what action (if any) should be taken to remedy or prevent these.

10.123. In addressing this task we have been mindful that the business of animal waste collection and rendering constitutes a vital public service as well as a commercial activity. We have also noted the continuing substantial concentration that has taken place in the industry over many years (see paragraph 2.16). Against this background we considered going to the lengths of subjecting the industry to a comprehensive system of regulation, including perhaps the creation of an Office of Animal Waste. Such a regulatory body might be given responsibility for regulation of prices; licensing of renderers and collectors of animal waste; environmental controls and the associated monitoring; and the monitoring of our recommendations.

10.124. We have rejected this approach. As regards the public service aspect of the industry, there is already in place an adequate regime to protect the public health and control environmental pollution, and large and small firms alike have impressed us with the progress they have made in meeting the stringent requirements being placed upon them. The problems arising from concentration are dealt with in the recommendations which follow.

PDM

Remedying the adverse effects on competition

10.125. We have found that the adverse effect of PDM's discriminatory pricing is the restriction of competition in rendering in England and Wales. We considered whether a pricing formula should be imposed on PDM for its purchase of raw materials which took account of yield and selling prices of end products; costs of transport and processing of the raw materials, and related overheads; and a reasonable level of profit.

10.126. PDM told us that in negotiating prices it already took account of such variables. But the price paid for each category of animal waste was influenced by other significant factors: quantity, quality, method of handling, location, collection service required, nationally negotiated contracts (covering, in particular, multiple collection points) and considerations of competition. Although there were a few formula-based contracts, general imposition of a pricing formula would, in PDM's view, be impossible to apply objectively and would unduly distort the competitive process. It also considered that determining a reasonable level of profit raised very considerable problems.

10.127. We acknowledge that imposing a pricing formula on PDM alone in England and Wales would distort competition, even though it could help to redress the competitive balance in a market already distorted by PDM's dominance. We also recognize that the implementation of a pricing formula would be difficult in this market and it would in our view be justified only if no other remedy were available.

10.128. We believe that other pricing remedies are available, and we considered two in particular, both of which would enhance competition by increasing the transparency of PDM's pricing of raw materials. One is a system of *posted prices*, under which PDM would be required to post in advance the ranges of prices for raw materials which it would offer. The other is a system of *published prices*, under which PDM would be required to publish in arrears details of prices recently paid.

10.129. PDM argued that because of the great variability between batches of raw material, *posted prices* could at best be merely a broad starting point for negotiations; a rigidly enforced posted price would preclude PDM from negotiating a price which more closely reflected the real economic value of the particular material.

10.130. We believe that a *posted price* system would need to be detailed. The main drawback of such a structure is that it would require not only that a new pricing system be implemented throughout the industry but also that there should be a much greater degree of separation of materials at the abattoir. This would impose on the abattoir an additional and exacting task, solely for the purpose of implementing the pricing system. We do not consider that this additional burden for the suppliers and the extra costs that would be entailed would be justified.

10.131. A *published price* system would not require as detailed a pricing structure, as it would be designed not to determine prices, but to provide information, in particular to suppliers and competing renderers, to assist the market to work more effectively. But even for this purpose of providing information the current system of pricing by main categories of material would be insufficiently precise. For example, it would not be of great advantage to a supplier to know what had been the range of prices paid by PDM during the previous week for best fat: he would have little idea what point on that range was appropriate to his own circumstances given the quality of his material and the cost of collecting it.

10.132. An effective *published price* system would therefore require additional detail to be provided regarding each contract and the prices to be reported in order to indicate in particular the quality and quantity of material purchased. A possible system is outlined in Appendix 10.1. We expect that such a system would provide suppliers with additional useful information on price and would place them in a stronger position in negotiating with PDM. It would be more difficult for PDM to pay particularly high or low prices to one supplier but not to others in similar circumstances.

10.133. PDM told us that it would be willing to publish a summary on a monthly basis of prices which it had paid for generic categories of animal waste if we came to the conclusion that such information would better enable all suppliers of animal waste to know what 'the approximate going rate' was for animal waste material. However, it believed that at best such information could only indicate general rather than specific levels of prices being paid. In our view such general information will not go far enough.

10.134. To diminish the effects of discriminatory pricing (see paragraph 10.118), we recommend that PDM should be required to publish weekly, together with detailed related information, a representative sample of prices and charges it has negotiated in the preceding week, commencing with the week ending 9 October 1993, in a form approved by the DGFT.

10.135. We also considered whether the divestment of one or more of PDM's major rendering facilities would be an appropriate remedy for the adverse effects on competition. PDM told us that 'the forced break-up' of its rendering organization would put at risk the integrated, safe and efficient system currently prevailing in England and Wales. We do not accept that the divestment of a major plant would have the dire effects predicted by PDM, but believe that such a requirement would be disproportionate to the adverse effects we have found.

236197 I

10.136. Divestment of the Market Harborough plant, however, is another matter. The plant has been moth-balled and is clearly not central to PDM's needs. Nevertheless, in the hands of another renderer this recently refurbished plant is likely to augment the competition faced by PDM. The attraction for an existing renderer or a new entrant is that the plant already has a licence to process animal waste and many of the difficulties associated with starting a rendering activity may therefore be avoided.

10.137. In order to diminish the adverse effects of discriminatory pricing (see paragraph 10.118), we recommend that PDM should be required to dispose of its Market Harborough plant including its rendering capacity within six months from the publication of our report to a purchaser (not associated directly or indirectly with PDM) approved by the DGFT and that, pending disposal, the plant should be kept in good repair but not be operated.

10.138. We have described in paragraphs 10.42 to 10.46 and 2.82 to 2.92 a number of barriers to entering the rendering industry. If, as a result of these, or for any other reason, no bid is forthcoming from a new entrant or from an existing renderer within the six-month period, we recommend that the Market Harborough plant should be decommissioned and the machinery sold by public auction, with a prohibition on sale to a PDM company or related organization or person. The licence for animal waste processing at Market Harborough should be surrendered at the same time.

Breaches of the 1986 undertakings

Gut-rooms

10.139. In order to remedy the adverse effects identified (see paragraph 10.118), we recommend that PDM should be required to transfer all its gut-room operations to a separate subsidiary limited company and should adopt and operate accounting systems and accounting procedures in the manner required in undertaking 1. We have made detailed suggestions as to such systems and procedures in Appendix 10.2.

10.140. If, within three months after the publication of our report, the DGFT is not satisfied that PDM is carrying on its gut-room business on an arm's length basis, or if there is a breach of any undertaking given by PDM in respect of its gut-room operations, we further recommend that PDM should be required to dispose of its gut-room business within a further six months to a purchaser approved by the DGFT.

Prior approval of acquisitions

10.141. In order to remedy the adverse effects identified (see paragraph 10.118), we recommend that PDM should be prohibited from acquiring all or any part of an animal waste enterprise, unless the DGFT has approved the acquisition in advance as being in the public interest.

Lack of transparency in published accounts

10.142. Towards the end of our inquiry, PDM told us that it would be prepared to publish consolidated accounts for its rendering activities, subject to continuing to keep private its service company, which paid directors' salaries. It argued that the results of the entirety of its business were irrelevant. In our view it will be necessary to look at the totality of PDM's business and the results of reference and non-reference activities, and for PDM to provide information which explains how overall results have been apportioned across business segments.

10.143. In order to remedy the adverse effects identified (see paragraph 10.118), we recommend that PDM should file with the DGFT, within nine months of the end of each accounting period, consolidated accounts for that period for the PDM enterprise as defined in paragraph 3.6. These consolidated accounts should as far as possible meet all the reporting requirements of the Companies Acts for a single holding company and its subsidiaries. In addition, they should include in accompanying notes a segmental analysis distinguishing between three categories of activity: red meat waste rendering, poultry waste rendering and all other PDM businesses. For each category the following items should be reported:

(a) end-product sales (reconciled to turnover);

(b) operating profit before interest and tax;

(c) capital employed as defined at paragraph 3.63 of this report; and

(d) number of employees;

and the analysis should set out the manner in which revenues, costs, assets and liabilities have been calculated and apportioned between segments.

10.144. The notes accompanying these consolidated accounts should also include details of any loan (whether interest-bearing or not), commission, consultancy fee or similar payment made by PDM, its directors, managers, proprietors, agents or related parties to any person engaged in the animal waste or related industries.

10.145. All the information described in paragraphs 10.142 to 10.144 should be covered by the report of the auditors of Prosper De Mulder Ltd, or such other registered auditors as may be specified by the DGFT, and should be made available for public inspection. In addition PDM should deliver to the DGFT within three months of its half-year an unaudited consolidated profit and loss account, and this also should be made available for public inspection.

Forrest

10.146. We put the same pricing formula to Forrest as we had put to PDM (see paragraphs 10.125 to 10.127). Forrest's reaction was similar to PDM's. Forrest argued in addition that a pricing formula would remove any degree of flexibility in the prices it offered to its suppliers. For example, suppliers might attach differing values to the categories of raw materials which they supplied. The effect of this was that whilst the overall package offered to abattoirs was broadly the same, the individual prices would vary. Again, we believe that implementation of a pricing formula would be difficult and would only be justified if no other remedy were available.

10.147. The considerations regarding a *posted price* system and a *published price* system, discussed earlier (see paragraphs 10.128 to 10.132) in relation to PDM, apply equally to Forrest. To diminish the adverse effects of discriminatory pricing (see paragraph 10.120), we recommend that Forrest should be required to publish weekly, together with detailed related information, a representative sample of prices and charges it has negotiated in the preceding week, commencing with the week ending 9 October 1993, in a form approved by the DGFT (see Appendix 10.1).

10.148. We expect that the remedy we have proposed in respect of Forrest's discriminatory pricing will be a sufficient restraint on the company's excess profits to remove the need for any additional remedy.

Overview

10.149. We have been concerned about the high levels of concentration in the animal waste industry in England and Wales and in Scotland. There are no compelling reasons (eg economies of scale) to suggest that only a large firm can survive in the industry. On the contrary, the evidence indicates that efficient smaller firms can continue not only to survive but to flourish. What is required at present, therefore, is the minimum amount of additional regulation necessary to curb the over-zealous protection of their supplies of animal waste by the two monopolists, and to stimulate competition. The other renderers make a valuable contribution to the rendering industry and should be encouraged to continue to do so; the preservation of competition for supplies of animal waste is likely to be the best way of ensuring that the public service performed by the industry is provided economically. Our recommendations have been framed with these considerations in mind.

P H DEAN *(Chairman)*

C C BAILLIEU

A L KINGSHOTT

P K R MANN

J S METCALFE

    S N BURBRIDGE *(Secretary)*

29 June 1993

Glossary

Abattoir	Slaughterhouse for cattle, sheep or pigs (not poultry).
Anaerobic digestion	Fermentation of organic matter in the absence of air, producing methane gas.
Anglo-Dutch Meats	Anglo-Dutch Meats Ltd.
Animal by-products	The products of slaughtering other than carcase meat and edible offal: includes hides and skins, casings, etc in addition to **animal waste**.
Animal waste	Animal material, including poultry waste, most of which is acquired for processing in **rendering** plants.
BATNEEC	Best Available Techniques Not Entailing Excessive Cost: the standard required by Part I of the **EPA**.
Beeson	Beeson Brothers (Crewe) Ltd.
Biggar	Biggar Quality Meats Ltd.
Boning plant	Establishment where carcase meat is boned and/or cut into joints or other packs for retail sale, or prepared for storage under the EC intervention buying programme.
BSE	Bovine spongiform encephalopathy, a disease of cattle.
Buchan Meat	Buchan Meat Producers Ltd.
Cattle unit	A measure of **abattoir** throughput common to all species (1 cattle unit = 1 adult cattle beast, or 3 calves, or 5 sheep or 2 pigs).
Cheale	Cheale Meats Ltd.
Chetwynd	Chetwynd Animal By-Products Ltd.
Clutton	E Clutton & Sons (Marchwiel) Ltd.
Collector	An independent dealer who buys and collects **animal waste**, principally fat and bone from butchers' shops, for sale to renderers.
Croda	Croda International plc.
The Croda report	*Prosper De Mulder Ltd and Croda International plc: a report on the merger situation* (HMSO, Cmnd 1611, August 1991).
DoE	Department of the Environment.
DGFT	Director General of Fair Trading.
Dundas Brothers	Dundas Brothers Ltd.
Dundas Chemical	Dundas Chemical Company (Mosspark) Ltd.
Elgin	Elgin Animal By-Products Ltd.

EPA	Environmental Protection Act 1990.
EUROP	Trading name of European Organic Processing Ltd.
FAP	Faversham Animal By-Products Ltd.
Fats & Proteins	Fats & Proteins (UK) Ltd.
FFA	Free fatty acids.
FMC	FMC plc.
Forrest	William Forrest & Son (Paisley) Ltd.
Frank Gysels	Frank Gysels Ltd.
Gallygoo	Reclaimed land on which **PDM's** Widnes plant is sited.
G H Klein	G H Klein & Son Ltd.
Gilberts	Gilberts Animal By-Products Ltd.
Greaves	Part-processed material, after extraction of **tallow**, but before final drying and milling to produce **meat-and-bone meal**.
Gut-room	That part of an **abattoir** where, after the beast has been slaughtered, its abdominal mass is segregated, to a greater or lesser degree, into by-products of a higher value than **animal waste**.
Hi-Cal	Hi-Cal Proteins Ltd.
Hillsdown	Hillsdown Holdings plc.
Hughes	A Hughes & Son (Skellingthorpe) Ltd.
IMC	Imperial Meat Company Ltd.
Incineration	Burning of waste material in an enclosed incinerator, as distinct from on-farm burning of animal carcasses.
ISM	Inverurie Scotch Meat Company, part of **FMC**, owned by **Hillsdown**.
Knacker	Licensed slaughterer of casualty animals and collector of fallen stock from farms, for salvage and disposal.
Landfill	Burying waste material, eg non-toxic industrial waste and house hold refuse, on land.
LASSA	Licensed Animal Slaughterers and Salvage Association.
MAFF	Ministry of Agriculture, Fisheries and Food.
Meat-and-bone meal	The dry and milled high-protein product of **rendering**, used principally for animal feed (hyphenated in this report to avoid ambiguity, although this is not the normal trade practice).
MCP	Midland Cattle Products Ltd.

MLC	Meat and Livestock Commission.
NFU	National Farmers' Union of England and Wales.
NFU Scotland	National Farmers' Union of Scotland.
Nortech	Nortech Foods Ltd.
OFT	Office of Fair Trading.
Pathogenic	Causing disease.
PBIT	Profit before interest and taxation.
PDM	Prosper De Mulder Ltd, its subsidiary and related companies.
Pears	J G Pears Ltd.
Peninsular	Peninsular Proteins Ltd.
Poultry plant/factory	Slaughterhouse for poultry.
Rendering	Mechanical and heat processing of **animal waste** to extract the fat content as **tallow**, and to dry and mill the high-protein residue as **meat-and-bone meal**.
ROCE	Return on capital employed.
Ruminants	Cattle and sheep.
Specified bovine offals (SBO)	Certain bovine offals (brain, spinal cord, thymus, spleen, tonsils, intestines), specified in regulations as those most likely to contain the causative agent of **BSE**; not permitted to be used in food for humans, animals or poultry.
S J Chandler	S J Chandler Ltd.
Smith	Smith Brothers (Hyde) Ltd.
Specialpack	Specialpack Ltd.
Strong & Fisher	Strong & Fisher (Holdings) plc.
Tallow	Fat extracted from **animal waste** by **rendering**.
The 1985 report	*Animal Waste: a Report on the supply of animal waste in Great Britain* (HMSO, Cmnd 9470, April 1985).
The 1986 undertakings	Undertakings given by **PDM** to the Secretary of State following **the 1985 report** (Appendix 1.2).
Tyneside Butchers	Tyneside Butchers By-Products Ltd.
UKRA	United Kingdom Renderers' Association.
Wildriggs	Wildriggs Proteins Ltd.

The references and conduct of the inquiry

1. On 30 September 1992 the Director General of Fair Trading sent to the MMC the following two references:

The Director General of Fair Trading in exercise of his powers under sections 9(1), 47(1), 49(1) and 50(1) of the Fair Trading Act 1973 hereby refers to the Monopolies and Mergers Commission the matter of the existence or the possible existence of a monopoly situation in relation to the supply of animal waste in England and Wales.

The Commission shall investigate and report on the questions whether a monopoly situation exists and if so

(a) by virtue of which provisions of section 6 to 8 of the said Act that monopoly situation is taken to exist;

(b) in favour of what person or persons that monopoly situation exists;

(c) whether any steps (by way of uncompetitive practices or otherwise) are being taken by that person or those persons for the purpose of exploiting or maintaining the monopoly situation and if so by what uncompetitive practices or in what other way;

(d) whether any action or omission on the part of that person or those persons is attributable to the existence of that monopoly situation and if so what action or omission and in what way it is so attributable; and

(e) whether any facts found by the Commission in pursuance of their investigations under the preceding provisions of this paragraph operate or may be expected to operate against the public interest.

For the purposes of this reference:

'the supply of animal waste' means the supply of animal material which is acquired for processing in rendering plants; and

'animal' does not include any bird or fish except in so far as these are included in butchery waste.

The Commission shall report upon this reference within a period of nine months from the date hereof.

(signed) BRYAN CARSBERG
30 September 1992   *Director General of Fair Trading*

The Director General of Fair Trading in exercise of his powers under sections 9(1), 47(1), 49(1) and 50(1) of the Fair Trading Act 1973 hereby refers to the Monopolies and Mergers Commission the matter of the existence or the possible existence of a monopoly situation in relation to the supply of animal waste in Scotland.

The Commission shall investigate and report on the questions whether a monopoly situation exists and if so:

(a) by virtue of which provisions of section 6 to 8 of the said Act that monopoly situation is taken to exist;

(b) in favour of what person or persons that monopoly situation exists;

(c) whether any steps (by way of uncompetitive practices or otherwise) are being taken by that person or those persons for the purpose of exploiting or maintaining the monopoly situation and if so by what uncompetitive practices or in what other way;

(d) whether any action or omission on the part of that person or those persons is attributable to the existence of that monopoly situation and if so what action or omission and in what way it is so attributable; and

(e) whether any facts found by the Commission in pursuance of their investigations under the preceding provisions of this paragraph operate or may be expected to operate against the public interest.

For the purposes of this reference:

'the supply of animal waste' means the supply of animal material which is acquired for processing in rendering plants; and

'animal' does not include any bird or fish except in so far as these are included in butchery waste.

The Commission shall report upon this reference within a period of nine months from the date hereof.

(signed) BRYAN CARSBERG
30 September 1992   *Director General of Fair Trading*

2. On 1 December 1992 the Director General of Fair Trading made the following variations to the terms of the two references:

Whereas by a reference dated 30 September 1992 the Director General of Fair Trading in exercise of his powers under sections 47(1), 49(1) and 50(1) of the Fair Trading Act 1973 referred to the Monopolies and Mergers Commission the matter of the existence or the possible existence of a monopoly situation in relation to the supply of animal waste in England and Wales:

Now therefore the Director General of Fair Trading in exercise of his powers under section 52(1) of the said Act hereby varies the said reference by substituting for the definition of animal the following definition:

'animal' includes any bird but does not include any fish except in so far as fish are included in butchery waste.

(signed) BRYAN CARSBERG
1 December 1992   *Director General of Fair Trading*

Whereas by a reference dated 30 September 1992 the Director General of Fair Trading in exercise of his powers under sections 47(1), 49(1) and 50(1) of the Fair Trading Act 1973 referred to the Monopolies and Mergers Commission the matter of the existence or the possible existence of a monopoly situation in relation to the supply of animal waste in Scotland:

Now therefore the Director General of Fair Trading in exercise of his powers under section 52(1) of the said Act hereby varies the said reference by substituting for the definition of animal the following definition:

'animal' includes any bird but does not include any fish except in so far as fish are included in butchery waste.

(signed) BRYAN CARSBERG
Director General of Fair Trading

1 December 1992

3. The questions in the reference concerning the supply of animal waste in England and Wales are answered in the following paragraphs of the report:

Whether a monopoly situation exists: paragraph 10.4;

    (a) paragraph 10.4;

    (b) paragraph 10.5;

    (c) paragraph 10.118;

    (d) paragraph 10.119; and

    (e) paragraph 10.118.

4. The questions in the reference concerning the supply of animal waste in Scotland are answered in the following paragraphs of the report:

Whether a monopoly situation exists: paragraph 10.6;

    (a) paragraph 10.6;

    (b) paragraph 10.7;

    (c) paragraph 10.120;

    (d) paragraph 10.121; and

    (e) paragraph 10.120.

5. The composition of the Group of members which was responsible for this inquiry and report is indicated in the list of members in the preface.

6. Notices advertising the references and inviting interested parties to submit evidence to the MMC were placed in:

Meat Trades Journal
Butcher & Processor
Meat Manufacturing & Marketing

7. In addition we sought information and views from trade associations, abattoirs, renderers, gut-room contractors, poultry producers, brokers of fats and proteins, the TUC, the CBI, Government departments and other interested parties. We held two hearings with MAFF and one with DoE. We also held 15 other hearings in England and seven in Scotland. The evidence we received is summarized principally in Chapter 7. During the inquiry members and staff visited various abattoirs, gut-rooms and rendering plants throughout Great Britain.

8. On 15 March 1993 we informed Prosper De Mulder Ltd of our provisional conclusion that a monopoly situation as defined in section 6(1)*(a)* of the Fair Trading Act 1973 existed in favour of

Prosper De Mulder Ltd and its subsidiaries and related companies (PDM) in relation to the supply in England and Wales of animal waste for rendering. On 15 March 1993 we also informed Hillsdown Holdings plc (Hillsdown) and William Forrest & Son (Paisley) Ltd (Forrest) of our provisional conclusion that a monopoly situation as defined in section 6(1)*(a)* of the Fair Trading Act 1973 existed in favour of Forrest and its parent company, Hillsdown, in relation to the supply in Scotland of animal waste for rendering. We notified PDM, and Hillsdown and Forrest, of the grounds for these provisional conclusions and outlined the points which the MMC would need to consider when assessing the effect of the monopoly situation on the public interest. A supplementary letter was sent to PDM, and to Hillsdown and Forrest, on 29 March. We received written submissions from PDM and Forrest in reply to our letters of 15 and 29 March. Representatives of Hillsdown and Forrest attended a hearing on 13 April and representatives of PDM attended a hearing on 14 April for the purpose of discussing these matters with us.

9. Additional hearings with representatives of PDM, and of Hillsdown and Forrest, were held on 6 May 1993 to discuss further those issues which might have a bearing on the public interest.

10. Some of the evidence received during the course of our inquiry was of a commercially confidential nature and our report contains only such information as we consider necessary for a proper understanding of our conclusions.

11. We thank all those who helped with our inquiry, particularly the companies principally involved.

The 1986 undertakings

Prosper De Mulder Limited (PDM) hereby undertakes to the Secretary of State that it will and will procure that its subsidiaries will:

1.   (i)   not enter into or offer a price for any gut-room contract unless, on the basis of reasonable estimates, the total expected revenue (calculated in accordance with undertaking (iii) below) accruing from the performance of such contract exceeds the total expected direct and indirect costs (calculated in accordance with undertaking (iii) below) attributable to the entry into and performance of such contract;

    (ii)   conduct all gut-room business in a manner which avoids any cross-subsidy between that business and any other business of PDM or any of it subsidiaries or between one gut-room contract entered into by PDM or any of its subsidiaries and another such contract;

    (iii)   in particular and without prejudice to undertaking (ii) above, adopt and operate accounting systems and accounting procedures so that the accounts of each gut-room contract entered into by PDM or any of its subsidiaries and of the gut-room contract entered into by or business of PDM and its subsidiaries will be:

        (a)   charged with all direct and indirect costs reasonably attributable to the conduct of that business; and

        (b)   credited with all revenue deriving from the conduct of such business;

        such costs and revenue in any case where they arise out of a transaction otherwise than at arms-length being equal to the costs and revenue that would be charged or credited in respect of any equivalent transaction at arms-length; and

    (iv)   provide the Director General of Fair Trading (DGFT) with such information as he may reasonably require from time to time to monitor compliance with the foregoing undertakings, and in particular:

        (a)   a statement of its gut-room contracts in operation at the date of these undertakings, specifying separately each abattoir or abattoirs in respect of which a gut-room contract is then in operation;

        (b)   in respect of each gut-room contract which it is proposed to enter into a statement showing:

            (i)   estimated throughput of, by number and type, animal and price to be paid for each type of animal;

            (ii)   estimated yield of product by weight from each type of animal and price of yield of product;

            (iii)   estimated direct expenses;

            (iv)   in the case of a gut-room contract relating to more than one abattoir, estimated amount and basic of apportionment of any common direct expenses;

            (v)   estimated indirect expenses and their basis of allocation;

(c) an audited annual statement, within three months of the end of the relevant accounting reference period, of the profit and loss of its gut-room business, together with reconcilable management accounts showing the profit and loss of each gut-room contract separately.

2. Not purchase or collect, or offer to purchase or collect, any grade of animal waste from any person on condition that such person supplies or will supply animal waste of a higher grade or grades to PDM or any of its subsidiaries.

3. (i) notify the DGFT at least one month before the date on which PDM or its subsidiaries (as the case may be):

    (a) acquire directly or indirectly or do anything with the intent that an associated person will acquire directly or indirectly any animal waste, enterprise, or

    (b) do anything alone or with others which would result in any animal waste enterprise ceasing to be distinct (within the meaning of Section 65, interpreted, where appropriate, in accordance with Section 77, of the Fair Trading Act 1973) from any enterprise carried on by or under the control of PDM or any of its subsidiaries.

(ii) on notifying the DGFT in accordance with undertaking (i) above any proposed action, provide him with details of such action, which shall include:

    (a) the identity of the animal waste enterprise or enterprises in relation to which such action is proposed;

    (b) where available, a profit and loss account for the most recent year's trading of such enterprise, or each such enterprise, and a balance sheet showing the financial position of such enterprise, or each such enterprise, at the end of that year;

    (c) details of any consideration proposed to be paid, specifying the amount, if any, attributable to the acquisition of the goodwill of such enterprise or each such enterprise; and

(iii) provide the DGFT with such further information as he may reasonably require with respect to any proposed action which is notified in accordance with undertaking (i) above.

In these undertakings:

'subsidiary' has the same meaning as in section 736 of the Companies Act 1985;

'associated person' means any person who is associated within the meaning of section 77(14) of the Fair Trading Act 1973 with PDM or any of its subsidiaries;

'enterprise' means, in relation to PDM and its subsidiaries, the activities or part of the activities of a business;

'animal waste enterprise' means the activities or part of the activities of rendering or collecting business carried on by or under the control of any person other than PDM or its subsidiaries;

'gut-room contract' means a contract for the operation of a gut-room in an abattoir or a contract for the operation of gut-rooms in abattoirs under common ownership;

'gut-room business' means the business of operating gut-rooms under gut-room contracts;

'animal waste' and 'animal' have the meanings attributed to them in the reference to the Monopolies and Mergers Commission dated 23 November 1982 of the matter of the existence or the possible existence of a monopoly situation in relation to the supply of animal waste in Great Britain.

PDM companies

Prosper De Mulder Ltd
    De Mulder (Mkt Harborough) Ltd
    Granox Ltd
    James Jennings and Company Ltd
        Jennings (Darlington) Ltd*
        Wear Refining Company Ltd*
    John Knight (Animal By Products) Ltd
    The Matlock and District Hide and Skin Company Ltd*
      De Mulder & Sons Ltd
    G E and H Mitchell Ltd
    J L Thomas & Co Ltd
    Webster Craven Ltd (formerly P Webster Ltd)
    Wells By Products Ltd (67%)
    Beacon Research Ltd (50%)
    Stannard & Co (1969) Ltd (50%)*

    Barbers Animal Products Ltd†
    R Bennett and Sons (Grampound) Ltd†
    S E & M Blowers Ltd†
    Wing and Dixon Ltd†

    Bacon Brothers (Animal Waste) Ltd*
    A C Beresford & Sons Ltd
    Boons of Stafford Ltd*
    Cluttons Animal By Products Ltd*
    Coopers (Farm Services) Ltd*
    Craven Calvert Ltd*
    Curtis (Animal By-Products) Ltd*
    De Mulder (Derby) Ltd*
    Hales (By-Products) Ltd*
    Haynes (Helston) Ltd*
    F H Jung (Transport) Ltd*
    Kerson (Holdings) Ltd*
    Luton and District Butchers Waste Contractors Ltd*
    Prosper De Mulder (Anglia) Ltd*
    Springfields Ltd*
    Springfields Protein Ltd*
    Swallow Bait Ltd*
    C Vaughan and Sons Ltd*
    James Williamson and Son (Gloucester) Ltd*

Frazer (Butchers) Ltd
    Chettles Ltd

Prosper De Mulder Transport

Prosper De Mulder Services

Oracle Motors Ltd

Francis Investments Ltd

---

*Non-trading company.
†Company with investment income only.

PDM: consolidated accounts for the year ended 31 March 1992

Consolidated profit and loss account for the year ended 31 March 1992

	Notes	1992		1991	
					£'000
TURNOVER	1		99,127		82,829
Change in stocks of finished goods			(661)		(364)
Other operating income			215		180
Own work capitalized			7		11
			98,688		82,656
Raw materials and consumables			36,806		30,533
			61,882		52,123
Staff costs	2	17,441		15,030	
Depreciation		3,435		2,914	
Other operating charges		33,688		30,384	
Share of loss of associated company		37		4	
			54,601		48,332
OPERATING PROFIT	3		7,281		3,791
Income from investments		0		0	
Interest receivable	4	75		83	
Interest payable	5	(854)		(1,148)	
			(779)		(1,065)
PROFIT BEFORE TAX			6,502		2,726
Taxation			2,270		1,263
PROFIT AFTER TAX			4,232		1,463
Minority interests			132		-
PROFIT ATTRIBUTABLE TO SHAREHOLDERS			4,100		1,463
Extraordinary items	6		222		128
PROFIT AVAILABLE FOR DISTRIBUTION			4,322		1,591
Dividends			183		137
RETAINED PROFIT FOR YEAR			4,139		1,454
Retained profit brought forward			17,951		16,498
Goodwill written off	7		(607)		-
RETAINED PROFIT CARRIED FORWARD			21,483		17,952

Consolidated balance sheet at 31 March 1992

£'000

	Notes	1992		1991	
Fixed assets					
Intangible assets		2		2	
Tangible assets	12	24,091		21,454	
Investments		(25)	24,068	47	21,503
Current assets					
Stocks		2,885		3,502	
Debtors	8	13,046		13,476	
Cash		121		93	
		16,052		17,071	
Creditors due within one year	9	15,203		17,381	
Net current assets (liabilities)			849		(310)
Total assets less current liabilities			24,917		21,193
Creditors due after one year	10		2,023		2,235
Deferred tax			906		852
Minority interests			351		-
			21,637		18,106
Capital and reserves					
Called-up share capital			104		104
Capital redemption reserve			50		50
Profit and loss account			21,483		17,952
			21,637		18,106

Notes to the consolidated accounts for the year ended 31 March 1992

		Notes	1992	£'000 1991
1	**Turnover**			
	Sales of end products		86,285	69,991
	Collection charges		11,921	12,557
	Sales of raw materials		511	371
	Other sales		410	(90)
			99,127	82,829
2	**Staff costs**			
	Wages and salaries		15,798	13,636
	Social security costs		1,571	1,345
	Other pension costs		72	49
			17,441	15,030
	The average weekly number of employees during the year was made up as follows:			
	Office and management		261	232
	Collection and processing		770	685
			1,031	917
3	**Operating profit**			
	This is stated after charging or crediting:			
	Directors' remuneration		770	487
	Hire of plant and vehicles		156	95
	Amortization of trade marks		1	1
	Auditors' remuneration			
	— Audit fees		45	47
	— Other services		164	124
	Net rental income		149	124
4	**Interest receivable**			
	Bank Interest		15	12
	Loan and mortgage interest		4	5
	Credit sale agreements		49	55
	Sundry interest		6	2
	Corporation tax repayment supplement		1	9
			75	83
5	**Interest payable**			
	Bank loans and overdrafts		631	912
	Other loans wholly repayable within five years		223	236
			854	1,148
6	**Extraordinary items**			
	Extraordinary income:			
	Profit on sale of freehold property		305	78
	Profit on sale of trade marks		-	85
			305	163
	Less: taxation on the above		46	35
			259	128
	Associated company (50%)			
	Profit on sale of goodwill		5	-
	Profit on sale of building		1	-
	Loss on investment in subsidiary		(10)	-
	Loan written off		(33)	-
			(37)	-
			222	128
7	**Goodwill written off**			
	Goodwill purchased during year		39	-
	Goodwill on consolidation		568	-
			607	-

139

Notes to the consolidated accounts for the year ended 31 March 1992 (continued)

			£'000
	Notes	*1992*	*1991*
8 Debtors			
Trade debtors		9,878	10,709
Mortgage loans		68	91
Credit sale agreements		171	285
Prepayments and accrued income		351	394
Amounts owed by associated company		-	26
Other debtors		2,578	1,971
		13,049	13,476
9 Creditors falling due within one year			
Current instalments on loans	11	1,769	2,101
Bank overdrafts		2,330	5,704
Leasing and hire purchase		276	320
Trade creditors		7,167	6,820
Amounts owed to associated company		-	26
Current corporation tax		2,458	1,049
Other taxes		552	489
Other creditors		463	718
Accruals		170	127
Proposed dividend		18	27
		15,203	17,381
10 Creditors falling due after one year			
Loans	11	1,915	1,967
Leasing and hire purchase		107	268
		2,022	2,235

				£'000
		1992		*1991*
11 Loans	*Within one year*	*After one year*	*Within one year*	*After one year*
Bank loans	800	1,700	800	1,550
ICFC	74	-	74	74
Pension fund	550	-	900	-
Ashworths	44	132	44	176
Craven Calvert	83	83	83	167
Winnerleigh Finance	55	-	55	-
P F De Mulder (re Francis Investments)	163	-	145	-
	1,769	1,915	2,101	1,967

12 Tangible fixed assets

	Land and buildings	*Plant and machinery*	*Motor vehicles*	*Total*
Cost or valuation:				
At 1 April 1991	11,520	31,764	6,562	49,846
Acquisition of subsidiary	365	1,087	285	1,737
Additions less grants	803	2,739	1,764	5,306
Disposals	(258)	(658)	(819)	(1,735)
At 31 March 1992	12,430	34,932	7,792	55,154
Depreciation:				
At 1 April 1991	3,547	20,321	4,524	28,392
Acquisition of subsidiary	47	289	125	461
Provided during the year	326	2,331	778	3,435
Disposals	(67)	(546)	(612)	(1,225)
At 31 March 1992	3,853	22,395	4,815	31,063
Net book values:				
At 1 April 1991	7,973	11,443	2,038	21,454
At 31 March 1992	8,577	12,537	2,977	24,091

Source: PDM.

Forrest's capital expenditure and cost projections

1. At our request Forrest supplied projections for the three years to 1995. Operating results are shown in Table 1.

TABLE 1 **Forrest's projected financial results, 1993 to 1995**

			£'000
	1993	*1994*	*1995*
End-product sales	[		
Material purchases			
Transport Processing Administration			
		*	
PBIT			
Tangible fixed assets Investment grants			
Net current assets Year-end capital employed			
Average capital employed			]
			per cent
ROCE	[	*	]

Sources: Forrest and MMC.

2. Forrest told us that it expected an increase in capital expenditure in the next three years. One of its cookers was 18 years old and would need to be replaced. The requirements of the EPA would also lead to expenditure of £650,000, principally for the installation of a bio-filter to handle foul air. Forrest also supplied a forecast of operating cash flow, as shown in Table 2.

TABLE 2 **Forrest: projected cash flow and fixed asset purchases, 1993 to 1995**

			£'000
	1993	*1994*	*1995*
PBIT	[		
Depreciation Investment grants Change in working capital		*	
Operating cash flow			
Purchases of fixed assets			]
			per cent
% of operating cash flow	[	*	]

Sources: Forrest and MMC.

*Figures omitted. See note on page iv.

236197 K2

3. Forrest's budgets show a small decline in materials processed compared with 1992, and a substantial decrease in greaves processed from 11,000 tonnes to 5,000 tonnes. Forrest believes that it is most unlikely that, either there will be adequate supplies of greaves available for purchasing, or that they will be available at a price which would offer an adequate rate of return. However, if greaves volumes and prices are restored to their 1992 levels, there is an immediate improvement in PBIT and cash flow of £300,000 and ROCE increases to over 40 per cent.

APPENDIX 3.4
(referred to in paragraph 3.46)

The financial results of three smaller renderers

1. In this appendix we set out the financial results of three of the smaller renderers and a brief account of their operations. As with PDM and Forrest, the sources of our information were the statutory accounts, completed questionnaires and discussions with the companies. The three companies are:

Fats & Proteins (UK) Ltd (Fats & Proteins)
Smith Brothers (Hyde) Ltd (Smith)
Gilberts Animal By-Products Ltd (Gilberts).

Financial information was also received from A Hughes & Son (Skellingthorpe) Ltd and Dundas Chemical Company (Mosspark) Ltd but was not in a form suitable for inclusion in this appendix.

Fats & Proteins

2. This business was established by Edmund Metcalfe Senior and subsequently transferred to a company owned by him and his family. It operates from a site in Lancaster. Because it has plentiful storage space, it is able to carry on a substantial trading activity in end products, the only renderer engaged in this activity. The company's financial results for the five years to 31 March 1992 are set out in Table 1. Because we need to compare its results with those of other renderers, we have apportioned its sales of end products between those which it has processed and those which were bought in, and we have calculated separate profits for trading and processing.

TABLE 1 **Fats & Proteins: summary of financial results**

£'000

Year to 31 March

	1988	1989	1990	1991	1992
Processing					
End-product sales	[				
Cost of raw materials					
Transport in					
Processing					
Other operating costs					
Processing profit					
Trading		Figures omitted. See note on page iv.			
End-product sales					
Cost of end products					
Trading profit					
PBIT					
Tangible fixed assets					
Net current assets					
Average capital employed					]

per cent

ROCE					
Processing	[				
Trading		Figures omitted. See note on page iv.			
Total					]

Source: MMC using Fats & Proteins' data.

143

3. Equivalent information in terms of £ per tonne for the rendering operation is set out in Table 2.

TABLE 2   **Fats & Proteins: summary of financial results per tonne processed**

£

			Year to 31 March		
	1988	1989	1990	1991	1992
End-product sales	[				
Cost of raw materials					
Transport in					
Processing					
Other operating costs					
			Figures omitted. See note on page iv.		
Processing profit					
Tangible fixed assets					
Net current assets					
Average capital employed					
Tonnes processed					]

Source: MMC using Fats & Proteins' data.

4. In addition to its purchases of end products for trading, Fats & Proteins buys a large quantity of greaves, for processing when the kill is at its seasonal low. Purchases of materials for rendering are set out in Table 3.

TABLE 3   **Fats & Proteins: volumes and values of rendering materials purchased**

£

			Year to 31 March		
	1988	1989	1990	1991	1992
£'000					
Cost of materials	[				
Less: Greaves					
Cost of materials collected					
Tonnes					
Materials processed					
Less: Greaves			Figures omitted. See note on page iv.		
Materials collected					
£ per tonne					
Greaves					
Other materials					]

Source: MMC using Fats & Proteins' data.

5. Most materials are collected from a relatively small area (97 per cent of materials are collected from within 100 miles) in the company's own vehicles, although outside contractors are used when necessary. About 30 per cent of materials are delivered to the plant by independent collectors.

6. [

Details omitted. See note on page iv.

]

7. [

Details omitted. See note on page iv.

]

144

Smith

8. The company is owned by two cousins, John and Robert Smith, and their families and operates from a site in Hyde on the outskirts of Manchester. In addition to the rendering business there is a substantial investment business, both of which were carried on in the same unlimited company. On 1 April 1991 the company was reorganized, and the rendering business was transferred into a new limited company. We have been able to separate the results of the rendering business from the rest of the group's activities, and the results of the rendering business for the five accounting periods to 31 March 1992 are shown in Table 4. The financial year-end was changed from 31 December to 31 March, so that the results to 31 March 1990 are for a 15-month period.

9. Part of the remuneration of the directors is attributable to the investment activities of the group. For the purposes of our analysis we apportioned their remuneration between the rendering and investment businesses.

TABLE 4   Smith: summary of the financial results of the rendering business

£'000

			Year to 31 March*		
	1987	1988	1990	1991	1992
End-product sales	[				
Cost of raw materials					
Transport in					
Processing					
Other operating costs			Figures omitted. See note on page iv.		
PBIT					
Tangible fixed assets					
Less: Net current liabilities					
Average capital employed					]
					per cent
ROCE	[		Figures omitted. See note on page iv.		]

Source: MMC from Smith's data.

---

*Year to 31 December for 1987 and 1988 with a 15-month period to 31 March 1990. ROCE for 1990 has been adjusted to an annualized basis.

10. Equivalent information in terms of £ per tonne processed is set out in Table 5.

TABLE 5   Smith: summary of financial results per tonne processed

£

			Year to 31 March*		
	1988	1989	1990	1991	1992
End-product sales	[				
Cost of raw materials					
Transport in					
Processing					
Other operating costs			Figures omitted. See note on page iv.		
PBIT					
Tangible fixed assets					
Less: Net current liabilities					
Average capital employed					
Tonnes processed					]

Source: MMC using Smith's data.

---

*Year to 31 December for 1987 and 1988 with a 15-month period to 31 March 1990. Components of capital employed for 1990 have been adjusted to an annualized basis.

11. Smith uses its own vehicles to collect materials, almost all of it from within 100 miles of Hyde with about 60 per cent from within 50 miles. Independent collectors supply approximately 30 per cent of materials. Smith has the lowest transport costs of any of the renderers for which we obtained detailed information. SBO material is sent to Gilberts for processing.

12. [

Details omitted. See note on page iv.

]

Gilberts

13. Gilberts is owned by the Pointon family and occupies a site near Leek in Staffordshire. Since 1988 the company's financial year-end has been 31 July. Audited accounts for the three accounting periods to 31 July 1990 were available in addition to draft accounts for 1991, the audit of which had not been completed. At May 1993, preparation of statutory accounts for 1992 was awaiting resolution of the treatment of a sale of building land. The company was able to provide us with information on volumes and costs for the three years to 31 July 1991.

14. [

Details omitted. See note on page iv.

]

TABLE 6   **Gilberts: summary of financial results**

			£
		Year to 31 July	
	1989	*1990*	*1991**
End-product sales	[		
Cost of raw materials			
Transport in			
Transport out			
Processing			
Administration		†	
Consequential loss claim			
PBIT			
Tangible fixed assets			
Net current liabilities			
Average capital employed			]
			per cent
ROCE	[	†	]

Source: MMC using Gilberts' data.

*1991 results are based on draft accounts.

15. As with the other renderers, equivalent information in terms of £ per tonne processed has been calculated by us and is set out in Table 7.

†Figures omitted. See note on page iv.

TABLE 7 **Gilberts: summary of financial results per tonne processed**

£

Year to 31 July

	1989	1990	1991*
End-product sales	[		
Cost of raw materials			
Transport in			
Transport out			
Processing			
Administration		*Figures omitted.*	
Insurance claim		*See note on page iv.*	
PBIT			
Tangible fixed assets			
Less: Net current liabilities			
Average capital employed			
Tonnes processed			]

Source: MMC using Gilberts' data.

*1991 results are based on draft accounts.

16. Gilberts obtains only about 5 per cent of its materials from independent collectors. Gilberts told us that it had always collected materials from a large area. In 1992 two of its large abattoirs closed and it lost other sources of materials to PDM (Gilberts alleged predatory behaviour on the part of PDM, see Appendix 6.2). In the ensuing price war, Gilberts was forced to cover even greater distances for full loads from large abattoirs. The price war must have been expensive for Gilberts, but the effects will not be visible until the accounts to July 1993 are available.

17. [

Details omitted. See note on page iv.

]

18. [

Details omitted. See note on page iv.

]

APPENDIX 3.5
(referred to in paragraph 3.46)

Comparison of the results of the renderers, 1989 to 1991

1. In the tables below we have set out the costs, revenues and capital employed for each of the five renderers for which we have detailed information. For the three smaller renderers we have calculated averages, weighted by tonnes of material processed, for inclusion in Chapter 3.

Operating costs, revenues and profitability

2. In Table 1 we have set out the transport costs for each of the five renderers during 1989 to 1991 in £ per tonne. PDM, Forrest and Fats & Proteins buy significant quantities of greaves, which we have eliminated so that transport costs are based more closely on £ per tonne collected.

TABLE 1   **Comparative inward transport costs per tonne of materials collected**

				£
	1989	*1990*	*1991*	*1989–91*
PDM	17.46	18.79	18.92	18.40
Forrest	17.42	20.95	21.24	20.03
Gilberts	[			
Smith		*Details omitted. See note on page iv.*		
Fats & Proteins				]
Weighted average	10.33	10.67	11.60	10.88

Source: MMC from data supplied by the companies.

3. In Table 2 we have set out the processing costs of these renderers in £ per tonne for 1991.

TABLE 2   **Processing costs per tonne, 1991**

			Fats &		£
	PDM	*Forrest*	*Proteins*	*Smith*	*Gilberts*
Labour	6.30	4.97	[		
Energy	7.43	8.71			
Repairs and maintenance	8.44	8.82			
Odour and effluent control	2.95	2.01		*Figures omitted.*	
Depreciation	2.15	2.37		*See note on page iv.*	
Other costs	3.02	4.54			
	30.29	31.43			]

Source: MMC from data supplied by the companies.

4. In Table 3 the renderers' operating costs for 1989, 1990 and 1991 are shown. We show three components of cost in the table: transport (both inward and outward); processing; and other operating costs (mostly administration). In Table 3 transport costs are calculated on the basis of £ per tonne processed, not per tonne collected as in Table 1.

TABLE 3 **Comparative operating costs per tonne of materials processed**

£

	1989	1990	1991	1989–91
Transport costs				
PDM	19.53	21.78	23.13	21.52
Forrest	14.57	17.56	18.70	17.09
Gilberts	[			
Smith		*Figures omitted. See note on page iv.*		
Fats & Proteins				]
Weighted average	10.11	10.43	12.10	10.88
Processing costs				
PDM	25.49	29.26	30.29	28.40
Forrest	31.61	31.92	31.43	31.65
Gilberts	[			
Smith		*Figures omitted. See note on page iv.*		
Fats & Proteins				]
Weighted average	22.42	24.00	26.62	24.33
Other operating costs				
PDM	7.76	8.27	7.37	7.79
Forrest	4.67	4.46	4.97	4.70
Gilberts	[			
Smith		*Figures omitted. See note on page iv.*		
Fats & Proteins				]
Weighted average	4.64	5.36	5.63	5.20
Total operating costs				
PDM	52.78	59.31	60.79	57.71
Forrest	50.85	53.94	55.10	53.44
Gilberts	[			
Smith		*Figures omitted. See note on page iv.*		
Fats & Proteins				]
Weighted average	37.17	39.79	44.35	40.41

Source: MMC from data supplied by the companies.

5.   In Table 4 we have calculated the 'processing margin' for PDM and the other companies. This margin is the difference between total operating costs and end-product sales and is available to cover the cost of raw materials and profit.

TABLE 4 **Comparative profits per tonne of materials processed**

£

	1989	1990	1991	1989–91
Total operating costs				
PDM	52.78	59.31	60.79	57.71
Forrest	50.85	53.94	55.10	53.44
Gilberts	[			
Smith	*Figures omitted. See note on page iv.*			
Fats & Proteins				]
Weighted average	37.17	39.79	44.35	40.41
End-product sales				
PDM	78.55	63.80	72.26	71.49
Forrest	101.61	79.18	69.92	82.50
Gilberts	[			
Smith	*Figures omitted. See note on page iv.*			
Fats & Proteins				]
Weighted average	86.59	63.27	60.90	70.46
Processing margin				
PDM	25.77	4.49	11.47	13.78
Forrest	50.76	25.24	14.52	29.06
Gilberts	[			
Smith	*Figures omitted. See note on page iv.*			
Fats & Proteins				]
Weighted average	49.42	23.48	16.55	30.55
Cost of raw materials				
PDM	22.79	0.03	4.23	8.84
Forrest	42.66	16.07	5.37	20.10
Gilberts	[			
Smith	*Figures omitted. See note on page iv.*			
Fats & Proteins				]
Weighted average	39.32	17.64	13.07	23.54
PBIT				
PDM	2.98	4.45	7.24	4.94
Forrest	8.10	9.17	9.15	8.96
Gilberts	[			
Smith	*Figures omitted. See note on page iv.*			
Fats & Proteins				]
Weighted average	10.10	5.84	3.48	6.51

Source: MMC from data supplied by the companies.

6. The costs of raw materials included in Table 4 include purchases of greaves by PDM, Forrest and Fats & Proteins; also, purchases of additives by PDM. The average price per tonne purchased, after eliminating these items, is set out in Table 5.

TABLE 5   Comparative costs of rendering materials per tonne purchased

£

	1989	1990	1991	1989–91
PDM	20.55	-2.17	0.57	6.14
Forrest	26.30	5.02	-5.32	7.37
Gilberts	[			
Smith		Figures omitted. See note on page iv.		
Fats & Proteins				]
Weighted average	30.39	13.60	9.66	17.90

Source: MMC from data supplied by the companies.

Capital employed and profitability

7. In Table 6 we set out an analysis of average capital employed.

TABLE 6   Comparative capital employed and ROCE per tonne of materials processed

£

	1989	1990	1991	1989–91
Plant and machinery				
PDM	11.23	10.71	10.29	10.74
Forrest	15.15	13.97	11.86	13.66
Gilberts	[			
Smith		Figures omitted. See note on page iv.		
Fats & Proteins				]
Weighted average	24.90	27.95	28.76	27.20
Other fixed assets				
PDM	8.33	8.12	8.63	8.36
Forrest	7.13	6.47	6.27	6.62
Gilberts	[			
Smith		Figures omitted. See note on page iv.		
Fats & Proteins				]
Weighted average	24.91	26.63	28.45	26.66
Tangible fixed assets				
PDM	19.56	18.83	18.92	19.10
Forrest	22.28	20.44	18.13	20.28
Gilberts	[			
Smith		Figures omitted. See note on page iv.		
Fats & Proteins				]
Weighted average	49.81	54.58	57.21	53.87
Capital employed				
PDM	25.12	25.08	23.93	24.71
Forrest	22.14	20.91	18.64	20.56
Gilberts	[			
Smith		Figures omitted. See note on page iv.		
Fats & Proteins				]
Weighted average	44.56	50.28	53.54	49.46
				per cent
ROCE				
PDM	11.9	17.8	30.3	20.0
Forrest	36.6	43.8	50.7	43.5
Gilberts	[			
Smith		Figures omitted. See note on page iv.		
Fats & Proteins				]
Weighted average	22.7	11.6	6.5	13.2

Source: MMC from data supplied by the companies.

151

8. Fixed assets in Table 6 are shown after deducting accumulated depreciation but, in the case of Forrest, before deducting investment grants. Gilberts and Smith have much higher values for land and buildings than PDM and Forrest.

Interpretation of comparative results

9. PDM has high operating costs and, in spite of paying moderate prices for raw materials, the lowest profit per tonne processed of any of the five renderers except Gilberts.

10. Of the smaller renderers, Fats & Proteins has the lowest costs and by paying modest prices for materials achieves by far the highest profit of any renderer. Smith also has relatively low costs. Compared with PDM, Smith has a similar ROCE for the three years and that of Fats & Proteins is higher. Gilberts' results reflect its higher costs from using batch processing (although lower than those of PDM and Forrest), its high costs of materials and the high book value of its land and buildings. Gilberts also suffered from the fire damage to its milling machinery in 1991.

Summary of the MMC's 1985 report on *Animal Waste*

1. The following is a summary of the conclusions and recommendations of the MMC's earlier report *Animal Waste: A Report on the supply of animal waste in Great Britain* (Cmnd 9470, April 1985). References below in parentheses are to paragraph numbers in that report.

Conclusions

2. Prosper De Mulder Ltd and its subsidiaries (PDM) processed about half a million tonnes of animal waste in 1982, which represented about 44 per cent of the total supply in Great Britain. A monopoly situation therefore existed in favour of PDM. (9.2–9.3)

3. The effects of that monopoly situation on the public interest had to be considered against the following public interest requirements:

(a) First, that the essential service of waste disposal provided to the meat industry by the rendering industry should be, and should continue to be, carried on effectively and reliably; without it abattoirs would have to cease slaughtering and there would be far-reaching effects on the supply of meat and livestock farming. (9.5–9.6)

(b) Second, that rendering should be carried on without unduly polluting the environment; the extent to which the industry operated to acceptable standards depended on the willingness and ability of renderers to invest in effective equipment. (9.7)

(c) Third, that the industry should be economically efficient. (9.8)

4. No evidence had been received of shortcomings in the service provided by PDM to abattoirs. PDM well satisfied the first public interest requirement. (9.10)

5. There was no evidence that PDM's operations gave rise to any greater degree of pollution than did those of renderers generally. Indeed if the industry had remained less concentrated the degree of environmental pollution would probably have been greater than it was; this was because some of the businesses which had closed or sold out had done so because they were unable or unwilling to incur the expense of installing effective control equipment. There was no evidence that the distances over which PDM collected material caused additional environmental problems at any of its plants. PDM therefore satisfactorily met the second public interest requirement. (9.11–9.13)

6. PDM did not feel itself insulated by its dominant position in the industry from a need to maintain and improve its efficiency. The company appeared to have a positive attitude towards development and investment likely to lead to cost savings. There was no basis on which to criticise the company's processing efficiency. (9.14–9.15)

7. PDM claimed that measures taken to reduce collection costs, and economies of scale resulting from fewer but larger plants, offset the cost of transporting material over greater distances. This claim might be correct, but had not been demonstrated. There was a lack of formal information systems to enable management to make decisions based on objective criteria rather than on intuition. The company appeared to be aware of the need for changes in its management style. (9.17–9.18)

8. There was nothing in the dominant position held by PDM that conflicted with the public interest criteria identified above. (9.19)

9. PDM's dominant position did not imply any special risk of disruption to the essential service provided. If the company were to find itself in financial difficulties, some of its plants were likely to

be sold as going concerns. PDM's industrial relations record had been good, and there was no special risk of disruption by industrial action. (9.20–9.22)

10. The monopoly situation identified did not, and might not be expected to, operate against the public interest. (9.23)

11. However, certain forms of behaviour alleged against PDM might, if substantiated, be against the public interest. (9.24) The first related to the way in which PDM had grown. This had been achieved partly by organic growth, but it had also been a willing buyer of other rendering and collecting businesses. It had expanded in the knowledge that, since the supply of raw material was approximately static, this must inevitably increase its market share. It had the capacity to increase its market share in Great Britain from about 44 per cent to around 55 per cent. Although not averse to eliminating a competitor when opportunity presented itself, there was no evidence that PDM had pursued a policy of doing so. Although PDM's expansion and acquisition policy tended to diminish competition in the rendering industry, there was no evidence that this had been to the detriment of abattoirs. PDM's acquisitions had resulted in a considerable degree of rationalisation of the rendering industry and reduction in surplus capacity, mainly by elimination of the less efficient renderers and those most likely to cause environmental pollution. (9.26–9.28)

12. PDM's selling prices were largely determined by the price of commodities over which PDM had no control. Any issue concerning PDM's pricing policy related only to the prices paid to its suppliers. It was felt impossible to judge whether particular prices were unreasonably low, or on the other hand unreasonably high, in order to capture supplies from competitors. No complaint about low prices were made by abattoirs, apart from objections to the imposition of charges for the removal of low-grade material for a period in 1980 to 1982 when renderers' profits declined sharply. PDM conceded that it had paid unreasonably high prices on occasions as a defensive measure to avoid losing a supplier, to regain lost suppliers, or to gain new suppliers from a competitor to whom other suppliers had been lost. There was no clear evidence that aggressive pricing was started by PDM. But, once challenged by a competitor, PDM was quick to respond with vigorous and aggressive pricing tactics including the paying of prices which PDM itself recognised as unreasonable. (9.30–9.33)

13. PDM's pricing, if not predatory in the sense of being aimed at eliminating competitors, was at least highly successful in defence of its market position. Because of its wide geographical spread PDM was able to do exceptionally profitable business in some areas where competition from other renderers was weak, and could thus afford to outbid its competitors for supplies in other areas, accepting a loss if necessary. Although PDM's pricing tactics might be regarded as defensive there was little doubt that they were effective in preserving its position. The evidence suggested that the company had reacted to loss or threatened loss of suppliers by engaging in price wars on occasions of its own choosing and against selected competitors, one at a time. (9.34)

14. PDM had used its powerful position to outbid competitors in a way not open to smaller renderers with much lower market shares. Moreover it was prepared to accept particular business at a loss in pursuance of such tactics against any individual competitor by whom it believed it was threatened. (9.35)

15. PDM's attitude to pricing and its competitors was the same both in connection with the acquisition of material for rendering and in connection with obtaining gut-room contracts. (9.36)

16. Cross-subsidisation of gut-room operation by rendering was likely generally to be anti-competitive and against the public interest because it would enable PDM to pay prices which a gut-room operator who was not also a renderer might not be able to match. (9.42)

17. A formal conclusion was reached that the implementation of PDM's pricing policy both for material for rendering and for gut-room contracts was a step taken for the purpose of exploiting or maintaining the monopoly situation. It operated and might be expected to operate against the public interest. (9.44)

18. If cases of predatory pricing again came to light in the future, inquiry under the anti-competitive practices provisions of the Competition Act 1980 might be appropriate. (9.45)

19. It had been suggested that PDM might be exploiting its position as the dominant renderer of low-grade material by refusing or threatening to refuse to collect such material from abattoirs unless it could also have their higher-grade material. Behaviour of this kind, if substantiated, would on the face of it be restrictive of competition and therefore contrary to the public interest. However, in the absence of specific evidence, and in view of the fact that PDM listed the names of over 100 abattoirs from which it collected only low-grade material, the company's statement was accepted that it never refused to collect low-grade material and that it would not in the future do so. (9.47–9.48)

20. PDM's profits, whether expressed as a return on capital employed or as a percentage of sales, were not excessive. (9.50–9.51)

21. PDM was not yet in a position fully to protect its profits when market conditions were adverse. (9.55)

22. If PDM were persistently to make very high profits it would be largely at the expense of the slaughtering industry; the larger companies would be able to protect their interests by themselves going into rendering. If the degree of exploitation was insufficient to induce abattoirs to take such defensive action, any renderer would be able to make high profits, and PDM's profits would not then be attributable to its monopoly position. Moreover if the effect on abattoirs of exploitation was so slight as to produce no countervailing action, the adverse effect on the public interest could be no more than minimal. (9.56)

23. There were therefore no adequate grounds for imposition of restraint on the level of PDM's profits. (9.58)

24. The formal conclusions were therefore that the monopoly situation which had been found to exist in favour of PDM and its subsidiaries did not, and might not be expected to, operate against the public interest, but that the implementation of the company's pricing policy was a step taken for the purpose of exploiting or maintaining the monopoly situation and that it operated and might be expected to operate against the public interest. (9.59)

Recommendations

25. The only recommendation made was in connection with PDM's pricing policy. The Director General of Fair Trading should be asked to obtain an undertaking from PDM that it would not offer for or enter into gut-room contracts without first having established a reasonable expectation that the operation of any particular gut-room taken on its own would be carried on at a profit, and that there should be no cross-subsidisation between gut-room business and other parts of the company's business or between any individual gut-room operations. (9.45, 9.60)

Further suggestions

26. However, certain factors that had led to a substantial concentration of the rendering industry since the 1960s seemed to favour further concentration in the future. It was suggested that if any further acquisitions by PDM of renderers or collectors were proposed, consideration should be given to referring these for investigation because of PDM's already dominant position in the market. (9.62)

27. One of the factors that had already led to concentration of the rendering industry, and could in the future make more difficult the maintenance of competition, was the tendency of local authorities to seek stricter enforcement of anti-pollution measures. It was suggested that there might be a system of voluntary arbitration under which a member of the Institution of Environmental Health Officers and a member of UKRA should visit plants experiencing odour problems and suggest remedies. (9.63)

Summary of the MMC's report on the PDM and Croda merger situation

1. The following is a summary of the conclusions of the MMC's report, *Prosper De Mulder Ltd and Croda International plc: a report on the merger situation* (Cm 1611, August 1991). References in parentheses in this appendix are to paragraph numbers in that report unless otherwise stated.

The merger situation

2. In January 1991 PDM purchased the plant and equipment, stocks and business carried on at Croda's rendering plant at Market Harborough and took a ten-year lease on the site. Therefore an enterprise carried on by or under the control of Croda had, within the six months preceding the date of the reference, ceased to be distinct from enterprises carried on by or under the control of PDM. (6.3)

3. In 1990 some 51 per cent of the animal waste supplied for rendering in the UK was supplied to PDM and around 4 per cent to Croda. A merger situation qualifying for investigation had therefore been created, by virtue of section 64 (2) of the Fair Trading Act 1973. (6.4 and 6.5)

PDM

4. The principal activity of PDM was the production of tallow and meat-and-bone meal. PDM's rendering operations were carried on at plants at Doncaster, Widnes, Nuneaton, Silvertown, Exeter and—since January 1991—at Market Harborough. (6.6 and 6.7)

5. PDM's consolidated accounts covered the results of the parent company and its plant-operating subsidiaries but not the related companies, which were also relevant. In the year to March 1990 PDM made a pre-tax loss of £1.2 million on a turnover of £84.4 million; at 31 March 1990 it had £21.5 million of capital employed and its net borrowings were 96.3 per cent of shareholders' funds. The related companies had a pre-tax profit of £2.3 million on a turnover of £33.1 million, so that the PDM group was in profit to the extent of just over £1 million. The gearing figure for the group was 62.5 per cent. PDM estimated its group pre-tax profit for the year to 31 March 1991 at £3.5 million. (6.8 to 6.10)

Croda

6. Croda was a broadly-based group of chemical companies and its rendering division a small part of its activities. During the 1980s Croda sold two rendering plants and closed seven others, leaving only the Market Harborough plant which had been modernized in the early 1970s and had a capacity to handle around 1,000 tonnes of high-grade waste per week. Croda took in some 1,200 tonnes of fat and bones per week on average in 1990, much of it collected by independent dealers and supplied to Croda depots in various parts of the country; it sold on most of the excess to other renderers. (6.11 to 6.13)

7. Croda's rendering activities generated an operating loss of £1 million on a turnover of £5 million in 1990. (6.14)

The merger

8. The acquisition by PDM excluded the Market Harborough factory premises and a bone degreasing plant on the same site. The consideration for the assets acquired was £612,000 of which £365,000 was for plant and machinery. PDM paid a nominal £1 for the goodwill and contracts. Over 80 per cent of Croda's raw material was supplied by independent dealers under informal arrangements. For PDM's ten-year lease of the premises—terminable by either side on 12 months' notice—rent was payable only after the first two years. (6.15)

9. Under a separate agreement PDM undertook to supply for the bone degreasing plant the labour and services required to operate it, and a substantial weekly quantity of bones, and to buy from Croda the products of that plant other than the degreased bone. PDM regarded the profits thus forgone as part of the price paid for acquiring the Croda rendering business. (6.16)

10. Croda retained possession of its collection depots but in the case of that at Stratford undertook for five years not to sell it to anyone intending to use the plant for the processing, storage or distribution of animal waste, and thereafter not to sell it to such a person without giving PDM first option to buy it at the price offered. The Stratford site still held a licence for rendering, though full re-equipping would be necessary. (6.17)

The market

11. Abattoirs generated about 80 per cent of the animal waste supplied for rendering. The 10 per cent proportion formerly supplied by knackers had fallen sharply in the last year following renderers' imposition of collection charges for knacker waste and, in turn, knackers' charges for collecting carcasses, which had led fallen stock suppliers to seek cheaper alternatives. The total supply of waste in 1990 was some 1.16 million tonnes in Great Britain, of which just under 1 million tonnes arose in England and Wales. (6.20 to 6.22)

12. It had been PDM's strategy to concentrate its activities at a small number of large continuous process plants with a degree of specialization as to type of material handled. Its unit costs were therefore sensitive to the volume of material processed. (6.27)

13. The acquisition of Croda added 5 per cent to PDM's 60 per cent share of the market in England and Wales. There were four other companies with about 5 per cent each and about a dozen others with smaller shares, of which some were linked to abattoir companies. Forrest had two-thirds of the Scottish market. Both Forrest and Peninsular were part of Hillsdown, the biggest abattoir operator in the UK. (6.29)

14. Rendering provided the only current practicable means of dealing with the bulk of animal waste. (6.30)

15. The market price for end products was largely determined by world market prices for alternative commodities such as coconut oil and soya bean meal. Most renderers used brokers as their agents. PDM's share of UK consumption was around 49 per cent for tallow and 45 per cent for meat-and-bone meal. (6.31 and 6.32)

Developments since the 1985 report

16. The rendering industry had experienced difficult and turbulent trading conditions, owing to a fall in end-product prices compounded by the salmonella and especially the BSE scares. With their income thus severely reduced, renderers had to cut the prices they paid for high-grade waste and introduce progressively higher charges for low-grade waste. For renderers who wished to remain in business, higher standards of odour and effluent control required capital investment on a scale which was substantial in relation to the turnover and profits which they could reasonably expect to achieve. In these circumstances it was not surprising that there had been further concentration in the rendering industry. PDM had further developed its strategy of specialization over the same period. (6.38 to 6.42)

157

17. After 1984/85, PDM's published profits fell sharply. Following the 1985 report PDM had adopted a structure involving two unlimited companies in order not to show the full profits of its operations. While the position was better if one looked at the PDM group, the group return on year-end capital in 1989/90 was still only 8 per cent. Fats & Proteins earned pre-tax profits in 1989/90 which represented a margin of 14 per cent on sales, and Smith Brothers a margin of 9.5 per cent, compared with between 2 and 3 per cent for the PDM group. (6.43 and 6.44)

18. The OFT had received eight complaints since the 1985 report. Of the three specifically relating to PDM, all were from competitors and concerned PDM's pricing and acquisition tactics and its growing dominance in the market. (6.45)

Public interest issues

Competition

Effect on Croda's suppliers and customers

19. Since Croda's activities were confined to high-grade materials, which made up about half of the total, the effect in that part of the market was correspondingly greater. In 1990 Croda obtained only some 200 tonnes per week of material direct. Only a small proportion of all Croda's material came straight from abattoirs: abattoirs generally preferred to deal with renderers who could take the full range of their waste. Most of the dealers had no contracts to supply Croda and were free to supply to other renderers. Arguments that abattoirs were vulnerable to PDM's market power did not apply because collecting low-grade waste from abattoirs was not Croda's business. (6.47 to 6.49)

20. PDM said that it had succeeded in holding on to all the supplies which Croda had obtained from collectors and in some areas had raised the price paid to them. PDM argued that there was effective competition from other renderers in most of the areas where material was collected for Croda. (6.50 and 6.51)

21. While the Scottish market appeared largely separate from the rest of Great Britain, England and Wales could not be broken down into clearly defined regional markets. For individually large quantities of material a national market could be said to exist in England and Wales, while the market for smaller quantities tended to be more local, particularly following the departure of Croda. (6.52)

22. PDM had been able to supply the Market Harborough plant from nearer sources and thus to produce higher-grade tallow. It had also won back a major customer for meat-and-bone meal which Croda had lost owing to quality problems. These improvements in product quality were of benefit to customers. (6.53)

23. The merger had brought about some reduction in competition for high-grade waste in the South-West and South-East but the effect was limited to the collectors (and potentially the producers) who supplied Croda. Moreover Croda had for some years not actively competed with PDM even for bones and fat. (6.54)

Effects on competitors and other parties

24. Renderers, abattoir trade associations and the MLC said that it was PDM's practice to pay lower prices in areas of weak competition. Its average prices were therefore lower than other renderers'. This put it in a strong position to undercut competitors in areas of strong competition, and other renderers were deterred by fear of its ability to retaliate against them. (6.55)

25. PDM said that its policy was not to acquire additional market share by competing on price but to try to maintain friendly relations with its competitors so that they might one day be ready to sell their businesses to PDM. It was, however, prepared to react vigorously if, as often happened, others tried to capture sources which it regarded as its own. (6.56)

26. PDM's prices varied widely for material carrying the same description. It was not possible to establish a clear picture as to regional variations, or the reasonableness of individual prices, or who instigated competitive bidding in any particular case. The lack of transparency in prices left scope for discriminatory behaviour. (6.57)

27. PDM firmly denied that it engaged in selectively undercutting competitors in the end-products market: because of its reputation for reliability and product quality its prices were always comparatively higher. (6.58)

28. Abattoir trade associations argued that abattoirs were hesitant about switching to another renderer for fear that they might soon be obliged to deal again with PDM from a position of weakness, having lost PDM's goodwill. They also argued that the merger was important because it put another rendering site, at Market Harborough, in PDM's hands in circumstances where the only likely route for market entry was via acquisition of an existing operation on a site already licensed whose equipment could be acquired at a fraction of the cost of a new plant. PDM's policy of acquisition, which usually led to plants being closed and removed from the industry, blocked entry by this route. (6.59 and 6.60)

29. Although the Market Harborough plant was well located its potential competitive value before the merger was limited because it was only licensed to process high-grade waste. It was difficult to assess the likelihood of Croda's Stratford site (see paragraph 10) being acquired for rendering, supposing PDM was unable to prevent that. (6.61)

30. The only likely market entrants appeared to be abattoirs and meat companies, possibly in conjunction with renderers other than PDM. There did not appear to be any overriding reasons to prevent abattoir companies from acquiring available rendering plants in competition with PDM. (6.62 and 6.63)

31. In negotiating prices, waste producers were in a position of strategic weakness which, however, like the other distortions in competition considered in paragraphs 24 to 30, was a consequence of the existing structure of the industry. The merger itself made but a small difference to this structural deficiency. (6.64)

PDM's costs and profitability

32. PDM accepted that its average transport costs were higher than other renderers', but argued that they were offset by lower processing costs due to specialization, and that some of its collection activity was uneconomic because of its policy of providing a full waste collection service to the meat industry. PDM's figures showed its collection and operating costs rising from £51 per tonne in 1985/86 to £60 in 1989/90, broadly in line with the general rate of inflation. PDM considered that it probably incurred comparatively higher operating costs as a result of the thorough and comprehensive nature of its operations at all stages of the business. (6.66 and 6.67)

33. The merger could be expected to improve PDM's efficiency in two ways. First, PDM now had two plants specialising in high- and low-grade waste in each of the North, Midlands and South of England. Secondly, PDM said that the Croda plant was the ideal size and nature to enable it to supply new markets which it had identified for high quality tallow and for a new high-protein meal which it could not supply from other plants. (6.68)

34. PDM had not used its dominance to make high profits in the last few years, though given the adverse trading conditions it would have had great difficulties in doing so. (6.69)

Other public interest issues

35. There would be adverse consequences for the environment and possibly for health as a result of waste being illegally dumped or put with general refuse if PDM's waste collection service were to deteriorate. MAFF drew attention to the essential role which PDM had played and was continuing

to play in more specific respects, while DoE expected PDM significantly to improve the environmental performance of the Croda plant. There was no doubt that PDM's resources, responsible attitude and commitment remained of great importance to the industry's future. The improvements in PDM's efficiency and the value of its end products may themselves be regarded as contributing to the public good. (6.72 to 6.76)

Conclusions

36. The merger had an adverse effect on competition in the collection of high-grade animal waste in the South-West and South-East of England (see paragraph 23 above), but Croda had been a declining competitive force and was likely to disappear altogether. Moreover there were no adverse effects on purchasers of end products. (6.77)

37. The merger brought a modest enhancement of PDM's market position in England and Wales, strengthening further its market power in relation to other renderers, and weakening the prospects of new entrants to the market. (6.78)

38. These adverse movements in the competitive position were marginal in relation to the pre-existing structural defects in competition within the industry, which had developed over many years (see paragraph 31 above). (6.79)

39. The merger was likely to improve PDM's efficiency, and to lead to some wider public health and environmental benefits (see paragraphs 33 and 35 above). (6.80)

40. Taking into account the limited adverse effects on competition on the one hand, and the important public issues of health and the environment as well as efficiency gains on the other hand, the merger did not and might be expected not to operate against the public interest. (6.81)

General observations

41. Having made this finding the MMC had no authority to make recommendations. It was, however, a fragile situation that England and Wales should be so dependent on one private company for such an important service as the collection and rendering of animal waste. Exceptionally, therefore, three suggestions were made (paragraphs 42 to 44 below), although it was recognized that their adoption would be purely on a voluntary basis. (6.82)

42. A different kind of inquiry might be necessary to address the various questions relating to public health and the environment which the relevant Government departments currently had under consideration. (6.83)

43. It would be advantageous if, in the case of any future proposed acquisition by PDM of businesses engaged in the collection or rendering of animal waste, notification of PDM's intentions were given to the OFT rather longer than, as currently required, one month prior—possibly three months. (6.84)

44. A group of companies playing such a crucial role as PDM in an important market should arrange its financial affairs in such a way that its published accounts were sufficiently transparent and complete to give a full picture of its trading fortunes. (6.85)

APPENDIX 4.3
(referred to in paragraphs 4.48 and 10.70)

PDM's acquisitions, 1986 to 1992

This appendix summarizes a schedule of PDM's acquisitions from 1986 to 1992 provided to us by PDM. Details are included of the approximate weekly tonnage acquired, and the related goodwill recorded in PDM's accounts, in the case of each of 12 small acquisitions of goodwill which was not pre-notified to the DGFT in compliance with undertaking 3 of 1986. The total value of those 12 acquisitions was £168,250, and the approximate total weekly tonnage acquired was 182 tonnes.

Date of acquisition	*Business acquired*
8.9.86	Collection and pet food businesses of MCP and factory at Stoke Bardolph, near Nottingham
20.2.87	Collection business of Stoke Mandeville Animal Products Ltd
14.12.87	Rendering business of Norfolk Fat and Bone Company Ltd
30.11.90	Collection business of Ashworths Products Ltd
3.12.90	Fat refining and dripping manufacturing business of Craven Calvert Ltd
7.1.91	Rendering business of Croda International plc
8.9.86	Raw material collection round of approximately *5 tonnes per week* from P G Dakin, 79 Woodland Avenue, Hove, East Sussex *Purchased goodwill: £4,000*
Nov '87	Raw material collection business of approximately *45 tonnes per week* of Delaney of Watton (Animal By Products)), The Airfield, North Pickenham, Swaffam, Norfolk *Purchased goodwill: £50,000*
7.10.88	Raw material collection round of approximately *12 tonnes per week* of M Lister and Sons, 270 Pettits Lane, North Romford, Essex *Purchased goodwill: £14,000*
18.7.89 & 18.8.89	Goodwill payment of £40,000 to Ashworth Products Ltd to ensure that all raw materials collected by the latter were delivered exclusively to PDM companies
Aug '89	Raw material collection round of approximately *10 tonnes per week* from P Tappenden, Plaistow, East London *Purchased goodwill: £10,000*
Feb '90	Raw material collection round of approximately *15 tonnes per week* in York area from Northern Butchers (Yorkshire) Ltd, Pontefract Lane, Leeds *Purchased goodwill: £16,000*
1990/91	Fat and bone collection rounds of J P Redfearn and Sons Ltd
	Fat and bone collection business of approximately *7 tonnes per week* from J Gibbs, 1 Redwood, Thorpe, Surrey *Purchased goodwill: £5,000*
	Fat and bone collection business of approximately *20 tonnes per week* from M Evans, Mandalay, Milton Park, Stroud Road, Egham, Surrey *Purchased goodwill: £20,250*
	Fat and bone collection business of approximately *12 tonnes per week* from P Say, 411 Stroud Road, Gloucester *Purchased goodwill: £10,000*
	Fat and bone collection business of approximately *10 tonnes per week* from N Dewey, 8 Bracken Drive, The Highlands, Rugby, Warwickshire *Purchased goodwill: £12,000*

Fat and bone collection business of approximately *15 tonnes per week* from P Davis, Rose Cottage, Bridgend, Aveton Gifford, Nr Kingsbridge, Devon
Purchased goodwill: £5,000

Goodwill of Sheppy (Wilton) Ltd of approximately *25 tonnes per week* purchased from Grays Waste Services Ltd, 8 Barbers Road, Stratford, London
Purchased goodwill: £20,000

Fat and bone collection business of approximately *6 tonnes per week* from C Scammell, Lancashire ABP, 26 Moor Way, Poulton le Fylde
Purchased goodwill: £2,000

Source: PDM.

Forrest group structure

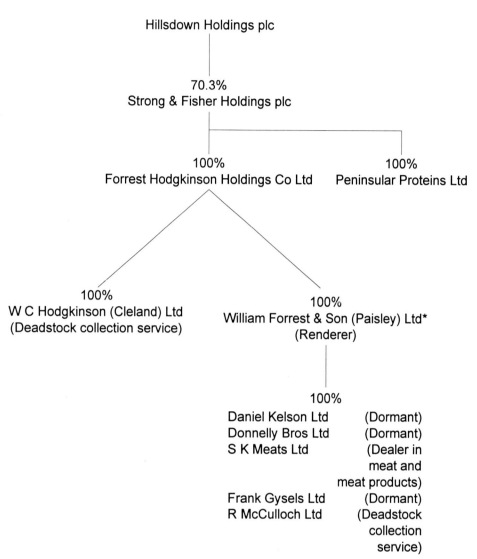

Source: Forrest.

*Forrest also has an 80 per cent holding in John Moran Ltd (Natural Sausage Casings).

APPENDIX 6.1
(referred to in paragraphs 6.5, 6.9, 6.11, 10.54, 10.55(a), 10.56
and paragraph 6 of Appendix 6.3)

Analysis of PDM's prices

The data set

1. We asked PDM for its quantities of best fat, bones, SBO and other offal collected from abattoirs (and some boning out plants belonging to the same group of companies) during the months of May and October 1992, together with the amounts paid or charged for these materials. Depending on the type of material this accounted for between approximately 49 and 75 per cent of PDM's total supplies of this material. We used this data to calculate prices or charges per tonne for each of the 185 and 188 suppliers respectively. The resulting ranges of prices or charges were very large indeed. (Hereafter, we refer to 'prices' only, but 'prices' should be taken to include 'charges'. In particular, a 'price' with a minus sign indicates a charge.)

2. For each material, we asked PDM for an explanation of the ten highest and ten lowest prices. We also gave it graphs showing every price per tonne plotted against tonnage collected. PDM's comments on the graphs and the top and bottom ten prices made it clear that there was a number of special cases which should be ignored. We accepted its arguments. We also removed many small suppliers at the lower end of the price ranges. This affected best fat and other offal in particular. 'Small suppliers' are defined as those supplying less than 10 tonnes per month.

3. Even after making these allowances the resulting ranges of prices or charges were still very wide, the smallest being £35 per tonne (bone May 1992) and the largest £140 per tonne (best fat October 1992). The full ranges are set out in Table 1. PDM also said that during these months the most intensive price war known to the industry was taking place, and that this had had a significant effect on prices charged. The line 'Other offal [1]' includes all small suppliers at the bottom of the range. 'Other offal [2]' shows the effect of removing them.

TABLE 1 **Initial ranges of raw material prices found in PDM data**

£ per tonne

	May 1992			October 1992		
	From	*To*	*Range*	*From*	*To*	*Range*
Best fat	0	132	132	0	140	140
Bones	0	35	35	-5	39	44
SBO	-110	0	110	-91	0	91
Other offal [1]	-110	15	125	-110	21	131
Other offal [2]	-87	15	102	-87	21	98

Source: MMC from PDM data.

4. PDM countered that the principal reason for the variation of prices was quality of the material and the resulting effects on the values of the end products derived from them. It gave us a lengthy list of the reasons why quality varied (see Appendix 8.2) and information on the difficulty of assessing quality and yields, and gave us several examples of prices which had been significantly affected by quality considerations. Variations in the quality of a material produced a wide variation in its yield of end products. Prices negotiated with individual abattoirs took these factors into account, along with experienced managers' judgment of quality: quality could only be assessed exactly by testing a sample. In particular, the 'best fat' category in Table 1 included material processed into edible fat. If this were eliminated, the highest prices paid for best fat for tallow production were £105 and £123 in May and October 1992 respectively. However, prices paid for raw material were never solely due to variations in yield.

Costs of collection and transport

5. We also asked PDM whether any of the observed differences in prices or charges were related to the cost of collection, for example in terms of the tonnage collected or the distance travelled. It replied that paradoxically distance may sometimes have the reverse of the effect which one would expect. For example, it estimated that it was £10 more expensive to collect 26 tonnes of raw material from a succession of small butchers' shops within 20 miles of one of its plants than to collect the same tonnage in one load from a large abattoir involving a motorway journey of 100 miles.

6. Prices also varied with the number of times that material had to be handled, but PDM said that this had a significant effect on no more than 3 per cent of the tonnage collected, all of which was for supplies of SBO and other offal. In any case it did not calculate the cost of collecting individual loads. Any necessary differences in prices were based on the assessments of experienced managers. However, PDM carried out special calculations for us of the cost of collecting small loads of material by means of a lorry visiting a succession of butchers' shops and that of collecting other material. The results are given in paragraph 3.19. PDM stated that part loads from small abattoirs were also collected by the same lorries that served butchers' shops.

7. We allowed for the additional collection costs from small abattoirs by simply omitting them from the data unless they belonged to a group of abattoirs or had their offal charges offset against payments for other materials (paragraph 18 below).

Quality of material

8. In response to further questions PDM produced the following Tables 2, 3 and 4, to illustrate variations in the ranges of combined yields of finished products which could be obtained from selected generally described raw materials when processed in each class of its plants. The tables also show the ranges of maximum gross saleable value of the materials based on finished product prices for January 1992. We also noted in Table 2 that for edible beef fat the theoretical value range was £93.40 per tonne (£291.60 minus £198.20). However, the ranges of prices actually paid for such materials by PDM in May and October 1992 were only £44 and £46 respectively. PDM stated that this was because fats purchased for edible production were carefully selected and were of the higher-yielding types. Since the processing of edible fat is not within the scope of our inquiry, we eliminated all edible fat from the data. Clearly, however, PDM's theoretical gross value ranges for edible fat were very poor guides to the actual ranges of prices charged in the months in question. PDM was unable to estimate for us the range of yields actually obtained from other materials in May and October 1992, since such figures were not normally collected because of the physical impracticability of so doing. However, PDM said that one of the features of its integrated and specialized rendering systems was that it was able to produce finished products with enhanced quality and therefore value compared with its competitors.

9. On the basis of this information we calculated a range of yields of meat-and-bone meal and tallow which would be implied by the ranges of prices actually paid by PDM in May and October 1992 and showed that if variations in prices were to be explained entirely by yield, a number of theoretical yields would result which were outside the ranges quoted in Tables 2 to 4. PDM then explained that the yield ranges given in these tables were not the maximum possible ranges of yield by weight, but those which gave the maximum range of gross saleable value in January 1992. PDM added that there were other combinations of meal and tallow yields for each raw material type which would give gross sales values within the maximum and minimum values cited. It also pointed out that within each raw material category there would be individual yields of either meat-and-bone meal or tallow which were outside the percentage yields quoted, but that any achievable yield combination within the maxima and minima shown in the tables would yield a sales value equivalent somewhere between the lowest and smallest sterling values quoted.

TABLE 2 **Best fat**

Edible plant

	Edible beef fat		Fat greaves		Total	
	Yield %	Value £	Yield %	Value £	Yield %	Value £
From	50.00	175.00	10.00	23.20	60.00	198.20
To	80.00	280.00	5.00	11.60	85.00	291.60

Finished product prices (£/tonne)

Edible beef fat	350.00
Edible greaves	232.00

High-grade plant

	Grade 2 tallow		Meat-and-bone meal		Total	
	Yield %	Value £	Yield %	Value £	Yield %	Value £
From	50.00	105.00	10.00	12.50	60.00	117.50
To	80.00	168.00	5.00	6.25	85.00	174.25

Finished product prices (£/tonne)

Grade 2 tallow	210.00
Meat-and-bone meal	125.00

Low-grade plant

	Grade 6 tallow		Meat-and-bone meal		Total	
	Yield %	Value £	Yield %	Value £	Yield %	Value £
From	50.00	74.50	10.00	12.50	60.00	87.00
To	80.00	119.20	5.00	6.25	85.00	125.45

Finished product prices (£/tonne)

Grade 6 tallow	149.00
Meat-and-bone meal	125.00

	£/tonne
Maximum gross value	291.60
Minimum gross value	87.00
Gross value spread	204.60

Source: PDM.

TABLE 3 **Bone**

High-grade plant

	Grade 2 tallow		Meat-and-bone meal		Total	
	Yield %	Value £	Yield %	Value £	Yield %	Value £
From	2.50	5.25	38.00	47.50	40.50	52.75
To	16.00	33.60	46.00	57.50	62.00	91.10

Finished product prices (£/tonne)

Grade 2 tallow	210.00
Meat-and-bone meal	125.00

Low-grade plant

	Grade 6 tallow		Meat-and-bone meal		Total	
	Yield %	Value £	Yield %	Value £	Yield %	Value £
From	2.50	3.73	38.00	47.50	40.50	51.23
To	16.00	23.84	46.00	57.50	62.00	81.34

Finished product prices (£/tonne)

Grade 6 tallow	149.00
Meat-and-bone meal	125.00

	£/tonne
Maximum gross value	91.10
Minimum gross value	51.23
Gross value spread	39.88

Source: PDM.

TABLE 4 **SBO and offal**

SBO

Low-grade plant

	Grade 6 tallow		Meat-and-bone meal		Total	
	Yield %	Value £	Yield %	Value £	Yield %	Value £
From	0.00	0.00	0.00	0.00	0.00	0.00
To	50.00	74.50	0.00	0.00	50.00	74.50

Finished product prices (£/tonne)

Grade 6 tallow	149.00
Meat-and-bone meal	0.00

	£/tonne
Maximum gross value	74.50
Minimum gross value	0.00
Gross value spread	74.50

Offal

Low-grade plant

	Grade 6 tallow		Meat-and-bone meal		Total	
	Yield %	Value £	Yield %	Value £	Yield %	Value £
From	5.00	7.45	17.00	21.25	22.00	28.70
To	14.00	20.86	36.00	45.00	50.00	65.86

Finished product prices (£/tonne)

Grade 6 tallow	149.00
Meat-and-bone meal	125.00

	£/tonne
Maximum gross value	65.86
Minimum gross value	28.70
Gross value spread	37.16

Source: PDM.

Note: Yields in Tables 2 to 4 are from materials as removed from the animal. PDM said that on average there was 5 per cent water contamination in this material.

Effects of fluctuations of prices of PDM's output

10. PDM also told us that prices of raw materials varied over time with the prices of the end products which they yielded. These prices were set by international commodity markets. However, larger abattoirs, particularly those belonging to groups, objected to price reductions for materials such as best fat, if the price of tallow declined on the international market. This meant that there was an appreciable time-lag before material prices were fully adjusted. Smaller abattoirs accepted price changes more readily. Therefore if one examined prices paid by PDM at any particular point in time, some abattoirs would be receiving the 'new', say, lower prices and others the 'old' or higher prices. There was no steady state.

11. We assessed the effect of this factor on prices for best fat in May 1992. These could reasonably be assumed to have declined by no more than £10 per tonne following the drop in tallow prices of about £10 per tonne between April and May 1992. We examined the abattoirs in the top £10 price band at that time and found that they did not consist entirely of large ones (defined as those supplying over 100 tonnes collected). Therefore none of the price bands could be eliminated by reason of this factor alone. In any case, prices in the top band of best fat of Table 1 would already be eliminated by omitting edible fat (see paragraph 8). For other raw materials any price lag effect can be assumed to be so small as to be negligible. PDM said that in any event, any possibility of reducing raw material prices to account for lower tallow values was negated by the effect of the 'price war'.

Effects of the 1992 'price war'

12. PDM put forward a number of other reasons for variations in prices or charges. The first was that from March to October 1992, which included the months for which we had sought detailed price information, a price war had been in progress. During this period it had found that competitors were offering 'unrealistically' higher prices to some of the large abattoirs normally serviced by PDM to win supplies of material needed to make up for supplies which they themselves had lost. PDM said that it had had to retaliate because it could not afford to lose, for example, 400 tonnes of material a week. Moreover it had, during this period, offered prices for some materials to win them away from a competing renderer. It added that rendering materials had been in particularly short supply in the spring of 1992, but that conditions for a renewal of a price war could easily recur in a future year.

1993 data

13. To help us compare prices between price-war and other periods, we asked PDM for the pricing data held in its computer for April 1993. These are the prices which would be applied to any transaction with the particular companies named therein. They are not necessarily prices actually charged in that month. However, they are the only data readily available for use. The resulting frequency distributions are given in Figures 1 to 4. It will be seen that the ranges of prices do not differ significantly from those shown in Table 1.

14. PDM commented that the data upon which Figures 1 to 4 were based were misleading because they did not include tonnages purchased in each price range. Moreover, even though the price war ended in November 1992, inevitably some residual price distortion remained. In particular, the average level of raw finished product prices increased significantly following the end of the price war. It would be simplistic, therefore, to conclude that because ranges of prices appeared similar between April 1993 and October 1992, this meant that the distorting effects on prices of the price war were less than had been thought.

Contracts covering several abattoirs

15. Secondly, PDM negotiated prices centrally for 14 groups which owned 80 abattoirs between them. In these cases a single price or charge was agreed for all abattoirs in the group for each type of raw material irrespective of the particular location, distance travelled or quantity collected. Abattoir groups preferred the simplicity of such a contract. We also noted that, within PDM's top ten suppliers of best fat (excluding edible) in May and October 1992, the highest price paid to a supplier belonging to a group exceeded the highest paid to a single independent supplier by £17 and £19 per tonne respectively.

16. For some group contracts prices were linked by a formula to the prices of end products. Prices would not, therefore, vary with the tonnage collected in a particular month.

Size of abattoir

17. Thirdly, some prices or charges were set in relation to the size of abattoir rather than to the quantities of particular material picked up on any particular occasion. Clearly, large abattoirs were more desirable to all renderers because they generally provided a steady, large source of supply in whole trailer loads, which were cheaper to collect.

Package deals

18. Finally PDM concluded deals at the request of an abattoir whereby for all materials taken together there was a net nil charge over the course of, say, a month. For some abattoirs this was much more convenient than to have to invoice PDM for certain materials and to pay PDM's invoices for others. For example, this would account for all the zero prices for best fat in May and October 1992. In other cases, at the supplier's request, a nil charge was made for offal and a reduced price was paid for other material.

FIGURE 1

Frequency of prices paid for best fat, April 1993

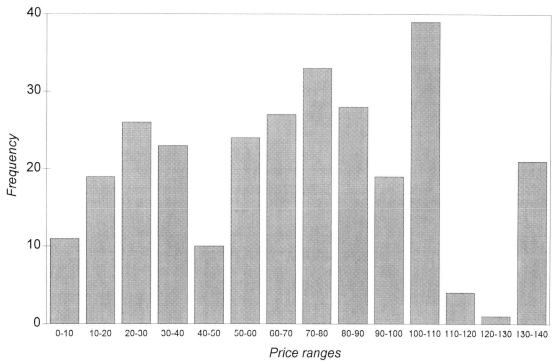

Source: MMC from PDM data.

FIGURE 2

Frequency of prices paid for bone, April 1993

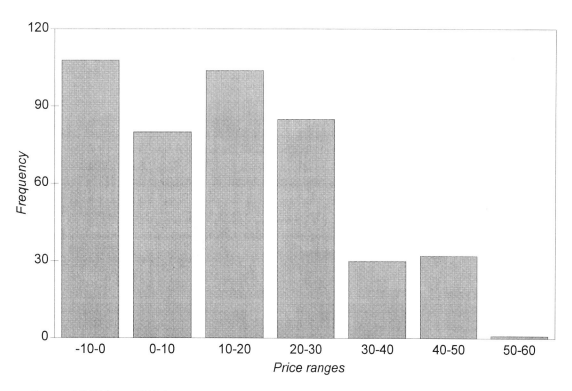

Source: MMC from PDM data.

Note: In the range -£10 to 0, three suppliers are charged -£10. The other 105 are charged/paid 0.

TABLE 5 **Estimated ranges about PDM's target prices as a function of the ranges of yields in Tables 2 to 4**

£ per tonne

	High-grade plant				Low-grade plant			
May 1992	Min	Max	Range	Target	Min	Max	Range	Target
Best fat	33	88	55	71	16	60	44	-
Bone	-24	16	40	10	-25	10	35	10
SBO	-	-	-	-	-106	-19	87	-64
Other offal	-	-	-	-	-57	-13	44	-40
October 1992	Min	Max	Range	Target	Min	Max	Range	Target
Best fat	51	115	64	94	21	67	46	-
Bone	-20	23	44	15	-22	14	36	15
SBO	-	-	-	-	-103	-14	89	-61
Other offal	-	-	-	-	-54	-10	44	-36

Source: MMC from PDM data.

23. If we compare the ranges in Figures 5 to 16 with the ranges of target prices in Table 5, we observe that in May 1992 the top price actually paid for best fat for low-grade production, £86 per tonne (Figure 6), was £26 a tonne higher than the theoretical maximum target price and that most of the medium and large quantities of best fat processed in these plants was above this maximum. A similar pattern is shown in Figure 12. It is difficult to accept that superior quality was the justification. Indeed, PDM said that, because of the price war, prices did not reflect as much as would normally be the case the full ranges of yields. It added that prices paid had never directly equated to the theoretical yields.

24. Similarly for bone in May 1992, the target price for all supplies was £10 per tonne, whilst the bulk of the tonnage in the figures was in the £20 to £30 price range, compared with the theoretical maximum target prices of £16 for high- and £10 for low-grade plant. There was also substantial tonnage in the £30 to £40 price range for both high- and low-grade plant. Quality does not appear to be a determinant of price in this case either.

25. In the case of SBO and other offal in May and October 1992, and of best fat in October, many prices are well outside the theoretical ranges of target prices (and in fact the ranges of actual prices paid exceed the theoretical ranges by from £14 to £70 per tonne, although at the extremes only small tonnages are involved). However, most of the tonnage of SBO in both months was priced at zero, ie well above the maximum target prices of -£19 in May 1992 and -£14 in October.

26. PDM said that the widest variations between actual prices and average target prices were on SBO and other offal. These were due to the following factors:

— the larger abattoirs with higher volumes achieved lower charges;

— these abattoirs significantly increased their slaughterings in October compared with May, and also compared with smaller abattoirs, so that the increased volume at the lower charges had the dual effect of increasing skewness (to the right) and bringing down the actual median and mean charges for low-grade materials;

— these larger suppliers were the ones particularly attractive to PDM's competitors; and

— the data under review referred to purchases made during an intense price war (see paragraph 12) when ordinary commercial considerations became of secondary importance to retention of business.

PDM said that it was therefore its contention that to carry out such a wide-ranging and detailed statistical exercise in an attempt to achieve an understanding of the complex issue of pricing in the animal waste industry was singularly inappropriate, when the raw data referred to a period when the whole market was wildly distorted and abnormal market conditions prevailed.

FIGURE 5

Tonnes of best fat processed by PDM high-grade plants, May 1992

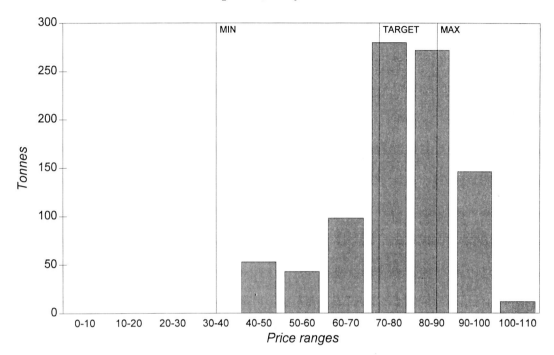

Source: MMC from PDM data.

Note: Medium and large quantities.

FIGURE 6

Tonnes of best fat processed by PDM low-grade plants, May 1992

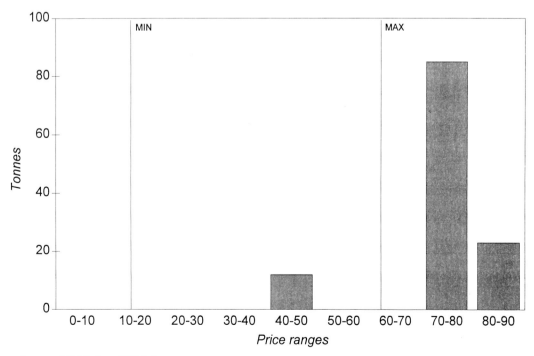

Source: MMC from PDM data.

Note: Medium and large quantities.

236197 M2

FIGURE 7

**Tonnes of bone processed by PDM high-grade plants,
May 1992**

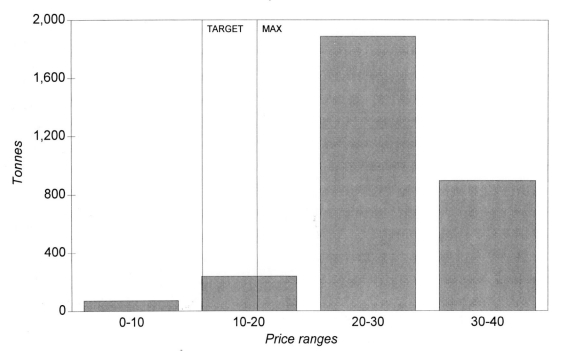

Source: MMC from PDM data.

Note: Medium and large quantities. Minimum = -£24 per tonne.

FIGURE 8

**Tonnes of bone processed by PDM low-grade plants,
May 1992**

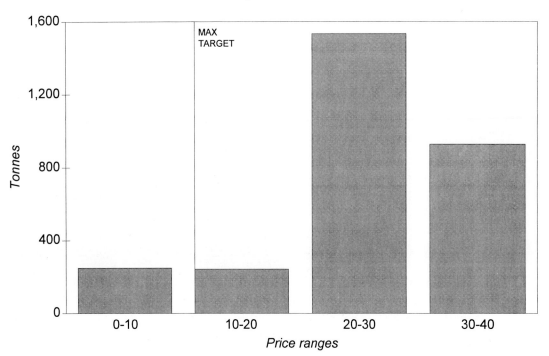

Source: MMC from PDM data.

Note: Medium and large quantities. Minimum = -£25 per tonne.

FIGURE 9

Tonnes of SBO supplied by abattoirs in each price range to PDM plants, May 1992

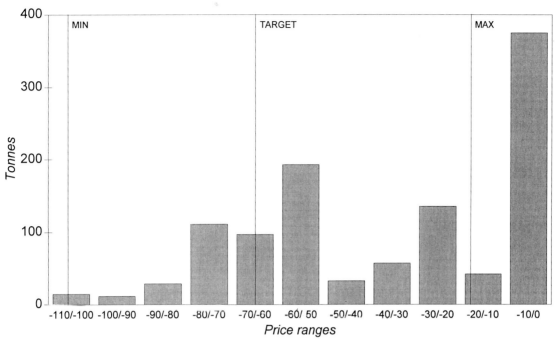

Source: MMC from PDM data.

Note: Medium and large quantities.

FIGURE 10

Tonnes of other offal supplied by abattoirs in each price range to PDM plants, May 1992

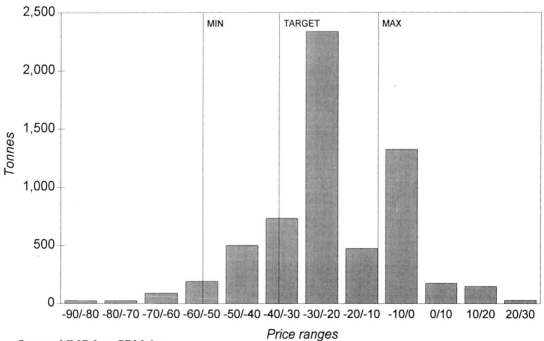

Source: MMC from PDM data.

Note: Medium and large quantities.

FIGURE 11

Tonnes of best fat processed by PDM high-grade plants, October 1992

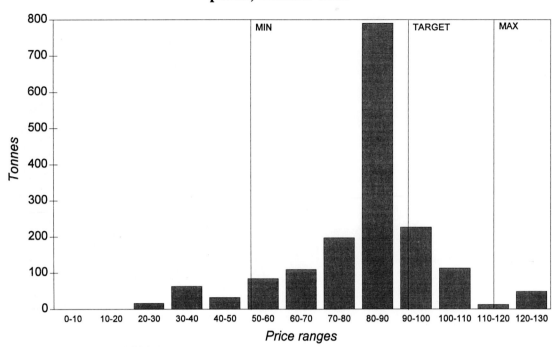

Source: MMC from PDM data.

Note: Medium and large quantities.

FIGURE 12

Tonnes of best fat processed by PDM low-grade plants, October 1992

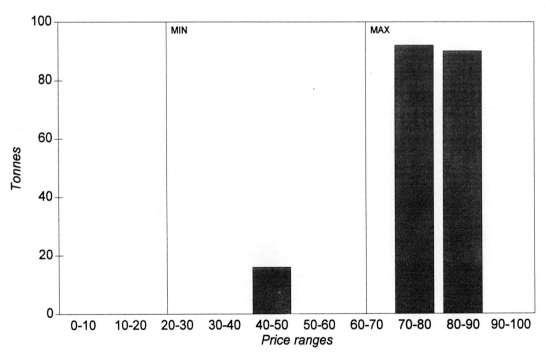

Source: MMC from PDM data.

Note: Medium and large quantities.

FIGURE 13

**Tonnes of bone processed by PDM high-grade plants,
October 1992**

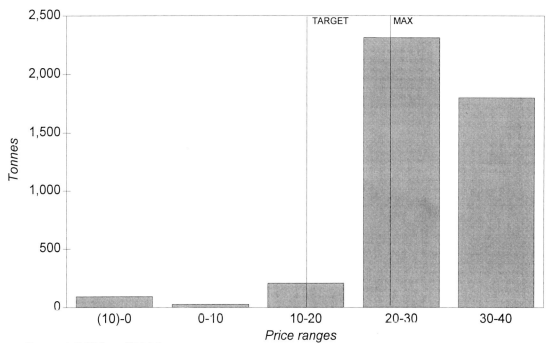

Source: MMC from PDM data.

Note: Medium and large quantities. Minimum = -£20 per tonne.

FIGURE 14

**Tonnes of bone processed by PDM low-grade plants,
October 1992**

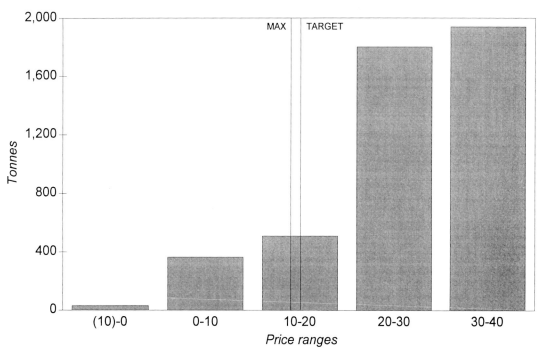

Source: MMC from PDM data.

Note: Medium and large quantities. Minimum = -£22 per tonne.

FIGURE 15

Tonnes of SBO supplied by abattoirs in each price range to PDM plants, October 1992

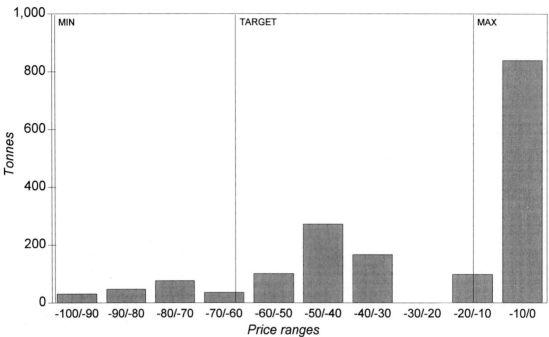

Source: MMC from PDM data.

Note: Medium and large quantities.

FIGURE 16

Tonnes of other offal supplied by abattoirs in each price range to PDM plants, October 1992

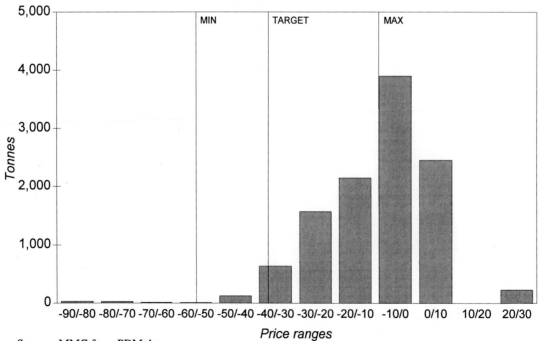

Source: MMC from PDM data.

Note: Medium and large quantities.

27. Table 6 shows, for high- and low-grade plants taken together, the medians of actual prices (medium and large quantities) and the modal price ranges. These are defined respectively as the price above and below which half the tonnage lies and the price range which includes the most tonnage. At the request of PDM, the mean prices were also included.

TABLE 6 **Actual prices (medium and large quantities), 1992**

All plant £ per tonne

| | Median price | | Mean price | | Modal price range | |
	May	Oct	May	Oct	May	Oct
Best fat	80	85	76	75	80–90	80–90
Bone	26	29	18	21	20–30	20–30
SBO	-25	0	-47	-42	-10–0	-10–0
Other offal	-24	-5	-28	-16	-30– -20	-10–0

Source: MMC from PDM data.

We noted that except for best fat in October 1992, all the median prices exceeded the target prices by handsome margins. PDM commented that, if all small quantities had been included, certain median prices would have been very different, eg the median price for SBO in May 1992 would have been -£50 per tonne and in October -£10 per tonne, as would have been the median price for other offal in that month. As explained in paragraphs 6 and 7 above, we omitted most small quantities collected since their low prices could be thought to be justified by higher than average collection costs. PDM claimed that our definition of small quantities (see paragraph 22 above) was inaccurate and misleading when applied to a supply point since a single supplier could be a 'large' supplier of other offal and a 'small' supplier of SBO, for example. On the other hand, we believed that it was better to make a greater allowance than necessary for small supplies than possibly to underestimate the effect of differential transport costs.

Price ranges by processing plant

28. PDM also gave us distributions of tonnages and prices for all best fat and bone in May and October 1992 separated between high- and low-grade processing plants. The ranges of prices paid are set out in Table 7 (excluding zero prices for best fat since these are the result of package deals).

TABLE 7 **Ranges of prices paid by processing plant**

£ per tonne

| | May 1992 | | October 1992 | |
	From	To	From	To
Best fat				
High-grade plant	45	105	24	123
Low-grade plant	40	86	40	95
Bone				
High-grade plant	0	35	0	39
Low-grade plant	0	35	0	35

Source: MMC from PDM data.

29. PDM stated that prices paid for raw material depended in large part on the value of the end products which was achieved by processing different grades of material in separate plants. There is some evidence from Table 7 that this is so in the case of best fat, although in October 1992 the lowest price for best fat processed in high-grade plants was £16 per tonne less than the lowest price for low-grade plants. However, for low-grade plants, the top prices well exceeded the maxima of the price ranges quoted in Table 5, corresponding to the maximum yields of Tables 2 and 3. Moreover there

appear to be no significant differences between high- and low-grade plants in the ranges of prices paid for bone. It is difficult to account for the differences therefore by any supposed higher quality and value of the high-grade material.

Imputed yields

30. We have noted above that PDM has no records of the yields which it obtains from raw materials supplied by particular abattoirs. So there exist no ranges of actual yields which could be compared with the theoretical yields in Tables 2 to 4. We therefore undertook the calculation of what yields would be implied by each of the prices paid for raw materials if all the price variation in the data had been due directly to variation in yields. This may appear to be a process of estimation which is worlds away from the practical business of rendering, but the calculations are based entirely on data given to us by PDM (again excluding suppliers of small quantities of material not belonging to groups of abattoirs and suppliers of edible fat).

31. Any price paid will, if it actually accords with PDM's system of calculating average target prices, imply a total yield. As an example, from Table 5 and Table 3, the price for bone of £16 in May 1992 implies, for a high-grade plant, a yield of 46 per cent of meat-and-bone meal if the yield of grade 2 tallow is 16 per cent, ie a total yield of 62 per cent. SBO is a material which yields only one end product and so a single price implies a single yield. However, where there is more than one end product a single raw material price will imply more than one total yield depending on the feasible combination of yields of individual products within the total.

32. We first of all added back the energy costs which we had subtracted from the maximum and minimum prices in Table 5. We then plotted points for the new maximum and minimum cost prices against their respective total yields taken from Tables 2, 3 and 4. We also plotted PDM's target prices against their respective average expected yields. The results are shown as the 'target' lines in Figures 17 to 28.

33. We then computed for total yield points at 2.5 per cent intervals maximum and minimum price values corresponding to the maximum and minimum possible yields of each finished product within the total yield. Limits on these yields are set by the maximum and minimum yields given in Table 8. It should be noted that the yields of tallow and meat-and-bone meal are not additive. For example, the maximum *total* yield of best fat is not (85 + 15) = 100 per cent. 90 per cent would be a more likely figure.

TABLE 8 **Estimated ranges of percentage yields of raw materials by weight**

	Tallow		Meat-and-bone meal	
	Min	Max	Min	Max
Best fat	50	85	5	15
Bone	2.5	16	35	55
SBO	0	50	-	-
Other offal	5	20	12	45

Source: MMC from PDM data.

34. For example, if we choose the 50.5 per cent total yield point for bone in May 1992, processed in a high-grade plant, the minimum yield of grade 2 tallow is 2.5 per cent and therefore the yield of meat-and-bone meal is (50.5-2.5) = 48 per cent. At the other extreme, the minimum yield of meat-and-bone meal is 35 per cent and the yield of tallow is (50.5-35) = 15.5 per cent. The corresponding prices are -£2.8 and £4.9 per tonne.

35. It is then possible to read off the Y-axis (price) of each figure the corresponding range of yields. Thus for best fat in May 1992, high-grade plant, £60 per tonne can be achieved by total yields between 69 and 73 per cent. SBO material yields only one end product—tallow—and so no ranges of yields need be computed. Thus for SBO in May 1992 each price has one corresponding yield, eg a price of -£30 corresponds approximately to a total yield of 40 per cent.

FIGURE 17

Price v total yield, high-grade plant, best fat, May 1992

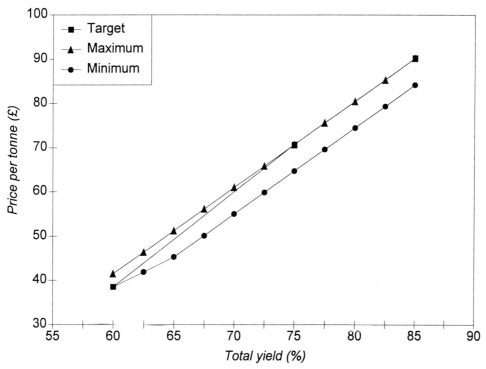

Source: MMC from PDM data.

FIGURE 18

Price v total yield, low-grade plant, best fat, May 1992

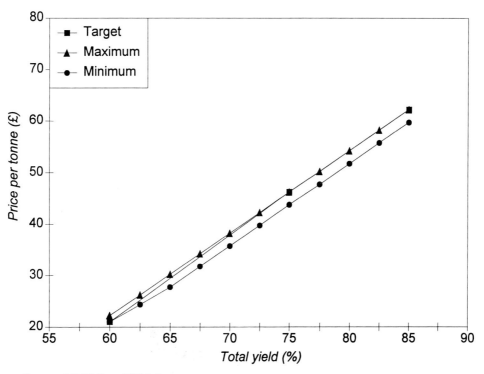

Source: MMC from PDM data.

FIGURE 19

Price v total yield, high-grade plant, bone, May 1992

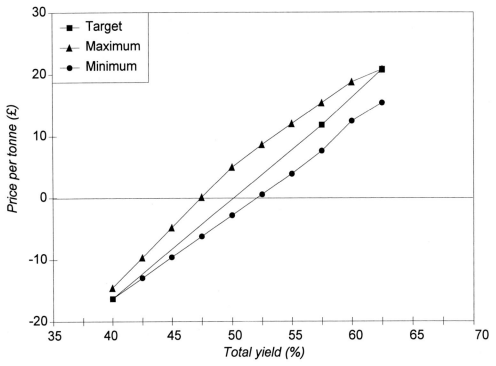

Source: MMC from PDM data.

FIGURE 20

Price v total yield, low-grade plant, bone, May 1992

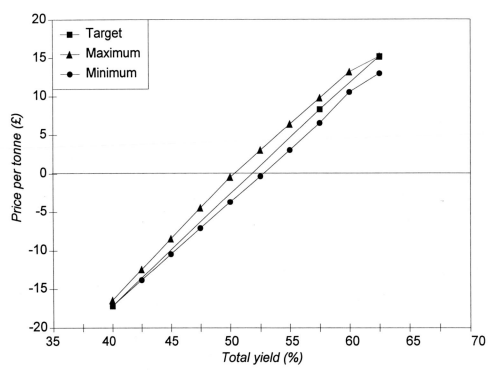

Source: MMC from PDM data.

FIGURE 21

Price v total yield, low-grade plant, SBO, May 1992

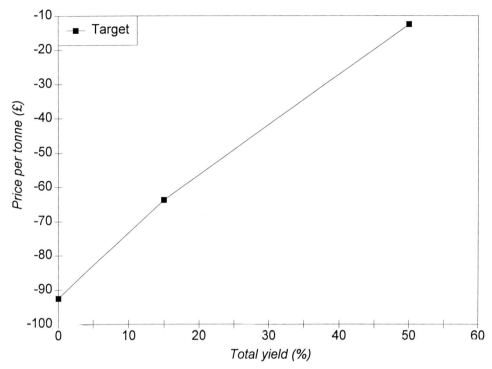

Source: MMC from PDM data.

FIGURE 22

Price v total yield, low-grade plant, other offal, May 1992

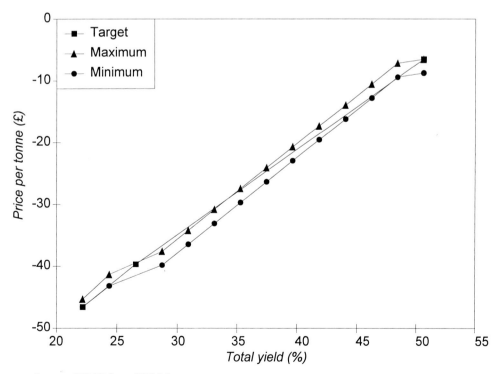

Source: MMC from PDM data.

FIGURE 23

Price v total yield, high-grade plant, best fat,
October 1992

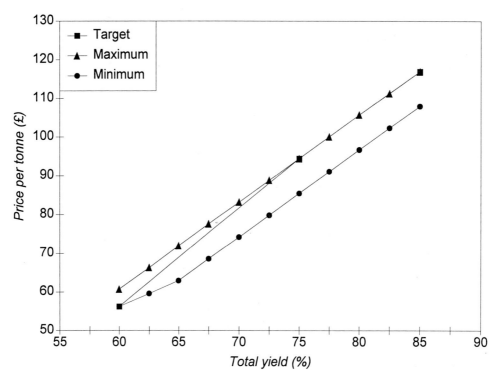

Source: MMC from PDM data.

FIGURE 24

Price v total yield, low-grade plant, best fat,
October 1992

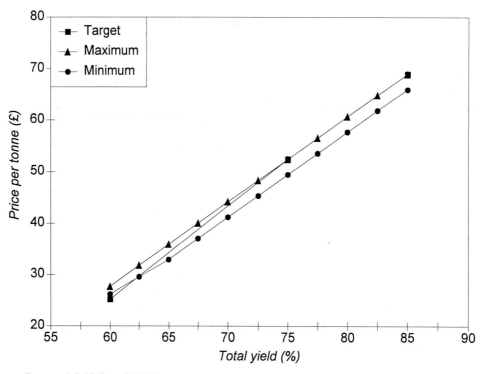

Source: MMC from PDM data.

FIGURE 25

Price v total yield, high-grade plant, bone, October 1992

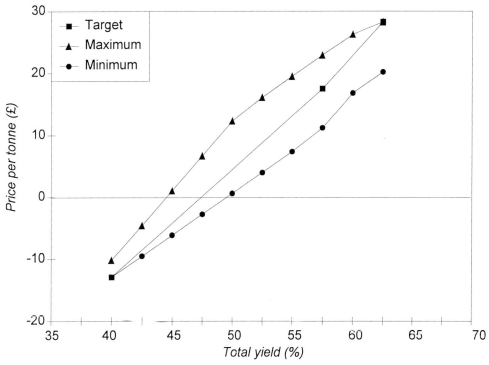

Source: MMC from PDM data.

FIGURE 26

Price v total yield, low-grade plant, bone, October 1992

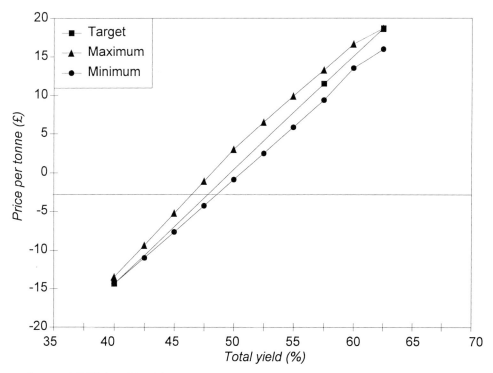

Source: MMC from PDM data.

FIGURE 27

Price v total yield, low-grade plant, SBO, October 1992

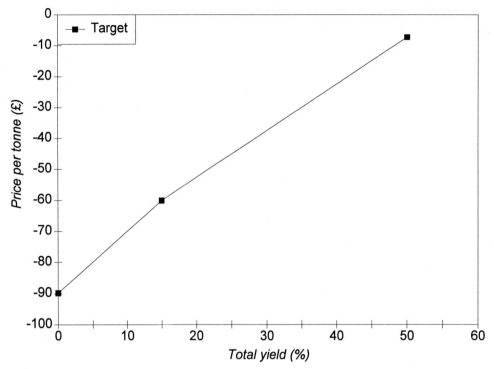

Source: MMC from PDM data.

FIGURE 28

**Price v total yield, low-grade plant, other offal, October
1992**

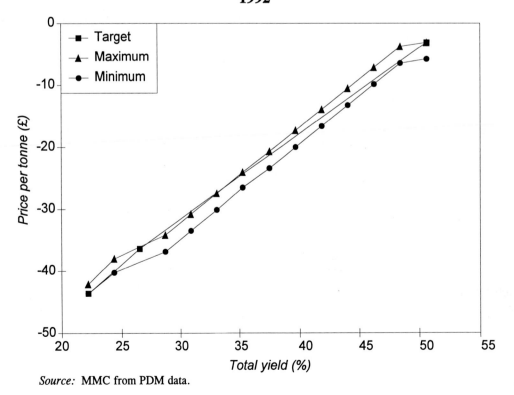

Source: MMC from PDM data.

36. Since the yield ranges calculated in this way for materials other than SBO are relatively small (in the range 2.5 to 7 percentage points), only a relatively small error is involved if we replace the £10 per tonne value ranges of Figures 5 to 16 with the corresponding total yield values from Figures 17 to 28. The results are plotted in Figures 29 to 40. Where the prices actually paid by PDM exceed the maxima or are less than the minima of Table 5, they cannot be explained by variations in yield. Outside these limits, therefore, tonnages are denoted as 'outside feasible range.'

37. It will be seen that each of Figures 29 to 40 contains tonnages outside the feasible range, chiefly above the upper limits of the ranges. This is particularly noticeable in the cases of best fat processed by low-grade plants, bone and SBO in both months; and of other offal in October only. The implication is that in these cases PDM is paying more for the material than could be justified on the basis of yield alone. PDM's comments at paragraph 26 above are noted. It added that it had never maintained that prices could be entirely linked to yield variations.

Summary

38. We compared prices paid by PDM for medium and large quantities of raw materials in May and October 1992 with the maximum and minimum theoretical target prices which would have been justified by the range of yields which gave rise to them. We found that there was a pattern in that prices actually paid tended to be above those that could have been explained by yield alone. Very large tonnages of bone and SBO, and of best fat processed by low-grade plants fell into this category.

39. We then approached the comparisons in a different way by calculating the theoretical total yields implied by the prices actually paid. We showed by this means too that, for the same raw materials as in paragraph 38 above, very large proportions of tonnages and in some cases the majority of tonnages fell outside the feasible range of total yields implied by the prices paid. It was possible to conclude from the comparison too that prices paid for large quantities of raw material could not be explained on the basis of their yields of end products.

40. We had extensive discussions with PDM about the facts and figures used in this analysis and about the methodology. PDM was highly critical of our approach and suggested a number of changes. Many of its comments are reflected in the foregoing paragraphs; others we have not accepted. After taking careful account of all PDM's representations we are satisfied that our analysis is robust. To a significant extent variations in payments/charges cannot be explained by reference to variations in yields of end products or by other physical factors.

FIGURE 29

**Tonnes of best fat supplied by abattoirs in each yield range
to PDM high-grade plants, May 1992**

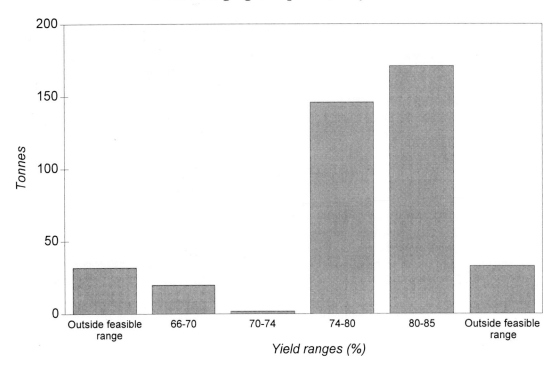

Source: MMC from PDM data.

FIGURE 30

**Tonnes of best fat supplied by abattoirs in each yield
range to PDM low-grade plants, May 1992**

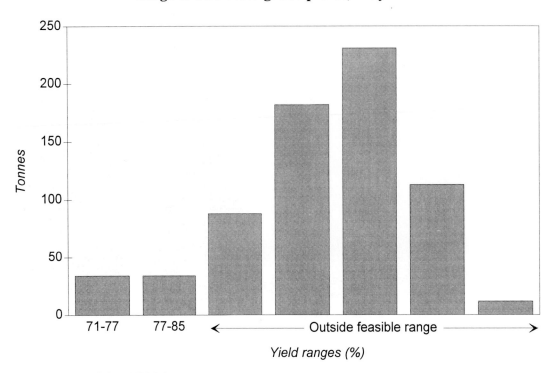

Source: MMC from PDM data.

FIGURE 31

**Tonnes of bone supplied in each yield range to PDM
high-grade plants, May 1992**

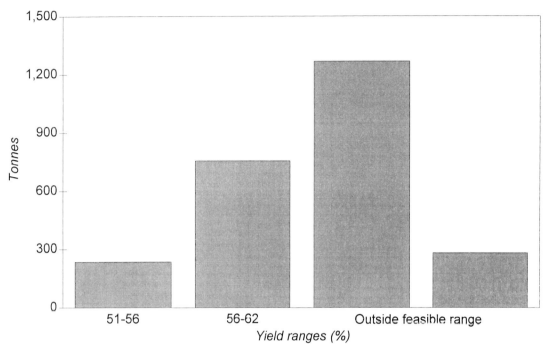

Source: MMC from PDM data.

FIGURE 32

**Tonnes of bone supplied in each yield range to PDM
low-grade plants, May 1992**

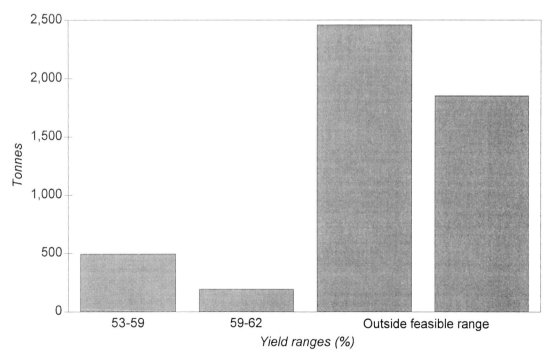

Source: MMC from PDM data.

236197 N2

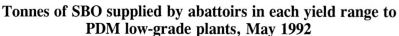

FIGURE 33

**Tonnes of SBO supplied by abattoirs in each yield range to
PDM low-grade plants, May 1992**

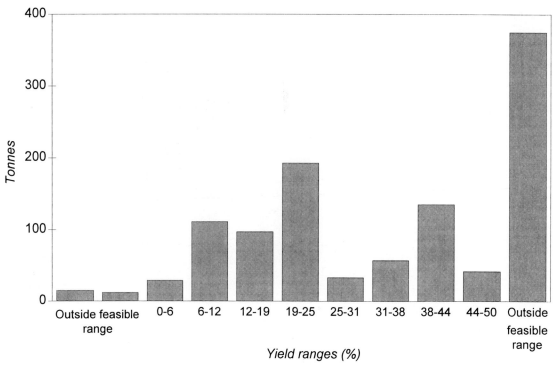

Source: MMC from PDM data.

FIGURE 34

**Tonnes of other offal supplied by abattoirs in each yield
range to PDM plants, May 1992**

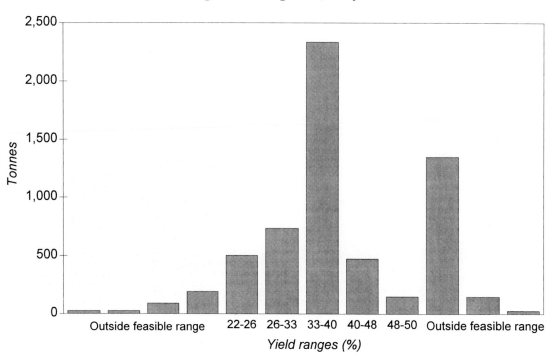

Source: MMC from PDM data.

FIGURE 35

**Tonnes of best fat supplied by abattoirs in each yield
range to PDM high-grade plants, October 1992**

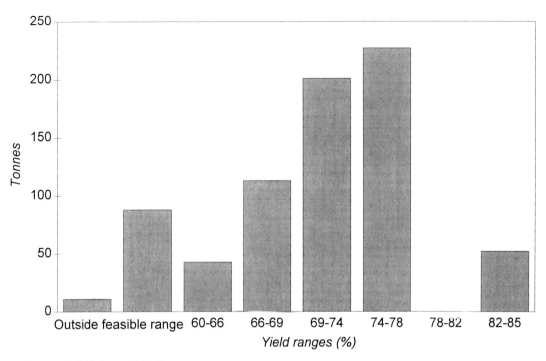

Source: MMC from PDM data.

FIGURE 36

**Tonnes of best fat supplied by abattoirs in each yield range
to PDM low-grade plants, October 1992**

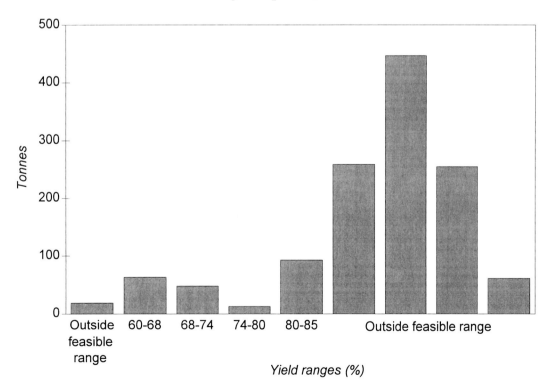

Source: MMC from PDM data.

FIGURE 37

**Tonnes of bone supplied by abattoirs in each total yield
range to PDM high-grade plants, October 1992**

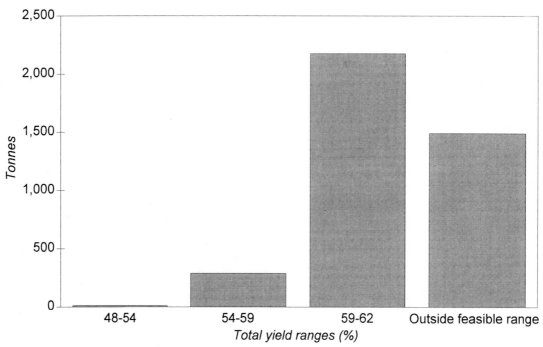

Source: MMC from PDM data.

FIGURE 38

**Tonnes of bone supplied by abattoirs in each total yield
range to PDM low-grade plants, October 1992**

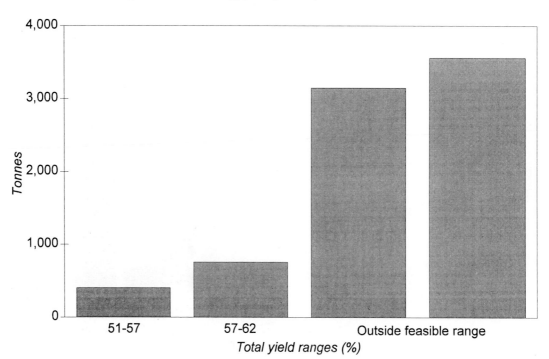

Source: MMC from PDM data.

FIGURE 39

Tonnes of SBO supplied by abattoirs in each yield range to PDM low-grade plants, October 1992

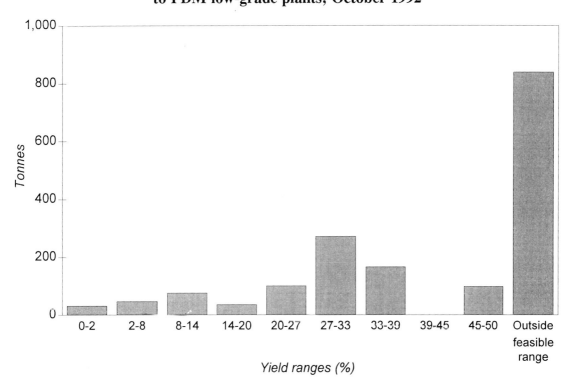

Source: MMC from PDM data.

FIGURE 40

Tonnes of other offal supplied by abattoirs in each yield range to PDM plants, October 1992

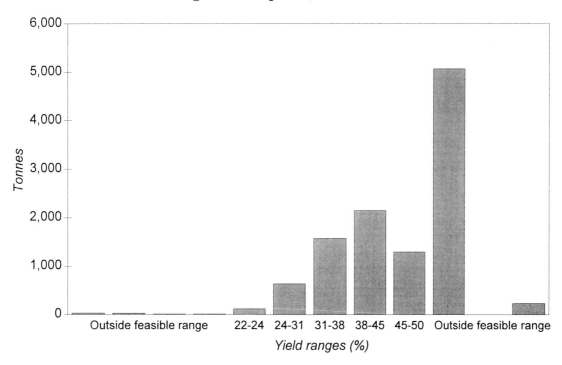

Source: MMC from PDM data.

Pricing cases: PDM

1. Four cases were investigated where we were told that particularly high prices had been paid for abattoirs' supplies of animal waste. All cases related to competition between PDM and Gilberts, and took place during the price war of May to October 1992. Each case is described below under the heading of the abattoir the supplies of which were being competed for, with the case of Anglo-Dutch Meats being considered in greater detail.

Anglo-Dutch Meats Ltd, Charing

Views of the complainant

2. Gilberts told us that during the price war PDM offered to beat Gilberts' prices if it thought that it would lose a contract at an abattoir, even if this meant offering unrealistic prices. At Anglo-Dutch Meats, Gilberts was charging the abattoir £20 per tonne to remove offal, a charge which was approximately £15 per tonne below PDM's. PDM then approached Anglo-Dutch Meats and offered to *pay* £25 per tonne for offal. Gilberts advised the abattoir to accept the offer since it believed that it resulted in a loss of £2,000 per week to PDM and would make the abattoir £3,000 better off per week. Anglo-Dutch Meats accepted the PDM offer and made a payment to Gilberts each week in the region of £500 to £700 by way of recognition that the price it had received for the offal was unrealistic.

The facts of the case

3. The abattoir at Charing was acquired by Anglo-Dutch Meats in 1985. Initially it gave the contract for animal waste disposal to PDM but in about 1986 transferred its contract to S J Chandler. Around late 1990, when it suspected that S J Chandler was about to cease trading, it transferred its business to Gilberts. Thereafter it transferred to Cheale for six months but then reverted to Gilberts for another six-month period.

4. In May 1992 Anglo-Dutch Meats was approached by PDM and awarded it a six-month contract on 18 May 1992, with collections commencing in the first week in June.

5. Anglo-Dutch Meats produces about 15 tonnes of fat per week and 70 tonnes per week of offal of all kinds (soft offal, SBO and hard offal from sheep's feet, pigs' heads and cows' udders).

Gilberts' prices

6. When Anglo-Dutch Meats transferred its waste products contract from S J Chandler to Gilberts, it suggested that the formula agreed with S J Chandler for paying for fat should be continued, and Gilberts agreed. The basis of the formula was 42.5 per cent of the tallow price in the previous week's *Meat Trades' Journal*. The advantage of the formula was that there was no haggling between the abattoir and the renderer and adjustments could be made every week based on an objective criterion. The offal price was left to negotiation.

PDM's offer

7. PDM agreed to pay for all the fat at £140 per tonne (compared with £95 per tonne that Gilberts was paying under the *Meat Trades' Journal* formula) and to pay £1,100 for all the offal irrespective

of quantity (compared with a charge of £9 per tonne for approximately 70 tonnes per week of offal, ie a charge of over £600 per week, levied by Gilberts).

A comparison of offers

8. At the time that PDM took the contract from Gilberts the approximate contract values were as shown in Table 1.

TABLE 1 **Value of contract at date of change of contractor**

	£ per week	
	Gilberts	*PDM*
Fat	1,800	2,520
Offal	-600	1,100
Total	1,200	3,620

Source: MMC and Anglo-Dutch Meats.

Given this very substantial difference Gilberts did not consider it worthwhile to counter-bid.

9. At the end of December 1992 PDM offered a less attractive deal but this was still worth considerably more than Gilberts could offer. It maintained the price of fat at £140 per tonne but stopped paying on all offal except for about 3 tonnes of udders, for which it pays £50 a tonne. The loss to Anglo-Dutch Meats was thus about £1,000 per week, but the abattoir is still receiving over twice as much as Gilberts was willing to pay.

Views of PDM

10. PDM said that it offered to make lump-sum payments for low-grade materials to Anglo-Dutch Meats because it had just lost another abattoir and needed to replace that tonnage. It claimed that, in profitability terms, it was marginal tonnage and should be seen in the context of the price war and PDM's need to retaliate against Gilberts for lost tonnage.

MMC comments

11. When the price war started, Anglo-Dutch Meats was paying Gilberts £9 per tonne for the removal of its offal and receiving for its fat an amount equivalent to a price of £95 per tonne, based on the price for tallow. Against this PDM offered to pay £140 per tonne for the fat and a lump sum of £1,100 per week for the offal. Since Anglo-Dutch Meats was producing about 70 tonnes of offal per week the payment per tonne was approximately £16.

12. PDM's break-even prices are compared with the offer to Anglo-Dutch Meats in Table 2.

TABLE 2 **PDM break-even prices and prices negotiated with Anglo-Dutch Meats**

	£ per tonne	
	PDM break-even prices October 1992	*Prices offered to Anglo-Dutch Meats Second half of 1992*
Fat	115 (best fat)	140
Offal	-5	
SBO	-30	16 } All offals

Source: MMC and Anglo-Dutch Meats.

195

Thus on the basis of these break-even calculations, PDM's offer implied a loss on both fat and offal, ie there was no offset from one product to another as is usual in a package deal.

Dalehead Foods Ltd, Cambridge

13. PDM improved its offer to remove Dalehead's offal by reducing the charge from £20 to £10 per tonne, and finally, we were told, it suggested a charge of £1 per tonne. It also offered to remove blood at no charge. We calculated PDM's break-even offal charge at £5 per tonne.

14. PDM did not, however, succeed in gaining the contract. It is the policy of Dalehead to employ more than one renderer and at one of its abattoirs it has replaced PDM with Peninsular.

W J Parker, Leicester

15. During the price war PDM reduced its collection charges to this abattoir by approximately one-half. Parker did not, however, give the whole of its business to PDM. It has a policy of dealing with more than one renderer and said that it was willing to support a small renderer in order to maintain competition.

Barratt and Baird (Wholesale) Ltd, West Bromwich

16. Over the period of the price war the price per tonne for bone offered and paid by PDM to this abattoir increased in the following way:

£20 from October 1991 to February 1992;
£25 in March 1992;
£30 from April to May 1992;
£35 from June to August 1992; and
£40 in September 1992.

It subsequently fell back in the following way:

£30 in October 1992;
£22.50 in November 1992;
£20 from December 1992 to February 1993; and
£25 in March 1993.

Our estimate of PDM's break-even price for bones is £43 per tonne. As the figures above show, this was not exceeded in the period from October 1991 to March 1993.

(referred to in paragraphs 6.16, 7.47, 10.64, 10.65,
paragraph 17(a) of Appendix 7.1 and Annex B of Appendix 10.2)

Gut-room contract at West Devon Meats, Hatherleigh

1. Imperial Meat Company Ltd (IMC) complained to the DGFT that in September 1991 PDM had taken on the gut-room contract at West Devon Meats, Hatherleigh, upon terms which could not be projected to be profit-making, given the market rates for rendering materials and for the removal of offal and SBO prevailing at the time PDM quoted for the contract, and that PDM was in breach of its 1986 undertakings. The DGFT invited IMC to provide estimates of PDM's costs and revenues from the gut-room contract. IMC's response indicated that the gut-room would be operated at a loss. The DGFT then received from PDM a budget for the Hatherleigh gut-room some 20 weeks after the beginning of the contract showing that it would operate at a profit. IMC's complaint was referred to us by the DGFT for our consideration.

2. Although there were many differences between IMC's estimate of the costs and revenues of the Hatherleigh gut-room and PDM's budget, we reduced the areas of disagreement to two issues. These were PDM's charges for administration, and the transfer prices for fats, offal and SBO between the gut-room operation and the rendering business.

Administration charges

3. PDM has been charging £50 per week to each of its gut-rooms which, it told us, was more than adequate to cover its administrative costs. IMC's charge to its own gut-rooms in 1991 was very much higher. We asked IMC to describe the minimum central organization required by an independent contractor operating several gut-rooms. IMC told us that a small office would be required, with one person permanently present to answer the telephone, deal with incoming mail, check the day's returns from the gut-rooms, prepare invoices and payrolls and carry out general office work. There would also be a proprietor or manager who would need a car. There would be audit and other professional fees. After discussions with its management, we estimated that this minimum organization would cost at least £75,000 per annum. PDM's £50 charge recovered approximately half of this amount in 1991/92, implying that a charge of about £100 per week for each gut-room would have been required to recover the minimum overheads considered appropriate by IMC.

4. PDM's undertaking 1.(iii)(a) requires it to charge each gut-room with all direct and indirect costs reasonably attributable to the conduct of that business. PDM's gut-rooms benefit substantially from PDM's organizational infrastructure. We therefore apportioned PDM's total overheads between its gut-room operations and its other businesses, using several different bases. The basis of apportionment which seemed to us to be the most reasonable was wages, and this gave a weekly charge per gut-room in 1991/92 of £342. We can accept that some of PDM's overheads are specifically related to other businesses and could have been excluded from our calculation, but PDM's weekly charge of £50 appears to fall far short of the amount required.

5. In our assessment of the Hatherleigh gut-room contract we have assumed that the weekly administration charge should be at least £100, and possibly as much as £342.

Transfer prices

6. PDM told us that it did not use third party prices for materials transferred from its gut-rooms to its rendering business, but used its own inter-company transfer prices. These transfer prices are mainly used within PDM for the large quantities of rendering materials collected by one plant but moved to another for processing. PDM told us that these transfer prices were calculated in exactly the same way as its target purchase prices (described in Appendix 6.1, paragraph 20), except that inward transport costs (from abattoir to first rendering plant/depot) were excluded; also a lower

average yield for best fat was used. The intention was that transfer prices would include more than the target profit, so that the company receiving the material would earn at least the full rendering profit while the company sending it the materials would earn no rendering profit at all (but could make a profit from astute buying).

7. The inter-company transfer prices are therefore meant to be low prices. PDM thought that by using these prices for transfers of raw materials from its gut-room operation to its rendering business, it would ensure that the latter was guaranteed the normal rendering profit and any cross-subsidy to the gut-rooms (which would breach undertaking 1.(ii)) would be avoided.

8. Because inter-company prices are intended for materials already delivered to a rendering plant, they cannot be applied to materials to be collected from an abattoir unless a transport charge is levied. PDM therefore charges each of its gut-rooms with the actual cost of transport. An independent gut-room contractor which does not have its own rendering facilities and sells its rendering materials to PDM receives a negotiated price and PDM pays the cost of transport from the abattoir to the plant. The system of pricing applied to PDM's own gut-rooms is therefore different from that applied to gut-rooms operated by most independent contractors.

9. A potential problem is that inter-company prices are not market prices. Like the target prices to which they are related, they are notional, PDM-determined prices. Undertaking 1.(iii) requires that 'each gut-room contract ... will be ... *(b)* credited with all revenue ... such revenue in any case where [it] arises out of a transaction otherwise than at arms-length being equal to ... the revenue that would be ... credited in respect of any equivalent transaction at arms-length'.

10. We asked PDM to provide various prices for the main categories of material for August 1991, which would have been the latest available to it for inclusion in a budget before the Hatherleigh abattoir opened in mid-September. Four prices were submitted for each category of material:

1. inter-company price (delivered to factory);
2. target price (collected from abattoir);
3. actual price (collected from abattoir); and
4. actual price (delivered to factory).

We also requested the same information for another month (February 1992) for purposes of comparison. When all these prices from both months were applied to our calculations for the Hatherleigh gut-room, they produced widely differing results, ranging from a loss of more than £600 to a profit of more than £900.

11. The actual prices for August 1991 and February 1992 provided by PDM were averages; PDM pays a very wide range of prices for the same materials. (PDM's pricing practices are dealt with in Chapter 6.) If we had taken the full range of actual prices paid or charged by PDM, the range of our results would have been even wider.

12. In its own calculations, IMC used a collection charge of £60 per tonne for offal, and £90 per tonne for SBO. These charges were higher than PDM's average charges, and resulted in a very large loss. Although it is possible that some abattoirs were paying such high collection charges, they may not have been employing independent gut-room contractors and in that case would not be totally comparable with the Hatherleigh abattoir.

Illustrative budget

13. In our calculations we have used the amounts paid by PDM to IMC for best fat and other fats; also, the charges made by PDM to the abattoirs, where IMC was operating the gut-rooms, for removing offal and SBO. From the point of view of IMC these would be the market prices for materials from a gut-room operated by an independent gut-room contractor. At our request, PDM provided us with these amounts for September 1991 (the month in which the Hatherleigh gut-room contract commenced), and we have applied them in an illustrative budget for this gut-room. This budget is set out in Table 1 together with those submitted to the DGFT by PDM and IMC.

TABLE 1 **Hatherleigh gut-room budgets**

	Volumes	PDM		IMC		MMC	
		Price	£	Price	£	Price	£
Headage revenue (expense)							
Cattle	700	-	-	(1.00)	(700.00)	-	-
Sheep	1,500	-	-	(0.10)	(150.00)	-	-
Pigs	600	-	-	-	-	-	-
			-		(850.00)		-
Pet food materials							
Tripes	700	1.50	1,050.00	1.00	700.00	1.50	1,050.00
Sheep paunches	1,500	0.05	75.00	-	-	0.10	150.00
Pigs maws	600	0.05	30.00	0.06	37.00	-	-
Sheep gut	1,500	0.20	300.00	0.25	375.00	0.21	315.00
Pig gut	600	0.12	72.00	-	-	-	-
			1,527.00		1,112.00		1,515.00
Rendering materials							
Best fat	15	72.50	1,087.50	80.00	1,200.00	70.00	1,050.00
Rough fat				47.50	-	45.00	-
Offal	40	(17.50)	(700.00)	(60.00)	(2,400.00)	(35.50)	(1,420)
SBO	13	(47.50)	(617.50)	(90.00)	(1,170.00)	(69.00)	(897.00)
			(230.00)		(2,370.00)		1,267.00
Less transport	68	5.88	400.00		-		-
			(630.00)		(2,370.00)		(1,267.00)
Expenses							
Wages	2	275.00	550.00		-	275.00	550.00
Wages	3		-	230.00	690.00		-
Administration	1	50.00	50.00	150.00	150.00	100.00	100.00
			600.00		840.00		650.00
Monthly profit/(loss)			297.00		(2,948.00)		(402.00)

Sources: PDM; IMC; MMC from information supplied by PDM and IMC.

14.   There are some differences between these budgets other than those arising from transfer prices and overheads. IMC's budget includes headage payments to the abattoir. We have confirmed that no such payments were made by PDM to West Devon Meats during the first six months of the contract, and so we have not included any in our budget. On pet-food materials, IMC accepted that a unit price for tripe of £1.50 was obtainable from a third party in Devon at that time, but told us that this price was above the market price then generally prevailing and that PDM was not necessarily in a position to use this price in its budget for the Hatherleigh gut-room. PDM operated the gut-room with two employees for the first six months, and only took on a third employee in April 1992 when the abattoir took on additional slaughtermen and the rate of killing increased.

15.   The widest differences between the three budgets in Table 1 arise from the different assumptions about the prices and charges applicable to the rendering materials. For the reason given in paragraph 13 above, we have used the actual prices received in September 1991 by IMC and the charges made to those abattoirs where it operated the gut-room, to evaluate its complaint. Using these prices and charges gives the loss of £402 shown in the table. The loss would increase to £644 if the higher weekly overhead charge of £342 suggested in paragraph 4 above were applied.

APPENDIX 6.4

(referred to in paragraphs 6.18, 10.100 and 10.101(a))

Analysis of Forrest's prices

1. MMC staff prepared tables of prices or charges made by Forrest for raw material in May and October 1992 from data supplied by that company. From these were derived the ranges of prices or charges shown in Table 1.

TABLE 1 **Price ranges of raw material**

£ per tonne

Material	May 1992			October 1992		
	From	To	Range	From	To	Range
Beef fat	35	100	65	38	113	75
Bone	0	20	20	1	35	34
SBO	(80)	(30)	50	(40)	0	40
Other offal	(55)	0	55	(40)	0	40

Source: MMC from Forrest data.

2. Forrest also provided a detailed commentary on the reasons for the particular prices or charges in October 1992. Forrest said that quantity supplied by an abattoir was the single most important factor, followed by quality and the size of load, and that these factors determined its prices or charges, together with particular features of a contract.

3. In order to test this statement we plotted prices per tonne for each type of material against quantity collected in the month and identified separately the approximate quality as assessed by Forrest in its detailed comments, and the quantity collected at any one time (the 'uplift'), where noted. There was a clear relationship between price and quality at the extreme of the quality ranges, but there still appeared to be a very wide range of prices paid for material classed by Forrest as 'medium quality'.

4. We put a series of graphs back to Forrest which replied that the approach to assessing prices by means of such broad categories was 'fundamentally flawed', despite the categorization being its own. It also provided more detailed explanations of the observed price differences for material in the medium-quality category. It gave examples of widely differing values of material in this category as a result of the differing yields of saleable products. It also argued that in the case of particular suppliers, low prices were paid because of the cost of transporting the material over long distances to the rendering plant.

5. In the case of beef fat, we accept that differences in quality and hence in yield of final products, and differences in transport costs, can explain almost the whole of the £75 range of prices found in October 1992. If so, however, the question arises whether a single description of 'beef fat' is appropriate for what is argued to be a material distinctly lacking in homogeneity.

6. In the case of bones, Forrest said that although it had previously indicated from which suppliers only small quantities were collected and from which large, quantity collected was not the sole determinant of price and variation of prices per tonne between abattoirs at which large quantities were collected were further explicable by quality differences. It quoted a number of examples where it suggested that quality was a significant variable and argued that the resulting price range for 'medium quality' was no more than from £13 to £30, ie £17 per tonne. We accept Forrest's arguments.

7. As to SBO, Forrest argued that a particularly low charge of £0 per tonne should not be taken into consideration since it was made for a short time in order to help an abattoir with top quality raw material and substantial daily uplifts that was being re-established after going into receivership. The charge was now £20 per tonne. We accept this and also its case that charges of £40 and £35 are

explained by the higher cost of collecting small quantities from remote abattoirs. The resulting range of charges is from £18 to £30. This may be compared with our estimate of Forrest's break-even charge for SBO in October 1992 of £36 per tonne. On this basis Forrest was making a loss of between £6 and £18 per tonne.

8. In the case of other offal, Forrest argued that charges of £30 and £20 should be eliminated from the range on the grounds that the quantities collected were small and in remote localities. The resulting range, which we accept, is from -£10 to £0. However, we estimate that in October 1992 Forrest's break-even price for other offal was £5 per tonne. On some contracts, therefore, it was making a profit of £15 per tonne and on the others only £5.

9. If we accept Forrest's arguments that particular prices are a function of quality and transport cost, as set out above, the remaining ranges of prices for October 1992 would become those shown in Table 2, in which they are compared with its estimated break-even prices.

TABLE 2 **October 1992 price or charge range not directly explicable by cost or quality variation**

					£ per tonne
	From	To	Range	Estimated break-even price	Estimated range of profit
Beef fat	90	97	7	94	+4 to -3
Bone	13	30	17	45	+31 to +15
SBO	(30)	(18)	12	(36)	-6 to -18
Other offal	(10)	0	10	5	+15 to +5

Source: MMC from Forrest data.

Pricing cases: Forrest

1. Four cases were investigated where we were told that particularly high prices had been paid for abattoirs' supplies of animal waste. Some related to competition between Forrest and Dundas Brothers and some to competition between Forrest and Dundas Chemical. Each case is described below under the heading of the abattoir the supplies of which were being competed for, with Buchan Meat and Biggar being described in greater detail.

Cases involving Dundas Brothers

Buchan Meat Producers Ltd, Turriff, Aberdeenshire

Views of the complainant

2. Dundas Brothers complained to the OFT on 22 September 1992 that it had lost its account at Buchan Meat as the result of an aggressive move by Forrest which it felt was of an unfair nature and outwith normal business practice. It was an account which it had gained in February 1992 and which had previously been Forrest's. Dundas Brothers asserted that the current difficulty being experienced by the meat trade generally and the publicized loss-making position of some groups including Buchan Meat led to Buchan Meat being pressurized by Hillsdown so that it moved its rendering account back to Forrest.

The facts of the case

3. Buchan Meat has traded since about the early 1960s and for many years it had dealt with Elgin Animal By-Products Ltd (Elgin), a rendering company which had one of Buchan Meat's directors on its Board. In 1989 Elgin's plant was burnt down, and it sold out to Forrest in 1990. Buchan Meat at that time decided to transfer its contract to Forrest because the prices seemed reasonable.

4. In 1991 Dundas Brothers offered Buchan Meat a deal which it accepted even though Forrest offered more afterwards. Buchan Meat told Dundas Brothers that this contract would run for six months from January 1992 and that it would then look at it again. The deal was settled at Christmas 1991 and Forrest was invited to re-tender after six months.

5. After six months Forrest did re-tender. It agreed to pay a base rate plus a bonus on a retro-active basis if volume targets were achieved. The base rates offered by Forrest were better than those offered by Dundas Brothers, and although Dundas Brothers came back with a counter-offer, Buchan Meat was not interested. Details of the various contract values are given in Table 1.

TABLE 1   **Contract values at time of change of contractor**

£ per tonne

	Average weekly volume (tonnes)	Dundas Brothers prices before change (ie until June 1992)	Forrest prices accepted*	Dundas Brothers counter-offer not accepted
Non-specified offal charge	31	[	-7.5	[
SBO charge	51		-25	
Bones income	50		25	
Fat income	29		99	
Cattle feet income	13	†	17.5	†
Average weekly charges (for offals)			-1,507.5	
Average weekly payments			+4,348.5	
Net payments		]	2,841.0	]

Source: MMC and Buchan Meat.

*In addition Forrest agreed to pay a £25,000 bonus on a retroactive basis if volume targets were achieved.

Buchan Meat said that it was the volume bonus which tipped the scales in favour of Forrest.

6. The contract with Forrest ran from June 1992 to the end of that year and since Buchan Meat was able to meet the volume target it was paid the £25,000 bonus, equivalent to about £960 per week or £5.50 per tonne. This additional payment should be seen in the context of an average weekly total payment to Buchan Meat of some £2,800.

Views of Forrest

7. Forrest claimed that there were two principal reasons for it being awarded the Buchan Meat contract. These were that:

(a) Buchan Meat had been a long-term supplier to Elgin, which was acquired by Forrest in April 1990; and

(b) Forrest offered a quality service at competitive prices.

8. Buchan Meat sought a quote from Forrest for the collection of its raw materials on 14 August 1992 and Forrest quoted in accordance with its usual prices, taking into account relevant market conditions and the significant tonnage expected to be available for collection. Buchan Meat indicated that the prices quoted by Forrest were higher than those it was currently receiving. Forrest understood that this was a result of the steady increase in market prices since Buchan Meat had concluded its contract with its then current renderer. Forrest was therefore led to believe by Buchan Meat that the quote would be accepted and on 17 September 1992 Buchan Meat telephoned Forrest and confirmed that it should resume collection of raw materials on 5 October 1992.

MMC comments

9. If it is assumed that the £5.50 reduction (mentioned in paragraph 6 above) was spread equally over all types of animal waste, the implied prices offered to Buchan Meat for each category of waste would be as set out in Table 2, in which they are compared with Forrest's break-even prices for 1992.

†Figures omitted. See note on page iv.

TABLE 2 **Forrest's break-even prices and prices negotiated with Buchan Meat**

	£ per tonne	
	Forrest's break-even prices Average 1992	Prices offered to Buchan Meat
Bones	30	30.5
Offal	-3	-2.0
SBO	-37	-19.5
Fat	74	104.5

Source: MMC.

While the charge for the offal and the payment for the bone was very near to Forrest's break-even, the charge for SBO material was much lower and the price paid for fat was much higher. On these figures it does not appear that Forrest covered its costs on the contract with Buchan Meat taken by itself.

Inverurie Scotch Meat Company, Inverurie

10. Dundas Brothers complained to the OFT on 22 September 1992 that it had lost its account at ISM, part of FMC, which is owned by Hillsdown. This was an account that it had serviced for many years. Dundas Brothers claimed that the move was not based entirely on price and service and referred to the relationship between Hillsdown and Forrest.

11. ISM said that all FMC abattoirs were independent trading units and that it was for local managers to decide which renderer to use. In this case, the net weekly payments available from Forrest were substantially better than Dundas Brothers' and were still higher when Dundas Brothers revised its prices to compete with Forrest's offer.

12. Prices per tonne for each category of material based on Forrest's offer are set out in Table 3, together with Forrest's break-even prices.

TABLE 3 **Forrest's break-even prices and prices negotiated with ISM**

	£ per tonne	
	Forrest's break-even prices Average 1992	Prices offered to ISM
Bones	30	22.5
Offal	-3	-10.0
SBO	-37	-
Fat	74	85 (pig) 100 (beef)

Source: MMC and ISM.

Forrest's offer involved a lower price for bone and a higher charge for offal compared with break-even, but also a higher price for fat.

Cases involving Dundas Chemical

Biggar Quality Meats Ltd, Biggar

Views of the complainant

13. Dundas Chemical told us that Biggar entered into an oral contract for its animal waste to be removed by Dundas Chemical but that Forrest increased its price to such an extent that Biggar remained with Forrest.

The facts of the case

14. Biggar has traded with Forrest for about ten years but in 1992 Dundas Chemical tried for the first time to obtain Biggar's animal waste. It offered a price which was an improvement on that being paid by Forrest and Biggar then approached Forrest. Forrest offered better prices than Dundas Chemical since it did not wish to lose Biggar's raw materials, the difference between the quotes amounting in total to £1,000 per week. Forrest agreed to pay the agreed prices retrospectively for one month to take account of the negotiation time, but insisted that Biggar should stay with it for the period July to December 1992, although it gave undertakings not to alter prices. In fact, the prices were not altered during 1992 and were kept at the July levels into 1993.

15. Table 4 shows the increase in prices paid to Biggar by Forrest.

TABLE 4 **Prices paid to Biggar at time of revision of contract**

		£/tonne
	Forrest's prices to 30.6.92	*Forrest's prices from 1.7.92*
Sheep heads/feet/ox feet	5	15
Fat	60	90
SBO	-50	-30
Sheep/cattle offal	-20	0

Source: Biggar.

Biggar is now being paid £90 a tonne instead of £60 a tonne for fat and is only having to pay £30 a tonne to have its SBO removed compared with £50 previously.

Views of Forrest

16. Forrest said that it had assessed the profitability of its contract with Biggar. [

Details omitted. See note on page iv.

]

MMC comments

17. The prices offered by Forrest to Biggar are contrasted with its break-even prices in Table 5.

TABLE 5 **Forrest's break-even prices and prices at time of revision of contract**

£/tonne

	Forrest's prices to 30.6.92	Forrest's prices from 1.7.92	Forrest's break-even prices Average 1992
Fat	60	90	74
SBO	-50	-30	-37
Offal	-20	0	- 3

Source: MMC and Biggar.

In addition, Forrest agreed to back-date the agreed prices by one month, which meant a discount to Biggar of some £4,300. Even if the discount is not taken into account, it is clear that Forrest's payments to Biggar were higher than would reflect break-even prices, and it would not therefore appear that Forrest covered its costs on this contract taken by itself.

British Beef Co Ltd, Hawick

18. Forrest competed with Dundas Chemical for the supplies of this abattoir. The abattoir manager was keen to have both companies collecting materials to maintain competition. Dundas Chemical now has a contract for the offals and fat and Forrest one for the bones.

APPENDIX 7.1
(referred to in paragraphs 4.49, 7.1, 10.50 and 10.78)

Summary of complaints and allegations against PDM and Forrest

PDM

Pricing: lack of alternatives to PDM

1. *(a)* Letters from six waste producers and three other third parties expressed the view that PDM's virtual monopoly, or dominance, of the animal waste market restricted free and fair competition and choice of disposal outlet; and that this forced animal waste suppliers to pay unrealistic collection charges. One of these, a Yorkshire abattoir owner, also claimed that price negotiation with PDM in areas where PDM had no competitor was difficult or impossible. Another, Tesco, explained that although it did not deal directly with PDM it had consulted with the majority of its own suppliers; although small, the value of waste still formed an integral part of an abattoir's return, and subsequent profit, and Tesco believed it would be unhealthy for the meat industry and commercially damaging to its suppliers if PDM was allowed to grow any larger. In the experience of Mole Valley District Council problems could arise when a waste producer had no alternative to collection by a monopolistic renderer which could, if it so chose, 'hold that producer to ransom'.

(b) Similar comments were made in the completed questionnaires we received from 11 abattoirs. Six of these particularly mentioned PDM's dominance and the lack of choice of outlet, including one which commented that PDM strongly resisted any opposition and that it had little choice but to deal with PDM as other renderers did not like to cross swords with PDM. The remaining five particularly mentioned prices/charges. One said that it used PDM many years ago but ceased to do so because an unsatisfactory service was provided and extortionate prices charged. Another said that there had always been price fixing by PDM and its main competitor, and that BSE had occurred to their advantage and prices had rocketed; charges for offal, which represented by far the biggest tonnage renderers had to remove, remained, and this was where a great deal of their profit lay. Another believed that the meat industry would be held to ransom if the concentration of outlets continued, just as it had been during the initial period of BSE. Apart from these 11, another abattoir told us that it had dismissed its General Manager partly on suspicion that by arrangement with PDM he had not completed and returned our questionnaire.

(c) *PDM pointed out* that it had explained the reasons for the very significant rationalization which had taken place in the rendering industry in recent years (see Chapter 8). Although this rationalization had inevitably reduced the choice of disposal outlets there was still very effective competition for quantity suppliers of animal waste. PDM maintained that the industry was now more efficient in its present rationalized form than had been the case when there were larger numbers of independent renderers scattered all over the country.

(d) *PDM denied* that it had ever forced animal waste suppliers to pay unrealistic charges. It also denied that price negotiation by suppliers in areas where it had no competitor was difficult if not impossible. It had demonstrated that in connection with significant supplies of waste material there were no areas where it had no competition. In connection with small collections from butchers' shops there was an alternative disposal route available to these suppliers via local authority waste disposal services. Thus in connection with this type of supplier the price which PDM could charge or must pay had to be competitive with the services provided by the local waste disposal authority. PDM had demonstrated by a very large number of small butchers' shops from which it still collected material that it did not exploit its monopoly in connection with what would individually be uneconomic sources of supply. PDM took a long-term view about the importance of shop collections and

believed it had a responsibility as the monopolist in the industry to service these sources of supply wherever they were as and when required to do so.

(e) *PDM believed* that the allegation made by Mole Valley District Council related to a small abattoir in Horsham which had persistently refused to pay charges to PDM for the removal of its low-grade material. The District Council's involvement was because of its concern, as the local environmental health authority, about the consequences of the non-removal of animal waste.

(f) *PDM told us* that its personnel had never discussed the matter of our questionnaire with the General Manager referred to at the end of paragraph 1(b).

2. In addition, Pears told us that abattoirs were frightened to switch even part of their tonnage from PDM because of the risk of PDM retaliating, first against the successful competitor and then, having dealt with that, against the abattoirs themselves when they had to go back to PDM cap in hand.

3. (a) The National Cattle Breeders Association argued that the continued imposition of removal charges might not be justified, as the rendering industry, dominated by PDM, no longer suffered from poor returns on its capital and the end-product market had also recovered.

(b) *PDM argued* that the continued imposition of removal charges was justified notwithstanding the rendering industry's improved returns on its capital and the recovery in the end-product market. The finished product market had very recently seen some long overdue improvement which would take effect from April 1993. Meal prices were expected to increase from £140 to £160 per tonne, grade 6 tallow prices from £160 to £185 per tonne and grade 2 tallow prices from £225 to £240 per tonne. As mentioned above, the 1992 price war had meant that there were still left in place some unrealistically high prices and low charges. PDM would expect its suppliers to use the very recent improvement in finished product prices as an argument for resisting the return of charges and prices to levels which PDM would still be able to justify based on its overall pricing structures.

4. (a) The National Farmers' Union complained that in November 1992 PDM reintroduced offal charges after a period of several months without them and despite the increase in soya bean meal prices at that time.

(b) *PDM agreed* that, in November 1992, following the end of the price war, it had sought to introduce more realistic levels of charges for low-grade material in spite of an increase in soya bean meal prices at that time. The modest nature of those price increases did not justify the maintenance of the unrealistic levels of charges and prices which had been secured by suppliers as a result of the price war in the summer of 1992.

5. (a) The Licensed Animal Slaughterers and Salvage Association expressed the view that the escalating costs of the removal service of PDM seriously threatened the knacker trade in England and Wales.

(b) *PDM emphatically rejected* the allegation that escalating costs of its removal service seriously threatened the knacker trade in England and Wales, and referred us to the Report of the Agriculture Select Committee at the House of Commons on the Disposal of Fallen Livestock of 17 July 1991. This report, said PDM, clearly demonstrated that PDM was in no way responsible for the difficulties being experienced by the knacker trade. Over the last 18 months charges for knacker material had fallen from £60 to £20 per tonne. PDM had played a major part in persuading the animal feed industry to abandon its prejudices against meal produced in part from fallen stock.

6. (a) An abattoir group argued that PDM based its pricing structure on its trading results rather than on the general trading conditions, and by allowing a purchase price movement to balance a low sales price insulated itself against the possibility of poor trading.

(b) *PDM denied* that flexibility in its pricing structure insulated it against the possibility of poor trading. As already indicated, it based its pricing structure, which it reviewed on a month-to-month basis, upon what it believed would be the principal factors affecting the trading conditions in the month ahead. This structure took into account anticipated value of finished products, costs of procurement, anticipated yield from material obtained and all other determinable or foreseeable market factors. The target prices for the various categories of raw material which resulted from such monthly assessments were then communicated to PDM's raw material purchasers, who then went out into the market and tried to achieve any necessary adjustments in charges made and prices paid. There was a considerable lag between a material change in PDM's budgeted pricing structures and the achievement of prices approximate to such structure in the market. This was because of natural resistance by suppliers to any changes proposed which were adverse to their interests. Conversely, however, where a significant supplier was of the opinion that he could achieve a better price or a lower charge, he would seek to implement an adjustment immediately. The system of pricing in the industry simply did not permit PDM even to attempt to claw back lost profit which had resulted from the many other factors affecting its complex business.

7. (a) Quaker Oats Ltd considered that PDM would use its market strength to obtain sole control of the poultry waste market, leading to higher prices and/or reduced efficiency, the cost of which would be passed on to consumers. Similar comments were made in the completed questionnaires we received from five poultry companies. Four of these particularly expressed concern at the lack of competition or choice of renderer for the by-products of their industry and three explicitly pointed to adverse price effects. One considered that bone prices did not always reflect increased meat-and-bone meal prices and stated that while increased prices for offal collection were imposed overnight, price decreases for offal collection came through only slowly.

(b) *PDM pointed out* that it had explained the circumstances in which it had fortuitously obtained its market position in relation to the supply of poultry waste (see Chapter 8). PDM denied that its dominance of this market had led to higher prices or reduced efficiency; indeed it claimed that the opposite was true. It also pointed out that no poultry material, whether feather, carcase or bones, could be used to produce meat-and-bone meal.

Price competition

8. (a) Initial evidence from one renderer, one independent collector and one knacker alleged that from time to time PDM selectively paid above market prices for its supplies in areas where it faced competition and then reduced its prices as soon as it had a stranglehold, while paying little or nothing in areas where it faced no competition; or that from time to time PDM selectively outbid competitors with the intention of eventually forcing them out of business.

(b) *PDM said* that, as a matter of general and specific policy, it had never at any time forced any of its competitors out of business, whether by selectively outbidding them or otherwise.

9. (a) Similar allegations were made in subsequent oral evidence received from two renderers, one collector and one abattoir operator. We were told of a small Manchester abattoir which PDM had won from one renderer during the price war by back-dating increased payments for previous supplies. This renderer also stated that PDM was able to obtain supplies at low prices in areas of no competition and to offer higher prices elsewhere, making its overall raw material costs significantly lower than those of other renderers. In this renderer's view, because of capacity barriers, competitors could have very little effect on PDM's total tonnage in any price war, but PDM seemed obsessed with tonnage and volume, so that losses always had to be replaced, whatever the consequences for PDM's profits.

(b) *PDM denied* that it had ever back-dated increased payments for previous supplies which it had already bought. However, in certain circumstances where there were outstanding charges owed to it by a supplier, it did sometimes agree to write these off as part of arrangements negotiated with the supplier for the continuance of supplies to it.

10. (a) Wildriggs was emphatic that PDM paid less for poultry waste where it had no competitor.

(b) *PDM strongly maintained* that the prices it paid for poultry waste were consistent throughout the UK.

11. (a) Pears noted that price wars and 'silly prices' occurred from time to time, and that it was 'just De Mulder's trying to get more tonnage all the time'. Pears also told us of an incident involving surveillance by PDM (see paragraph 7.56); and said that over the years it had been PDM's strategy to put competitors' margins constantly under pressure until they lost the will to continue. Although small competitors tried to keep the peace rather than rock the boat as Pears had done, they still eventually went out of business: their suppliers gradually disappeared because they were only small and PDM would not let them have any big ones.

(b) *PDM said* that it had demonstrated that it was compelled to pay unrealistically high prices and make unrealistically low charges for material during the 1992 price war. PDM accepted that as soon as the price war came to an end it had endeavoured to adjust prices and charges to more appropriate and realistic levels. However, there was a long period of adjustment which PDM had to endure before it could hope to return to the levels of fair prices and charges which existed prior to the price war.

(c) *PDM said* that the allegation about an incident involving surveillance of Hughes by PDM did not make sense. The investigation which PDM had carried out in relation to the Hughes rendering business in 1991 had been for the purpose of ascertaining whether SBO material was being used in production of meat-and-bone meal by that company contrary to the regulations banning that practice.

(d) *PDM reiterated* that it had never sought to put a competitor renderer out of business by engaging in predatory pricing or charging. It had always been PDM's policy to increase its market share by acquisition rather than by competition on price.

12. (a) One abattoir noted that the charges levied on it by Granox had fallen only since Gilberts had tried to win its contract, and questioned how they could fall from £50, to £25, to £15 within two months.

(b) *PDM admitted* to the charge adjustments referred to in this allegation and said that they were the direct result of the price war in 1992.

13. (a) In addition, a renderer told us of telephone calls it received from PDM from time to time signalling PDM's view of prices and the adjustments it intended to make. November 1992 was one such time, when charges were reintroduced after the price war.

(b) *PDM told us* that it was to the benefit of all renderers when the 1992 price war eventually came to an end. It did not deny that discussions took place at all times within the rendering industry about general trading, and said that obviously such discussions had included the price war at that particular time.

14. (a) Pears told us that if PDM perceived that a competing renderer was in a weak trading position, it would offer artificially low end-product prices in order further to weaken that competitor. Moreover, PDM had in the past forced it to compete by offering 12-month fixed price contracts for supplies of animal waste, and then squeezed it by releasing a huge amount of meal from stock to depress the price on the end-product market.

(b) *PDM maintained* that it supported end-product prices, the benefit of which accrued to all renderers. This it achieved through its significant export sales. If these export sales were made through the home market they would undoubtedly have a depressant effect on end-product prices. PDM never offered artificially low end-product prices to weaken a competitor.

15. (a) One small renderer complained that PDM controlled the feather and blood processing plants and that, while it had no proof that PDM blended the high protein outputs of those plants with its standard meal, it had encountered problems selling its meat-and-bone meal which was 46 to 48 per cent protein when PDM protein values were 50 per cent (quote guaranteed). Smaller renderers could only compete in selling to the large feed compounders by selling their meal cheaper—surely this was unfair competition across the board.

(b) *PDM pointed out* that under the Feeding Stuffs and Fertiliser Regulations renderers were not permitted to include either blood meal or feather meal in meat-and-bone meal products.

Profitability/viability of PDM

16. (a) Fats & Proteins expressed concern that PDM, according to its balance sheets and accounts over the years, might not be sufficiently profitable to warrant new investment, and also sustain its viability should the need for significant investment in plant renewal or replacement arise.

(b) *PDM said* that it had maintained throughout the inquiry that its plants were 'state of the art' in the rendering industry.

The 1986 undertakings

17. (a) IMC complained about the terms on which PDM had taken on the gut-room contract at West Devon Meats, Hatherleigh (Appendix 6.3). Another gut-room contractor told us of a lack of trust of PDM, as to whether it was offering the best deal, ie removal charges too high, fat prices not high enough or weights inaccurate. Pears explained that it was very difficult to win supplies where PDM operated the gut-room, and cited a recent example where it had failed despite offering 'a very good price'—there was, it said, no such problem where the gut-room was not operated by PDM.

(b) *PDM said* that it had satisfied the DGFT since giving its undertakings in 1986 that it had always operated its gut-rooms on an arm's length basis.

18. (a) A pet food company argued that distortions (by virtue of PDM's breaching undertaking 2) in the market for the supply of edible red and green offal would prejudice the interests of farmers as well as those of the ultimate consumer. This company and two others all complained that PDM was abusing its position as the dominant renderer to abattoirs to take their often long-standing supplies for edible (pet food) offal, in some cases by linking the availability of these supplies to free inedible (rendering) offal collection while paying less for the pet food materials than they had paid. Subsequently PDM had offered to sell frozen tripe to one of them. Pears believed that PDM had a definite advantage when bidding for pet food material because it could also clear the other by-products.

(b) *PDM said* that it believed that it had at all times complied with undertaking 2 of 1986. Without further detail of alleged breaches it was unable to comment on alleged distortions in the market for the supply of edible red and green offal potentially prejudicing the interests of farmer and consumer.

236197 P

Market arrangements and behaviour

19. *(a)* Three waste producers or collectors alleged that PDM used G H Klein to obtain animal waste from customers who would not knowingly deal with PDM.

    (b) PDM told us that it was not correct to say that it used G H Klein to obtain supplies from customers who would not knowingly deal with PDM. The business of G H Klein was well known to be closely associated with PDM. That business had a tenancy of some premises which were part of PDM's Silvertown factory complex. Although it was an independently-owned company, at one time it was a wholly-owned subsidiary of Stannard and Co (1969) Ltd in which PDM had a 50 per cent interest.

20. *(a)* Pears and two other competitors were clear that PDM enhanced its dominance of the supply of animal waste in England and Wales by informal links with other companies in the industry such as Clutton, G H Klein and Specialpack. Pears stated that PDM had admitted that it owned companies people did not even know about.

    (b) PDM admitted that it had close trading relationships with some other companies in the industry, including Clutton, G H Klein and Specialpack. Notwithstanding such links, G H Klein currently sold grade 6 material to Cheale. Specialpack rendered its own SBO material. PDM bought Specialpack's fat but its red offal material was supplied to Spillers. PDM charged Specialpack market price for clean offal. PDM had similar arm's length trading arrangements with Clutton.

21. *(a)* An abattoir group and LASSA noted that PDM and Forrest did not compete with one another and said that this unreasonably penalized the suppliers of animal waste and resulted in higher prices being passed on to the public as part of the cost of meat production.

    (b) PDM explained that the only reason why it did not trade in Scotland was because of the distances between its plants in England and any significant supplies of raw material in Scotland. Anyway it was not its practice to bid for supplies which had never been its own. It had once purchased a business in Scotland (Frank Gysels) with a view to carrying on rendering there but this had been an unsuccessful venture and the business had been sold to Forrest (see paragraph 8.15).

22. *(a)* Four renderers and a collector all told us that by forestalling the availability of the plant and equipment of former renderers for sale on the open market (procuring the cutting up, or the sale abroad, of such plant and equipment as PDM did not itself require), PDM prevented it from falling into the hands of any would-be or existing competitor.

    (b) PDM said that it did not understand the basis of, and knew of no evidence which would support, any allegation concerning foreclosing the sale of plant and equipment on the open market. PDM bought its own requirements for plant and equipment where appropriate in the market. If the allegations were based upon the closure of Beeson, these had already been dealt with by PDM (see paragraph 8.19).

23. *(a)* Quaker Oats Ltd alleged that PDM had come to dominate the poultry waste market through consistently either purchasing or paying for competing poultry waste rendering facilities to be closed, particularly those capable of processing feathers, which constituted a major part of the cost of processing poultry waste. Pears said that PDM had been delivering quantities of feathers to take up all of Hughes' feather-rendering capability, so blocking Pears' outlet for its feathers and jeopardizing its ability to provide the necessary full collection service to its customers.

    (b) PDM denied that it had purchased any competing poultry waste renderer or paid for any such rendering facility to be closed. Poultry stations had ceased to process their own waste because they had been compelled to do so by their own customers.

24. *(a)* A pet food company commented that as there was an exclusive agreement between PDM and Hillsdown covering the rendering by PDM of all poultry waste not required by Hillsdown (including items fit, if not intended for, human consumption), edible waste required by the pet food industry might in future be rendered.

(b) *PDM argued* that there was no commercial logic in PDM rendering material for which higher values could be obtained from pet food manufacturers. The agreement between PDM and Hillsdown was for a three-month period only, although it may be renewed. All material acquired from Hillsdown sources pursuant to the agreement which could go into pet food was used for that purpose. The pet food industry still imported significant quantities of its material requirements. Nor did PDM's competitors in the pet food supply industry have rendering plants which enabled them to process the surplus poultry material which was left after pet food materials had been extracted; and general renderers could not process such poultry material because, as a result of the specifications of the poultry retailers, this could not be used in the production of meat-and-bone meal for poultry feeds.

Forrest

Pricing: lack of alternatives to Forrest

25. *(a)* Two abattoirs, two trade bodies and a renderer commented on the dominance of Forrest. One abattoir expressed its concern at both Forrest's and PDM's dominance of the industry at large. Another felt that it had to be careful to keep Forrest happy and accept whatever it implemented, whether as regards price or waste collection times. Highland Venison was concerned that prices should be affordable, while LASSA expressed the view that the escalating costs of the removal service of Forrest seriously threatened the knacker trade in Scotland. Dundas Chemical pointed out that, while it and abattoirs from which Forrest collected had been struggling to survive, Forrest had made some £3 million profit in its last financial year.

(b) *Forrest stated* that it recognized the problems faced by knackers in Scotland, but these were not the result of its removal charges. Rather, they were due to the high costs incurred by knackers in collecting carcases from the farms, and the severe drop in the value of their products which knackers, in common with abattoirs and other suppliers, had had to withstand due to a fall in the value of end products. These problems were understood to be common to knackers throughout Europe. In contrast with other countries in Europe, however, the UK did not subsidize its renderers to collect knacker material. Not only Forrest and PDM but all renderers were understood to have been forced to impose charges for knacker material.

(c) *Forrest commented* that as to the allegation that in the last financial year Forrest had made a profit of £3 million, Forrest identified the financial year referred to as 1990, when the trading profit (even including dividends) was under £1 million. (Net interest received and extraordinary items, which it did not consider relevant to an assessment of the performance of Forrest, accounted for the balance of the total profit.)

Price competition

26. Complaints about possible predatory behaviour by Forrest were received from Dundas Brothers and Dundas Chemical. Case studies regarding these complaints are reported in Appendix 6.5.

Inefficiency of Forrest

27. *(a)* Dundas Chemical argued that Forrest was extremely inefficient. For an annual turnover of some £9 million it employed around 120 people. These included transport managers,

213

accountants, raw materials buyers and administrative staff, all on inflated salaries. In addition, employees had expensive company cars, good pension and holiday rights and a relatively short working day. All of this represented costs of some £500,000 to £750,000 before any direct operational costs began to be incurred.

(b) *Forrest maintained* that these allegations were wholly unsustainable and commented that:

— Forrest had one transport manager, one accountant and one raw material buyer and, like all other renderers, administrative staff;

— Forrest believed that the salaries paid were in line with the market-place for similar types of employees;

— Forrest did not run a fleet of expensive cars for its employees. It had nine cars (one Mercedes, one Volvo estate, three Nissan Bluebirds, two Vauxhall Cavaliers, one Ford Sierra and one Vauxhall Nova) and they were of a commensurate quality to those run by other renderers and other abattoir owners;

— pensions were only for senior employees and the entitlement was one-half of the final salary at age 65;

— holiday entitlement was four weeks plus statutory holidays per annum, which was in line with the industry in general. Very few of the management took up their annual entitlement due to volume of work, with a normal minimum week of fifty hours and more when required; and

— Forrest's 1990 accounts showed a total administration charge of £473,435 of which £238,136 referred to salaries and £53,976 to cars.

Market arrangements and behaviour

28. (a) An abattoir group and LASSA noted that Forrest and PDM did not compete with one another and said that this unreasonably penalized the suppliers of animal waste and resulted in higher prices being passed on to the public as part of the cost of meat production. Dundas Chemical commented that it would not be uneconomic for Forrest to obtain supplies from south of the border. Dundas Chemical itself serviced former PDM suppliers at Burscough and Garstang every day, as well as going as far north into Scotland as Fife; and PDM collected chicken waste from Scotland. Dundas Chemical suspected some understanding dating back to Forrest's purchase of Frank Gysels from PDM.

(b) *Forrest stated* that the fact that it did not currently operate in England resulted from its proper evaluation of a number of commercial and economic factors and not from any agreement or understanding with PDM (see paragraphs 9.11 and 9.16). Forrest also confirmed that it did not enter into any non-competition agreement with PDM at the time of its acquisition of Frank Gysels.

29. (a) A renderer told us that by forestalling the availability of the plant and equipment of former renderers for sale on the open market (procuring the cutting up, or the sale abroad, of such plant and equipment as Forrest did not itself require), Forrest prevented it from falling into the hands of any would-be or existing competitor.

(b) *Forrest supplied details* of equipment which it had obtained from renderers in the past and of the main items and plant which it had sold within the last ten years, including sales to Elgin and Tyneside Butchers. Forrest also confirmed that it did not buy the plant from Strathmore Meat Co Ltd, Grant Brothers Ltd or E Lewis & Sons Ltd when it acquired those businesses. Further, it had not been approached by any Scottish renderer to sell any equipment.

Rationalisation of the rendering industry in England and Wales: a paper submitted to the MMC by PDM

PDM's current position as by far the largest renderer of animal waste in England and Wales has come about through a gradual policy of acquisition and organic growth going back over a period of 25 years.

The acquisitions of rendering businesses made by PDM during this period are set out in part in Appendix 5.2 of the 1985 Report and (in part) in Appendix 2.4 of the Croda Report. There have been two very significant trends in the rendering industry during the last 25 years. First virtually every large public or private company interests in the meat trade which included rendering have withdrawn from this particular activity by either closing down or selling their rendering operations. Secondly during the same period a large number of small companies have also withdrawn from the industry, many of them selling their businesses to PDM either in whole or in part. PDM have been the principal beneficiary of these trends having some 20 years ago adopted a corporate strategy to become a country wide rendering business willing to collect animal waste from any source, whether large or small and wherever it arose. During the same period there has also been a very considerable rationalisation within the meat production and processing industries. This is continuing and will probably accelerate.

PDM's most significant acquisitions have been:—

in 1969, Unilever's collection and rendering businesses at Silvertown (in East London) and Exeter;

in 1974, Boons of Stafford Limited's rendering business at Derrington, near Stafford;

in 1976, Barbers Animal Products Limited's and its associate Haynes (Helston) Limited's rendering and knackers businesses at Chard and Helston;

in 1976, Swift & Company Limited's animal waste processing business at Beccles;

in 1978, Springfields Limited's animal waste businesses at Bristol, Blagdon, Gloucester, Swindon and Hendre (near Pencoed);

in 1979, Hypromel Products Limited's animal waste businesses at Wymington, Bourne and Ditchford;

in 1980, S & W Berisford Limited's rendering and knackers businesses at Widnes and Murton, near York and collection business based at West Drayton in London;

in 1986, Midland Cattle Products Limited's (a subsidiary of Thomas Borthwick Plc) national collection business and rendering plant at Stoke Bardolph, Nottingham; and

in 1991, Croda International Plc's remaining collection business and rendering plant at Market Harborough.

During the same period, the following large national companies have withdrawn from rendering:-

In the late 1980s, the Vestey organisation closed its rendering operations at Wootton, Northampton;

In 1980, The Fresh Meat Company Limited (a farmers co-operative) sold its rendering operations to Midland Cattle Products Limited (MCP) which had become a subsidiary of Thomas Borthwick Plc in 1976. In 1982/83 MCP had had four processing plants. By 1986 these had been reduced to its remaining factory at Stoke Bardolph which was sold to PDM in 1986.

Croda International Plc, which had entered the rendering industry by taking over British Glues and Chemicals Ltd in 1969 and subsequently had acquired several other rendering factories, had closed all but one of these plants by 1991, when it sold its remaining rendering and collection business to PDM and leased to PDM its remaining factory at Market Harborough.

In answer to question 6 of the MMC Questionnaire, PDM set out details of twelve other rendering plants which to PDM's knowledge had gone out of business in the last 7 years without being offered for sale. Included amongst these were poultry waste processing businesses which had been operated by Buxted Chickens, Fitch Lovell, Unigate and Hillsdown Holdings Plc.

During the same period the only instances of persons coming into the industry, as opposed to leaving it, have been:-

(a) Hillsdown Holdings' acquisition of the business of North Devon Meat Limited (a farmers' co-operative) in 1988/89. North Devon Meat Limited owned an existing rendering plant (known as Peninsular Proteins Limited) which had been commissioned in 1978.

(b) Cheale (Meats) Limited, a meat company, acquisition of the rendering plant of S & J Chandler Limited at Thruxted Mill near Canterbury in 1990.

(c) B & E (Rassau) Ltd opened a rendering plant in South Wales in 1988, but this closed down in 1989 as a result of financial problems.

With the exception of PDM, the only other independently owned rendering businesses of significance in England and Wales in 1993 are Fats and Proteins (UK) Limited of Lancaster, Smith Brothers (Hyde) Limited of Hyde, Cheshire, A Hughes & Son (Skellingthorpe) Ltd of Skellingthorpe, Lincs and Gilbert Animal Products Limited of Stoke, and the poultry processing business of Wildriggs in Penrith.

(referred to in paragraph 8.51 and paragraph 4 of Appendix 6.1)

Raw material pricing—factors affecting price:
a paper submitted to the MMC by PDM

Factor	No	Comment
QUALITY **Assessment** **(How do we assess quality)**	1.	Prices are fixed/agreed for a period in advance; (ie prior to receipt of material) based on the combination of factors already detailed, and knowledge of Raw Material Manager of the particular site/materials collected.
	2.	The PDM driver will alert the supplier's staff and/or our own Raw Material manager of any noticeable problems, as material is being collected.
	3.	Similarly, on his visit to site PDM's Raw Material Manager will often inspect the waste as it is being discharged into our containers, and take up any issue with site management
	4.	On receipt at plant the material is often already mixed with that from other sites, making identification impossible
	5.	However it can be seen that **unlike any other industry,** supplies of animal waste cannot be rejected and returned to the supplier, but must be dealt with.
	6.	Notwithstanding this, if any particular supply source of waste gives cause for serious concern and the problems have not been resolved as in (2) or (3) above, or through direct discussions between supplier and PDM management, it is possible to carry out yield or quality tests on PDM/s pilot plant test rig.
	7.	It is obvious therefore that any detailed Quality Assessment can only be carried out **retrospectively.**
	8.	The pursuit of adequate quality control of raw materials for rendering is a continual battle, with attention to this aspect of their operations usually being low on a supplier's list of priorities.
	9.	This is in some ways understandable, since to a supplier this material is his waste product, and the renderer's container is his 'dustbin'. Often following complaints from the renderer, quality control will improve for a short time but then deteriorate.
	10.	It must also be remembered that at the abattoir, the handling of waste is the most menial and dirty task and often the area of highest labour turnover, being the most unattractive of jobs.

Factor	No	Comment
QUANTITY	1.	Is the supplier (site) part of a regional or national group with central price negotiation?
	2.	Destination of material to be processed (does it have to be double or (in the case of SBO) triple handled?)
	3.	Special equipment (eg fork lift truck, hoppers etc) at supply site
	4.	Type (standard) of containers (eg stainless steel) at EC approved sites
	5.	Collection service and method most appropriate for supply source; (eg is it part of a 'milk-round' type service? Are there facility, hygiene, or storage constraints at the supply site affecting collection service required?)
	6.	Is there sufficient material within a category to allow for separate handling and subsequent processing?
	7.	Do we collect a range ('basket') of materials from the site, affecting collection system?

Factor	No	Comment
QUALITY **(a) Yield** **(by weight)**	1.	See attached summary sheet of raw materials classified under generic headings.
	2.	Individual **single species** abattoirs will classify and/or mix different proportions of the different types of fat; [eg One abattoir will sell Suet as a separate classification and others will not]
	3.	**Mixed Species** abattoirs may or may not mix the materials of each animal type
	4.	Slaughter patterns between species will vary both seasonally and on a daily basis
	5.	There will be varying degrees of contamination with excess moisture & blood etc
(b) Yield **(by value)**	1.	Rendering/Processing destination of the material: eg Best Fat processed into Grade 6 Tallow (Doncaster, Exeter & Hartshill); Grade 1/2 Tallow (Silvertown & Widnes} or edible (Leeds factories)
	2.	Degree of contamination (quality of handling) at source
	3.	Quantity sufficient for separate collection or container

Factor	No	Comment
DISTANCE	1.	Quantity being collected
	2.	Type of collection vehicle (eg part of a 'milk round')
	3.	Quality grade of rendering destination
	4.	Double handled? Supply point may be 30 miles from collection factory, but 150 miles from rendering destination.
	5.	Distance/time relationship (ie quality of road system). For example, 60 miles from Cornish supplier to Exeter, compared with 60 mile journey on motorway to say Hartshill.
	6.	Frequency or required time of collection related to distance. (eg Anglo Dutch Charing require clearance of bone before 6.00 am after night shift).
	7.	Is the collection site part of a national or regional group?

Factor	No	Comment
OTHER	1.	Some suppliers prefer to 'trade off' payments for some grades against no charge for others.
	2.	Some suppliers prefer to 'weight' prices and price adjustments between different types of waste for their own internal costing reasons
	3.	'Service v Price' considerations
	4.	Buyer/Seller relationship (strengths & weaknesses)??
	5.	Competitive influences on individual waste categories within the 'basket' supplied; eg where a competitor makes a selective [eg fat; or bone etc] bid which could affect the overall situation from a profitability point of view. (NOT selective predatory pricing)
	6.	Intensity of competition

Raw material classifications

(Possible Materials included within Generic Classifications)

BEST FAT

Beef	Lamb	Pig
Suet (Kidney & Heart Caul Fat Other Mesentary (Abdominal) Cod (Groin) Channel Cutting/Boning Slaughter Trimmings	Kidney Fat (Halal) Caul Fat Body Fat 'Mates'	Caul Fat Flare Fat Body Fat

BONE

Beef	Lamb	Pig
Mixed Bone Shank Bone Marrowbone Skulls Skinned Feet Feet	Carcasse Bone Skinned Heads Skinned Feet	Mixed Bone Shank Bone Feet Skulls

OTHER OFFALS

Beef	Lamb	Pig
Cattle Feet Hide Trimmings Condemned (mixed) 3d & 4th Stomachs Stomach & Gut Content Rough Offal Foetus	Unskinned Heads Unskinned Feet Whole (DOA) carcasse Rough Offal Stomach Stomach Content Skin Trimmings (wool)	Black Offal Whole dead Pigs Condemned carcasse Hair Stomach Stomach Content

SBO

Beef	Lamb	Pig
Intestine Intestine with Fat (Middles) Tonsils Brain Thymus Spinal Cord	N/A	N/A

A system of published prices

1. A system of published prices would aim to provide both suppliers and renderers with useful indicators of current price levels for animal waste as paid by the two leading renderers, PDM and Forrest. (Prices should be taken to include charges unless otherwise stated.) The main requirements of such a system are as follows:

(a) the price information should be up to date;

(b) the information should be easily accessible;

(c) the system should be simple enough to provide clear guidance to users; but

(d) the information provided should be sufficiently detailed to be applicable to the users' own businesses, and this means that indicators of quality and quantity need to be provided for each price;

(e) the system should be able to cater for 'package deals' (see paragraph 2.71), in addition to stand-alone price deals, and for overrider discounts; and

(f) the system should cope with contracts between renderers and abattoir groups (in addition to contracts with individual abattoirs).

2. A possible system of published prices reflecting these requirements might be along the following lines:

- *coverage:* a representative sample of contracts current with abattoirs and poultry plants; the sample to be selected from those contracts where a change in price has occurred in the preceding week;

- *timing:* information to be provided weekly by PDM and Forrest and to relate to the most recently negotiated contracts;

- *information to be provided:* in addition to the price per tonne for each of the categories of waste covered by the contract:

  - quantity purchased
  - number of abattoirs or poultry plants; and
  - estimated yields of tallows (grades 2 and 6 as appropriate) and meals (meat-and-bone, poultry, blood or feather as appropriate);

- *package deals:* where prices for individual categories of material within the package are available, each price to be reported with an indication that it forms part of a particular package; where there is only a price available for the whole package this price to be reported, together with the quantity, in a separate list of package deals;

- *overrider discount:* an indication to be provided where this is an element in the contract;

- *publication:* the information provided by PDM and Forrest to form separate sets of tables in the Market Update section of the *Meat Trades Journal*.

PDM's breaches of the 1986 gut-room undertakings: detailed recommendations

1. PDM should use a standard form for the monthly statement it prepares for each of its gut-rooms. Inter-company transactions should be shown separately from those with third parties, and volumes and unit prices should be recorded. Units of measurement, eg head, tonnes, kg, should be on a uniform basis between gut-rooms. A draft form is at Annex A.

2. PDM should continue to submit an audited annual statement to the DGFT, within nine months of the end of the relevant accounting period. For each gut-room contract PDM should submit to the DGFT a schedule on which the 12 monthly statements described in paragraph 1 above are summed to give annual totals. The sums of these individual gut-room schedules should agree with the audited accounts of the gut-room subsidiary, or be reconciled thereto. The statement should be audited by registered auditors specified or approved by the DGFT (the auditors).

3. The DGFT should agree with PDM a basis for allocating a fair proportion of its total overheads to its gut-room operation, on the lines set out in Annex B.

4. PDM should satisfy the DGFT that transfer prices between its gut-rooms and its other businesses are open-market prices, reconcilable with its published prices in order to help to ensure even-handed treatment:

(a) between PDM's own gut-rooms and those operated by its competitors; and

(b) between abattoirs which employ PDM in their gut-rooms and those which do not.

5. PDM should retain sufficient detailed records to support the transfer prices referred to in paragraph 4 above for three years or such other time as the DGFT may determine. These records should include all purchases of raw materials from, and sales of materials and products to, third parties.

6. PDM's undertaking to submit a budget to the DGFT in advance of taking on any new gut-room should continue in force. Prices for raw materials used in such budgets should be current open-market prices.

7. PDM should arrange with the auditors that they should, in their report on the annual statement to the DGFT, verify *inter alia* that:

(a) the statement is in agreement with the accounting records of the gut-room subsidiary; and

(b) the overhead charge has been computed in accordance with the formula agreed by the DGFT.

Monthly gut-room statement

Abattoir:		Month ended:		
	Units		*Price*	*Income (Expense)*
Headage income/(expense)				
Cattle		ea.		
Pigs		ea.		
Sheep		ea.		
Total headage				_____
				_____
Sales to third parties				
Sheep gut (runners)		..		
Pig gut (runners)		..		
Pig pancreas		Kg.		
Pigs maws		..		
Spleens		..		
Total third-party sales				_____
				_____
Inter-company sales/(charges)				
Best fat		Kg.		
Other fats		Kg.		
Offal		Kg.		
SBO		Kg.		
Other rendering materials:		Kg.		
Total rendering materials				_____
				_____
Tripes		ea.		
Manifolds		..		
Beef udders		..		
Reeds		..		
Sheeps paunches		..		
Total other materials				_____
				_____
Operating expenses third-party				
Wages		men		
National Insurance				
Laundry				
Water				
Waste disposal				
Transport				
Depreciation				
Inter-company				
Transport				
Overheads				
Total operating expenses				_____
				_____
Net profit/(loss)				_____

Allocation of overheads to gut-rooms

1. The DGFT should obtain from PDM a schedule listing its overheads for its most recent financial year, showing those which are directly attributable to gut-rooms, those which are indirectly attributable and those from which the gut-room operation of PDM derives no benefit.

2. Direct overheads should be charged to the gut-rooms concerned.

3. The portion of indirect overheads allocable to the gut-room operation should be calculated, on a basis to be approved by the DGFT, and charged by PDM to its gut-room operation and thence to individual gut-rooms.

4. In order to ensure that PDM's gut-rooms do not operate on terms that are likely to disadvantage its competitors unfairly, PDM should also submit to the DGFT a separate calculation of the overheads of its gut-rooms on a stand-alone basis (see paragraph 3 of Appendix 6.3). If the amount so calculated exceeds the sum of its direct overheads and indirect overheads allocated as above to its gut-rooms, this higher amount should be substituted as the charge by PDM to its gut-room operation.

Index

Printed in the UK by HMSO
Dd 0509839 C12 1474/1 9/93 326197 19542